T0246701

PRAISE FOR *THE JAPANESE ART OF LIVING SEASONALLY*

"Natalie Leon has been able to deftly articulate my awe for, and relationship with nature in ways that I have often struggled to put into words myself. Her curiosity is contagious, and will leave you with a feeling of tenderness after reading. If you've been feeling disillusioned or are simply looking for a bit of comfort, this is the perfect book to pick up to reconnect with your local environment and enrich the everyday life with natural, if not a bit ethereal, beauty."

Kaki Okumura, author of *WA: The Art of Balance*

"'Studying the art of tea awakens your sensitivity to the seasons.' Natalie Leon's practice of chado 'The Way of Tea' informs her writing in The Japanese Art of Living Seasonally, *but it is her innate perceptiveness, her sense of wonder and curiosity, and her wide-ranging research and knowledge which make this book meaningful on so many levels. Besides providing a wealth of information about so many aspects of Japanese culture, she also provides workable advice and guidance on how to enrich our everyday lives by celebrating the wonders of every day wherever we are."*

Bruce Hamana, student and teacher, Urasenke Tradition of the Way of Tea;

author of *100 Beautiful Words in the Way of Tea*

"This is a fascinating and authoritative book. From Spring's hanami (flower-viewing) celebrations to Winter's oshogatsu (new year) rituals, Natalie Leon explains the timeless symbols, rites, philosophies and observances that define Japanese life throughout the nation's 72 traditional micro seasons. Delve into The Japanese Art of Living Seasonally at any time of year and find often-unexpected and illuminating insights into Japanese manners and practices."

Naoko Abe, author of *'Cherry' Ingram: The Englishman Who Saved Japan's Blossoms*

"If any culture can be said to have perfected the art of observation, it is Japan. Whether in poetry, art, food, or ceremony, attention to the ever-changing phenomena of nature throughout the seasons is a Japanese hallmark. Natalie Leon offers here a guide for everyone to incorporate these delightful insights into everyday life with recipes, suggestions for carving out time and occasion, and cultural insight."

Liza Dalby, author of *East Wind Melts the Ice*

The Japanese Art of Living Seasonally

Natalie Leon

This edition first published in 2024
by Watkins, an imprint of Watkins Media Limited
Unit 11, Shepperton House
89–93 Shepperton Road
London N1 3DF

enquiries@watkinspublishing.com

1 2 3 4 5 6 7 8 9 10

Designed by Kate Cromwell. Typeset by JCS Publishing Ltd
Illustrations by Inko Ai Takita

Printed and bound in the United Kingdom by TJ Books Ltd

A CIP record for this book is available from the British Library

ISBN: 978-1-78678-785-9 (Hardback)
ISBN: 978-1-78678-786-6 (eBook)

www.watkinspublishing.com

The

Japanese

Art of

Living

Seasonally

An Invitation to Celebrate Every Day

NATALIE LEON

*For my mother, who taught me the names of all the flowers
and first introduced me to the wonders of Japan*

CONTENTS

Introduction

Chapter 1. *Shizen*: Japan and the Natural World

Seibutsu no Sekai: The World of Living Things   16
Shintō: The Way of the Gods   17
The Japanese Ritual Year   17
Kisetsukan: Cultivating a Sense of the Seasons   19
Dentō Sandō: The Three Ways   23
Wa: Harmony   24
Sources of Japanese Tradition   25
The *Manyōshū*: Collection of Ten Thousand Leaves   25
The *Kokinshū*: Collection of Ancient and Modern Poems   26
Genji Monogatari: The Tale of Genji   27
The Ancient Japanese Calendar   28
Seasonal Markers   29
Saijiki: The Book of the Seasons   29
Kigo: Seasonal Words   30
The Seasons of Japanese Poetry   31
Gosekku: The Five Sacred Festivals   31
Yama: Mountain   33
Seek Out Beauty in Every Season   35

Chapter 2. *Hanami*: The Ritual of Flower Viewing

The Roots of *Hanami*: A Celebration of Spring   41
The *Sakura Zensen*: The Cherry Blossom Forecast   42
Kyokusui No En: The Meandering Stream Banquet   43
Stages of Blooming   44
Mono no Aware: Sensitivity to the Impermanence of All Things 45
The Flower of the Soul   46
Sandaizakura: The Three Great Cherry Trees   47
Haru Matsuri: Spring Festivals   48
The Small Seasons of Spring   52
Sakura Kigo: Seasonal Words for *Sakura* Season   54
Konohana Sakura Hime: The Cherry Blossom Princess   56
Ippon Zakura: Solo *Hanami*   59
Japanese Micro Season No.11: The First Cherry Blossoms Bloom 59
Varieties of Cherry Blossom   60
Utamakura: Poetic Places   61

Haru Wagashi: Sweets for Springtime 62
Hanami at Home: How to Throw Your Own *Hanami* Party 64
Chirashi Sushi: Scattered Sushi 66
Oubaitōri: Bloom in Your Own Time 67

Chapter 3. *Shun*: Savouring the Seasons

Washoku: Traditional Japanese Cuisine 70
Ichiju Sansai: One Soup, Three Dishes 71
Itadakimasu: I Humbly Receive 71
Ohashi: Chopsticks 72
Gohan: The Importance of Rice 72
Kaiseki Ryōri: Eating the Seasons 75
Hashiri, Sakari and *Nagori*: Eating in Season 77
Obanzai Ryōri: Home Cooking in Kyōto 78
Moritsuke: The Art of Japanese Food Arrangement 82
Goshiki: The Rule of Five 84
Shōjin Ryōri: Buddhist Temple Cuisine 86
Foraging in Japan 87
Japanese Micro Season No.67: Parsley Flourishes 88
Naorai: Eating with the Gods 93
Lessons We Can Learn from *Washoku*: Eating with Intention 94
Growing a Japanese Kitchen Garden 95

Chapter 4. *Mottainai*: Zero-waste Living

Kamikatsu: Japan's First Zero-waste Town 101
Fashioned from Nature 102
Boro Boro: Visible Mending 104
Tsutsmi: Wrapping 104
Mingei: The People's Art 108
Kintsugi: A Vein of Gold 109
The Sustainable Japanese Home 111
Kokoro: The Heart of the Craftsperson and Spirit of Their Tools 117
Ōryōki: Just Enough 120
Kakinoha: Wrapping with Leaves 121
Kaisō: Sustainable Superfoods 122
Tsukemono: The Japanese Art of Preserving 124
Dōtoku: The Virtues of the Land 127

Chapter 5. *Mizu no Michi*: The Way of Water

Japan's Creation Myth 135
Kiyomizudera: The Temple of Pure Water 135
Temizu: Hand Water 136

Nagoshi no Harae: Summer Purification Rituals 137
Benzaiten: The Goddess of Everything That Flows 138
Kannon: The Goddess of Mercy 139
Mizu no Kamisama: The Shintō Goddess of Water 140
Ryū: Dragons 141
Ryūjin: The Dragon God 141
Shiki no Niwa: The Four Seasons Garden 142
Onsen: Bathing in Nature 142
Kyōkai: Liminal Spaces 143
Tsuyu: The Rainy Season 144
Natsu Matsuri: Summer Festivals 145
Ajisai Matsuri: The Hydrangea Festival 146
Tanabata: The Star Festival 146
Umi no Hi: Marine Day 150
Obon: The Festival of Returning Spirits 151
Ryoo o Mitsukeru: Finding Coolness 151
The Small Seasons of Summer 153
Natsu Kigo: Seasonal Words for Summer 155
Natsu Wagashi: Sweets for Summertime 156
Japanese Micro Season No.29: Irises Bloom 157
Onomatopoeia: The Sounds of Nature 158
Shinshō Fūkei: Recollected Vistas 159
Kibune 159
Shinroku: New Green 160
Finding Beauty in the Darkness 161

Chapter 6. Kimono: Wearing the Seasons

The "Thing to Wear" 164
Iro: The Traditional Colours of Japan 166
Gogyo Setsu: The Five Elements 167
Kasane: The Japanese Art of Colour Layering 173
Kusakizome: Natural Dyeing with Plants 177
Atelier Shimura: Weaving the Colours of Life 177
Japanese Micro Season No.22: Silkworms Start Feasting on Mulberry Leaves 179
Kimono Sustainability 179
Kamon: Family Crests 182
Kimono Motifs 182
Itchiku Kubota 184
Kitsuke: A Kimono for Every Season 184
Shikunshi: The Four Philosophers 188
Seijin no Hi: Coming of Age Day 188
Karyūkai: The Flower and Willow World 189
Kimono Accessories 189
Koromogae: The Seasonal Change of Clothing 190
Kimono no Hi: Kimono Day 191

Chapter 7. *Kadō:* The Way of Flowers

Living with Flowers 194
Ikebana: Giving Life to Flowers 196
Rinpa: Nature in Japanese Art 198
An Arrangement for Every Season 199
Tsutsuji: Azaleas 203
Kadō Matsuri: Flower Arranging Festival 204
Japanese Micro Season No.32: The First Lotus Blossoms 204
Jōdo: Pure Land Buddhism 205
Sōmoku Jōbutsu: The Buddhahood of Plants 205
Noh Theatre: The Flowering Spirit 206
Japanese Micro Season No.18: Peonies Bloom 209
The Japanese Floral Calendar: A Year in Flowers 210
Tsubaki: Camellia 211
Aisatsu: Seasonal Greetings 212
Hanachōzu: Flower Water Basin 214
Hanakotoba: The Japanese Language of Flowers 217
Hana Kigo: Beautiful Japanese Words for Flowers 218
Spend Time with Flowers 219

Chapter 8. *Otsukimi*: The Ritual of Moon Viewing

Hazuki Jūgoya: The Clearest Night 224
Tsuki no Usagi: The Moon Rabbit 225
Meigetsu: The Harvest Moon 226
Yearning for the Moon 228
The Beauty of Things Obscured 229
Japanese Micro Season No.50: Chrysanthemums Bloom 230
Kikumon: The Chrysanthemum Seal 230
Kiku no Sekku: The Chrysanthemum Festival 233
Niiname no Matsuri: The Imperial Harvest Ritual 237
Kuri no Sekku: Day of Sweet Chestnuts 238
Kaki: Persimmons 239
The Small Seasons of Autumn 240
Kannazuki: The Month without Gods 242
Japanese Micro Season No.41: Heat Starts to Die Down 242
Hana no: Autumn Fields of Flowers 243

Chapter 9. *Chadō:* The Way of Tea

The History of Japanese Tea 252
Wabi Cha: Tea of Quiet Taste 253
What is the Japanese Tea Ceremony? 254
The Four Guiding Principles of *Chadō* 256
Roji: The Dewy Path 257

Chaseki: The Tearoom   258
Calligraphy for the Tea Ceremony   260
Toriawase: Curated with Care   260
Tea and the Seasons   261
Chawan: Tea Bowl   262
Chasen: Tea Whisk   262
Mitate: To See Anew   264
Wagashi: Sweets for the Tea Ceremony   264
A Seasonal Guide to Japanese Tea   265
Taking Time for Tea   269
Ichigo Ichie: Once in a Lifetime   271
New Year in the Tea Room   272
Nodate: The Japanese Tea Picnic   273

Chapter 10. *Momijigari:* The Ritual of Leaf Hunting

Chinju no Mori: Shrine Forests   280
Shinboku: Sacred Trees   281
Shinrin Yoku: The Ritual of Forest Bathing   282
Domestic *Shinrin Yoku*: Bringing the Outside Inside   286
Six Beautiful Japanese Words Associated with Trees   287
Momijigari: Red-leaf Hunting   288
Aki Matsuri: Autumn Festivals   290
Jikkan Jūnishi: Ten Stems and Twelve Branches   292
Aki Kigo: Seasonal Words for Autumn   292
Japanese Micro Season No.54: Maple Leaves and Ivy Turn Yellow   293
Sika: Deer   294
Shichi Fukujin: Japan's Seven Lucky Gods   294
Aki Wagashi: Autumn Sweets   295
Ichō: Lessons from the Ginkgo Biloba   296
Tatsutahime: The Goddess of Autumn   297
A Goddess for Every Season   298
Japanese Woodland Botanicals   299

Chapter 11. *Oshōgatsu*: The Fifth Season

Shimekazari: Tied Rope Ornament   303
Engimono: Japanese Good Luck Charms   304
Kadomatsu: Gate Pine   305
Osechi Ryōri: Foods for the New Year   305
Hatsuyume: The First Dream   307
Hatsuhinode: The First Sunrise   308
Hatsumōde: The First Shrine Visit   308
Hatsugama: The First Tea Kettle   308
Nengajō: New Year Cards   309
Yuki Usagi: The Snow Rabbit   310

Shōchikubai: The Three Friends of Winter   312
Kitsunebi: Fox Fire   313
Fuyu Kigo: Seasonal Words for Winter   314
Setsugekka: The Three Beauties   315
Yukimi: Snow Viewing   315
Yuki Matsuri: Snow Festivals   316
Yuki Onna: The Snow Maiden   318
Tsuru: Cranes   318
The Small Seasons of Winter   319
Yuzu: Citrus Junos   322
Suisen: Daffodils   324
Japanese Micro Season No.55: Camellias Bloom   325
Fuyu Wagashi: Winter Sweets   325
Fuyogomori: Hibernation   327
Shitamoe: Sprouting Beneath the Snow   327

Resources

Acknowledgements   330
Japan's 24 *Sekki* (Divisions of the Solar Year) and 72 *Ko* (Micro Seasons)   332
Selected Bibliography   336
Permissions   341

INTRODUCTION

The exceeding beauty of the Earth, in her splendour of life, yields a new thought with every petal. The hours when the mind is absorbed by beauty are the only hours when we really live.

*BRITISH NATURALIST
RICHARD JEFFERIES (1848–1887)*

Growing up in a small village in Hertfordshire, England, I was innately aware of the changing seasons in the countryside, whether it was the sight of the first snowdrops in January, the joyous blossoming of cherry trees in spring, blackberry-picking in the summer, hunting for russet-coloured leaves in the autumn or cutting holly for Christmas decorations. I have always been happiest when surrounded by flowers and plants, foraging for ingredients for my latest seasonal recipe and spending hours drawing and photographing every tiny detail of the landscape. When I discovered traditional Japanese art, with its exquisitely rendered flowers and grasses that adorned the hems of silk kimono, graced gold-leaf folding screens and echoed across every conceivable medium, I fell in love with these symbolic seasonal motifs and the philosophies and ancient traditions behind them. They captured my heart long before I could experience them in person. Natural imagery is everywhere in daily Japanese life, represented in infinite elegant, traditional and modern forms.

Later on, after over a decade of city living and feeling increasingly disconnected from the seasons, I felt the pull of the wild. I longed for the countryside where I grew up. While living in my London flat, I often felt suffocated. I craved wide open spaces, vast expanses of green where I could wander, pick wild flowers, forage to my heart's content and fill an imaginary pantry with flower-infused delights as quickly as I filled sketchbooks with drawings of flowers as a teenager. I couldn't escape to the countryside, so instead I focused on surrounding myself with nature in myriad ways, inspired by Japan's 72 micro seasons and annual festivals. The many Japanese ways of honouring the seasons helped me to re-establish the connection that had been ever-present for me as a child. Celebrating each micro season, equinox and solstice as they collapsed into each other deepened my relationship with the seasons and the wider natural world.

Yet, for the first time in history, four billion people live in urban areas: more than half of the world's population. If these numbers continue as predicted, by 2050 approximately seven billion people will be living in urban environments (UN World Urbanization Prospects, 2008). Human beings are not designed to live isolated from nature, so in our move towards urbanization, we have inevitably lost something. We are more disconnected than ever before from the countless wonders of the natural world. As the urban sprawl exponentially increases, we lose air quality, areas of outstanding natural beauty and many precious plant and animal habitats.

Humanity is struggling with the mental and physical consequences of this on a grand scale, in what Florence Williams, author of *The Nature Fix,* calls "our endemic dislocation from the outdoors". As a result, we have lost our sense of wonder and connection; we are anxious, isolated and often depressed. We need to find ways to incorporate nature into our urban lives by participating in nature-based activities, eating more seasonally and re-engaging with our childlike sense of curiosity and joy. These practices can help form a prescription to combat our alienation from nature.

Throughout the years when travelling to my favourite places was impossible, I focused on finding new and different ways to tune into nature by introducing little touches inspired by Japanese seasonal living traditions into my everyday life – for example, by practising the rituals of *hanami* (cherry blossom viewing), *momijigari* (red-leaf hunting) and *tsukimi* (moon viewing). Practices like *hanami* are a beautiful way to celebrate spring and the promise of what's to come in the year ahead. Taking time out of our frantic lives to meet a friend for lunch under a blooming cherry tree reminds us of the passage of time. There are certain trees in my neighbourhood that I like to visit each year, taking a picnic, a bentō or bringing my utensils to make some tea for myself beneath the clouds of blossom. After all, you really only need yourself and *ippon zakura* – a single cherry tree – to participate in *hanami* and enjoy a quiet moment of calm in nature.

As we become more environmentally conscious and desire a slower pace of life, we choose to savour more and consume less. There is so much that the world can learn about the beauty of intentional seasonal living from Japan, something the country's great thinkers, poets, artists and craftspeople have known for over 1,000 years.

ABOUT THIS BOOK

Like marine biologist Rachel Carson (1907–1964), I have always been preoccupied with "the wonder and beauty of the Earth". Carson believed "natural beauty has a necessary place in the spiritual development of any individual or any society", and I can't disagree.

Over the last decade, my quest to uncover Japan's seasonal culture has led me to fabled temples, moss-covered gardens and hidden tearooms. I have attended a fox wedding in Kyōto, foraged for wild mountain vegetables in Yamagata, hunted for autumn leaves in Osaka, slept in a Buddhist monastery on Kōyasan, celebrated spring with countless cherry blossom viewing picnics, handpicked *yuzu* (my favourite Japanese citrus) in Kochi and experienced an earthquake in Kumamoto. The passages of this book whispered to me when I walked through ancient forests, visited Shintō shrines as petals fell all around me and strolled through Japanese gardens as koi swam languidly alongside me. I researched it in beautiful libraries, editing the manuscript in my favourite tea houses and by the light of candles under a blanket in the darkest days of January. I wrote it because I wanted to share my passion with you.

I hope it will become a companion, trusted friend and guide as you take your first steps toward the art of living seasonally. The contents are my humble offering to you, a selection of the Japanese seasonal rituals, foods, flowers and folklore that captured my heart and imagination. These are the traditions that have deeply impacted my relationship with the seasons and all living things. I hope they will enrich and inspire you, just as they did me. There is comfort to be found in the cyclical nature of time, life-affirming poetry in the ephemeral and beauty everywhere for those with eyes to see it.

I've organized the book by theme so you can dip in and out of whatever chapter piques your curiosity and return to it year after year when the season comes around again. In Chapter 1 I introduce some of the key concepts behind the book, such as my guiding principle, *kisetsukan*, a sense of the seasons. Chapter 2 focuses on the A-list celebrities of spring, Japan's world-famous cherry blossoms and the many wonderful traditions surrounding them, while Chapter 3 uncovers Japan's many ways of savouring the seasons through food, exploring foraging, *kaiseki* (an elevated multicourse meal of many small, exquisite dishes) and *obanzai* (Kyōto-style home cooking). In Chapter 4 we explore more sustainable ways of living and travelling inspired by the Japanese concept of *mottainai* (which means "what a waste!"). Chapter 5 is the unofficial summer chapter, which dives into Japan's many aquatic myths and Chapter 6 invites you to enter the world of the kimono, Japan's iconic T-shaped garment, to discover its special relationship to the seasons. Next comes Chapter 7, a wholehearted celebration of Japan's many floral traditions. In Chapter 8, we turn our eyes to the night sky, delighting in the beauty of the moon and all things lunar. Chapter 9 explores the world of *Chadō* or the Way of Tea, while Chapter 10 introduces the joyous late autumn activity of *momijigari* or red-leaf hunting. Finally, Chapter 11 delves into *Oshōgatsu*, the Japanese New Year – one of the nation's most important annual festivities.

Throughout the book I've shared suggestions of how we can enrich our days by taking inspiration from Japan's rich seasonal culture and implementing some of these ideas and traditions in our own ways, by engaging with local plants, trees, flowers and seasonal phenomena. Make living an art and capture your own seasonal moments in poetry, images, music and fashion. Please feel free to share them with me at #theartoflivingseasonally.

Enjoy whichever season you find yourself in – they all have their merits. Do not rush headlong into the future always looking toward the next thing and never pausing to enjoy this very moment. Slow down, practise the art of noticing and you will begin to see the manifestations of nature's beauty all around you. Find small ways to celebrate and savour the ripe, juicy flesh of the season. Drink in the golden light that drips over the landscape of late autumn – painting everything with a palette of citrine, amber and gold. The fading autumn leaves beneath you are the fragrant compost from which entire new worlds are born – food for your transformation, evolution and metamorphosis.

I hope that the Japanese traditions, rituals and philosophies I fell in love with will inspire you and demonstrate that it is possible to find a harmonious balance between our hectic modern lifestyles and our natural inclination to connect with nature, wherever we are. This book is my love letter to seasonal Japan.

Natalie Leon
London, 13–17 October 2023
Kiku no hana hiraku/ Chrysanthemums bloom

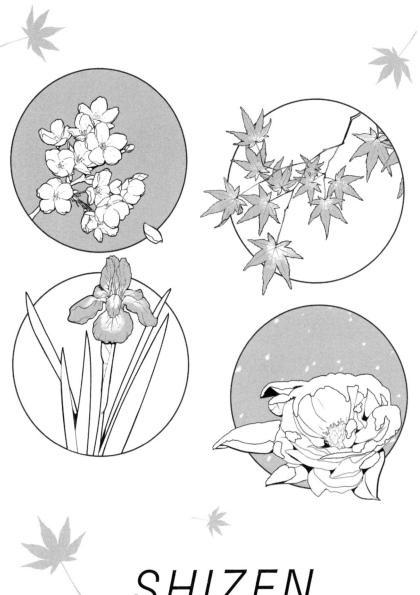

SHIZEN

Japan and the Natural World

There is nothing you can see
that is not a flower;
There is nothing you can think
that is not the moon.

MATSUO BASHŌ
TRANSLATED BY R H BLYTH

Humanity has an instinctive biological need to be near nature. We're drawn to it, just as flowers lean toward the sun. The further away we are from it, the more we suffer. We can't help but seek it out. Nature calls to something profound deep inside us, our wild selves, buried deep beneath our suits and ties, our busy city lives and all our technological distractions.

As British neurologist and naturalist Oliver Sacks said, the love of nature and living things is essential to the human condition. This concept, known as biophilia, asserts that we human beings are happiest when we feel connected to other living things, whether that's stroking our pets, cultivating a garden or watching the waves crash upon the shore.

Sacks has written about the spiritual, emotional, physical and neurological effects nature has on us, explaining it through our deep and abiding love for gardens, which perfectly expresses our desire to interact with and tend to nature. This is something I've felt keenly my whole life. Nature has always called to me, especially during the pandemic when the soothing act of tending my tiny patio garden kept me sane. Part of my morning ritual in the summertime is to get up and, prior to having breakfast, feed and water my garden before the day begins in earnest and the sun becomes too fierce. I like to walk barefoot on the cool patio slabs and, as I water, I pull out the odd weed, deadhead the roses and talk to my plants: "Look how much you've grown!"

SEIBUTSU NO SEKAI

The World of Living Things

In Japanese thought, humankind has a close relationship with nature. We are a part of it, not separate or distinct from it. This brotherhood includes the sea, the sky, the Earth and all those who swim in it, soar above it and walk upon it – the world of living things. Author Ninji Imanishi describes the enormity of life on Earth as our "great family of various members". This mindset differs from the views we often encounter in the West. Here, nature is something to be treated with reverence and respect, not conquered or controlled. As author Dani Cavallaro explains, "The belief that humanity cannot exist independently from nature lies at the core of the Japanese value system."

According to the Daijisen Dictionary, the word *shizen*, often translated as "nature" or "natural", comprises the entire cosmos. This means it encompasses everything between Heaven and Earth, including human beings. One of the fundamental teachings of Shintō, Japan's ancient indigenous religion, is the interconnect§edness of all things, while compassion for all sentient life is at the heart of another of Japan's great religions traditions, Mahayana (Pure Land) Buddhism.

SHINTŌ

The Way of the Gods

Still enshrined at the heart of Japanese society today, Shintō, Confucianism and Buddhism are three wellsprings of Japanese tradition. Over time, Shintō has incorporated elements of both of the others. Japan is home to countless gods, known as the *Yaoyorozu no Kami* (eight million gods), because there are simply too many to count. These nature guardians dwell in its free-flowing streams, august mountains and primeval forests. They control the weather and the tides and protect and watch over the land of the rising sun, whose supreme deity is the Sun Goddess Amaterasu Ōmikami (see page 232). Shintō worships *shinra banshō*, meaning "all things in nature". It personifies natural elements such as trees, lakes and rocks, imbuing them with sacred spirits called *kami*.

Shintō or *Kami no Michi* translates to "the Way of the Gods", and *Koshintō* (ancient Shintō), Japan's native religion, encompasses animism, folklore and ritual. At its core is nature worship, as well as the interconnectedness of all things, including humanity and the natural world, and the importance of maintaining balance and harmony. Shintō's nature worship can be described as a way of life.

While Shintō may be a uniquely Japanese faith, it has lessons to offer us that can enrich the lives of anyone. There are some 100,000 Shintō shrines in Japan, tucked away in tiny backstreets in the centre of Tōkyō, the world's biggest city; perched on the edges of cliffs; hidden in watery grottos along the coastline; and everywhere in between. Make the forest your green cathedral, the mountains your temple, the shining lake your shrine – and worship often.

THE JAPANESE RITUAL YEAR

Professor Mark Cody Poulton describes nature as "a cultural artefact" in Japan. In fact, in Japan nature *is* culture and vice versa – the two have become so interwoven that it's almost impossible to tell them apart and they are now inseparable. The nation has strong ties to its agricultural roots and every one of the 365 days of the calendar is packed with cultural traditions and seasonally focused communal events, celebrating the bloom of a flower or the beauty of the harvest moon. These ancient celebrations reinforce the rhythm of the year, attuning people to the changing seasons.

Many of you may already honour the changing seasons in some way, consciously or subconsciously. This book is my invitation to cultivate your sense of the seasons by observing and engaging with them regularly so that this becomes a practice, ideally an annual one.

Take inspiration from Japan's ancient traditions to create new rituals of your own that celebrate the first buds of spring and the spectacular colours of the changing autumn leaves. Mark these magnificent moments in the year in your own small way each and every year from now on. You could also dedicate a small table, a blank piece of wall or a single shelf as a *tokonoma* (display area for art, flowers and objects) that represent the seasons for you, then change them accordingly as the year progresses. We give meaning to things by creating rituals around them, repeating them over and over, day by day, little by little, making them real.

The small rituals we choose to make time for matter. These practices don't have to be grand affairs (unless you want them to be). As Casper ter Kuile shares in *The Power of Ritual*, they can be small, simple and private moments, just for you. Almost anything can become a ritual – for example, changing the artwork hanging on the walls of your home, placing a vase of seasonal flowers on your desk or pausing to notice the latest phase of the moon. Such small actions help us mark the passage of time, whether we are celebrating the blossoming of spring, the warmth of summer, the rich abundance of autumn or the stark allure of winter. Taking the time to commemorate these moments in the year – the unique beauty of each season – enriches our lives, lifts our spirits and re-energizes our creativity. So, cultivate seasonal awareness like a precious seed. If you nurture it, it will grow and you will flourish.

A wholehearted celebration of the innumerable gifts of the Earth, its flowers, trees, waters, mountains and plains can also be found in the traditional Japanese arts. Nature infuses Japanese culture at every level. According to tea instructor Bruce Hamana, seasonal references are the DNA of traditional Japanese culture. These recurring motifs are a part of the language of *kisetsukan*, an awareness or sense of the seasons, which is a thread that runs through the Japanese ways or arts, binding them all to each other and connecting them with nature itself in a symbiotic web of nature and culture. We are nourished by nature, literally, metaphorically and creatively. Echoes of the previous season, fallen leaves and scattered petals will become fodder for the next stage of life, fuelling nature's next creative endeavour. Why not let them fuel yours?

KISETSUKAN

Cultivating a Sense of the Seasons

According to Sen Soshitsu XV (born 1923), the Grand Master of the Urasenke School of Tea, one of the unique benefits of living in harmony with the seasons is developing an increased sensibility towards nature. When we nurture this sensitivity "we are awakened to the beauty that surrounds us every moment".

The word *kisetsukan* means "a sense of the seasons". When I first discovered this concept, it was as though everything finally clicked into place, it gave a name to a mindful practice I had been engaging with in my own small way for years. After attending *keiko* (tea ceremony practice) at the home of tea master Bruce Hamana in Kyōto, I sat down with him to talk about the nature of *kisetsukan*, a subject close to both of our hearts. Hamana sensei noted that over 1,000 years, Japan has carefully woven the symbols, sounds and tastes of the seasons into "a rich cultural tapestry". As a result, nature and its cycles have become so ingrained in Japanese culture that the two are now virtually indistinguishable from each other. The Japanese approach to nature perceives humanity as a part of nature's infinite variety, not separate from it. In Japan, nature has become culture, and culture is a part of nature. This symbiotic relationship can be observed throughout numerous Japanese art forms, rituals and traditions, repeated and refined over centuries, including literature, textiles and the tea ceremony.

That day in April, Hamana sensei displayed a scroll in the tearoom that read, "Spring enters a thousand forests – flowers everywhere". This is a Zen proverb or philosophical question known as a *kōan*, which is a brief, deceptively simple phrase that's shorthand for a much larger question to be contemplated by students. It's understandable then that Robert Aitken Roshi has described *kōan* as "the folklore of Zen". In this instance, spring is a metaphor for the teachings of the Buddha or enlightenment because, according to Soiku Shigematsu, priest of the Rinzai School of Zen, all nature is the manifestation of *satori* (enlightenment).

The notion of *kisetsukan* is about tuning in to the signs of the changing seasons, like turning the dials on an old-fashioned radio till you find the right station and everything clicks into place. To begin with, you have to actively work at it, making an effort to look for the signs, the buds of a certain flower or the ripening of a particular fruit, but soon this instinctual seasonal sense will become a part of you. Once that happens, you will begin to notice these heralds of the seasons wherever you go. By engaging with the present over the course of a year, the seasonal moments come together to form your own personal ritual calendar filled with festivals, foods, flowers and folklore celebrating every season of your life, big and small.

Cultivating Awareness

In Japan, the sights, sounds and signs of *kisetsukan* are like oxygen molecules in the air; they're everywhere, permeating everything. Although it's not something taught in schools, it is something you can learn, a practice you can develop by cultivating awareness. Once you begin to slow down and see the threads of *kisetsukan* that weave throughout traditional Japanese culture, you'll start to notice their evidence everywhere. If you follow those threads, they will guide you through the year. *Kisetsukan* is a deep green well of inspiration to draw from. It can bring us so much joy, nourish our creativity and, in the process, add a deeper layer of meaning to our daily rituals.

Hamana sensei explained that *kisetsukan* is, at its heart, about awareness, focus and living in the present. Cultivating an awareness or sensitivity to the seasons will also make you more aware in general.

Let nature be your teacher.

WILLIAM WORDSWORTH

Honing your awareness and understanding of those around you, which impacts both your relationships and inner world. Ultimately, that process leads us to the path of *satori* (enlightenment). The characters that make up the word *satori* include both "heart" and "self". So, in order to reach enlightenment, one must know their own heart. In the immortal words of poetess Mary Oliver (1935–2019), "attention is the beginning of devotion."

Directed Attention

We are all suffering from attention deficit. It is constantly being stolen from us by technology – the phone rings, yet another email arrives and endless notifications pop up on our screens. Naturalist Henry David Thoreau (1817–1862) knew that the key to noticing the subtle changes in the seasons happening all around us required what he called "directed attention". When we recalibrate our lives by tuning into nature and training ourselves to notice, for example, the slightest changes in the colours of the leaves or the blossoming of winter camellias under the snow, a whole new world opens up to us, revealing the distinct beauty of every season. I like to call this the art of noticing, the process of training your eye or "getting your eye in", as it was called in art school. When you start to actively practise the art of looking, you begin to see beauty and inspiration everywhere.

You can also learn to direct your attention by handling objects – turning them over in your hands and noticing their weight and how they are constructed. When you do this, try disconnecting from what the intended purpose for the object might have been. In your hands, what could it become? A vessel for flowers, perhaps? Something to contemplate while you enjoy your quiet tea moment? Inspiration for a haiku?

I find my treasures in nature. I collect pebbles, bracken and mosses, seed pods, fallen branches, leaves and flower heads. Each season offers its own riches, lessons and inspiration.

What We Can Learn from *Kisetsukan*

- Living in harmony with the seasons enriches our inner and creative lives.

- Seasonal traditions lead to a deeper appreciation of natural beauty in all its forms.

- Seasonal rituals help us develop a deeper understanding and gratitude for the natural world.

- Slowing down and noticing the rhythm of the year can lead to increased personal harmony and a sense of calm in our busy modern lives.

- Anyone anywhere can embrace these rituals and create seasonal traditions of their own.

- By practising the art of noticing, we can nurture and reconnect with the sense of wonder we felt as children.

- There is beauty everywhere. We only have to attune ourselves to it.

DENTŌ SANDŌ

The Three Ways

The word *do* or *dou*, means "road", "path" or "way". Practitioners of these ways, such as *Chadō* (the Way of Tea), *Kadō* (the Way of Flowers) and *Shodō* (the Way of Writing), which are known as the three pillars of traditional Japanese art or *Dentō Sandō* (the Three Ways), are especially sensitive to the changes that take place in the natural world throughout the year because the procedures, forms and philosophies behind the *geidō*, Japan's traditional arts, keep them grounded in the present.

To explore an example, much like practising any of the Japanese martial arts such as *Kendō* (the Way of the Sword), walking the path of the Way of Tea is much more than a hobby. The Way of Tea is a way of living that helps its devotees cultivate a keen awareness of the passage of time and a refined sensibility to the rhythm of the seasons. Grand Master Sen Soshitsu XV called *Chadō* "an art of the seasons" because "the tearoom mirrors the natural world, instead of competing with it, gently enhancing seasonal feelings". The changing seasons provide one of the foundational elements of the Way of Tea, and celebrating these subtle changes is one of the greatest joys of tea people.

I believe there are huge benefits, both to us as individuals and to society as a whole, to cultivating an awareness of the seasons. Beyond a more finely tuned sense of Japanese aesthetics, there's also a beneficial spiritual component. These mindful practices bring us comfort, calm and one step closer to enlightenment. Bringing our focus into the present positively impacts our interpersonal relationships with others and our relationship with ourselves, our thoughts and our consciousness.

One of the foremost teachings of Buddhism that many Japanese artists and intellectuals took to heart was impermanence. According to H E Davey, author of *The Japanese Way of the Artist,* one of the definitions of the word *furyu* expresses the concept of a moment of fleeting, transitory beauty that cannot be captured and will not last. An appreciation of the evanescence of life can be profoundly life-affirming; we are but shooting stars, after all. This knowledge is embodied by the concept of *mujōkan* or *mujō,* also known as *mono no aware* (see Chapter 2). *Shoshin*, the beginner's mind, is another benefit of practising a Way. It teaches us to approach everything as if it were the first time and to always be open to new opportunities for growth. This encourages modesty and humbles everyone, from the expert to the least experienced. In the beginner's mind, there are endless possibilities.

WA

Harmony

Long before Japan was called *Nihon*, it was known as *Wa* or *Wakoku* (the country of harmony). *Wa* is the oldest recorded name for contemporary Japan, given to the ancient people living in the southern part of the country. *Wa* represents the spirit of Japan, as well as the nation as a whole.

The kanji *wa* also means "togetherness or harmony", a key foundational element of Japanese culture. This concept originates from Confucian ideals of a cooperative society, which values the needs of the many over the desires of the individual. A respectful and harmonious relationship between nature and humanity often characterizes traditional Japanese culture. *Wa* is another expression of this. Even in our urbanized and technologically advanced age, Japan retains its connection to nature, celebrating the cycle of the changing seasons.

SOURCES OF JAPANESE TRADITION

Poetry is one of the building blocks of traditional Japanese culture, the embodiment of the nation's relationship with nature and a rich source of inspiration for the country's writers, artists, artisans and craftspeople. As anthropologist Liza Dalby wrote in her memoir *East Wind Melts the Ice*, "The entire Japanese poetic tradition is grounded in the observance of the passing seasons, and it is quite simply second nature to view human emotions through seasonal metaphors."

Kyōto-based ceramic artist Shinichi Miyagawa comes from a 330-year-old ceramics dynasty. He and his father still live and work in Kyōto. They are renowned specialists in producing exquisite *dōgu* (utensils) for the tea ceremony. During a visit to their family home and workshop, Shinichi san explained that when he creates a new artwork, he draws inspiration from *waka* (Japanese poetry), *kanshi* (Chinese poetry), the Rinpa school of Japanese art and the work of his ancestors. These works form a codex of seasonal motifs established over thousands of years. Each successive generation of the Miyagawa clan refines the work of those who came before them. The exceptional work of this family can be found in the Kyōto State Guest House, whose collection represents the pinnacle of Japan's art and crafts. It's also presented in international collections such as the British Museum, the Victoria and Albert Museum in London and the Boston Museum of Fine Arts.

THE *MANYŌSHŪ*

Collection of Ten Thousand Leaves

Throughout the book, I refer back to two fountainheads of Japanese poetry. The *Manyōshū* (*Collection of Ten Thousand Leaves*) is Japan's oldest existing collection of Japanese poems or songs, compiled during the Nara period (710–794) and the *Kokinshū* (*Collection of Ancient and Modern Poems*). The *Kokinshū* was defined by the aristocratic sensibilities of the Kyōto Imperial court and presented a utopian approach to nature. In contrast, as haiku expert William J Higginson eloquently put it, the *Manyōshū* suggests the "fresh breezes of the countryside".

Professor Hideo Shintani, curator of the Manyo Historical Museum in Toyama, credits the *Manyōshū* as one of the main sources of Japanese tradition and culture. The popularity of the cult of the four seasons in Japan began with this anthology. The *waka* poetry of the *Manyōshū* established the affinity between the wonders of the four seasons and Japanese poetry, setting the standard for the future of the Japanese poetic tradition. It immortalizes Japan as a dragonfly island, where heavenly rivers flow in the shadow of sacred mountains, protected by divine winds and perilous seas.

THE *KOKINSHŪ*

Collection of Ancient and Modern Poems

The *Kokin Wakashū,* also known simply as the *Kokinshū* (*Collection of Ancient and Modern Poems*), was compiled c.900 and is an Imperial anthology of Japanese poetry written in *tanka* form. *Tanka* is an ancient kind of short-form poetry. In the foreword, courtier Ki no Tsurayuki (884–946), who compiled the poems at the request of Emperor Daigo (885–930), wrote, "The songs of Japan take the human heart as their seed and flourish as myriad leaves of words … Hearing the cries of the bush warbler among the blossoms or the calls of the frog that lives in the waters, how can we doubt that every living creature sings its song?" Here, seeds, leaves and flowers are directly linked to human feelings and expressions, becoming key concepts in Japanese poetry.

One of the *Sanjūrokkasen* (Thirty-six Immortal Poets), Tsurayuki's lyrical words in the foreword are reminiscent of the words of British naturalist Richard Jefferies (1848–1887), written 1,000 years later. "Every blade of grass, each leaf, each separate floret and petal, is an inscription speaking of hope … My heart is fixed firm and stable in the belief that ultimately the sunshine and the summer, the flowers and the azure sky, shall become, as it were, interwoven into man's existence." This demonstrates the continuity of these ideas across time and different cultures.

GENJI MONOGATARI
The Tale of Genji

Another hugely influential piece of Japanese literature is the world-famous *Tale of Genji* (*Genji Monogatari*), written 1,000 years ago during the Heian period (794–1185), a time of peace and tranquility known as the golden age of the classical Japanese arts. It is arguably considered to be the world's first novel. Written by author and noblewoman Murasaki Shikibu at the height of the Kyōto Imperial court, it follows the life and loves of the disinherited son of the Emperor, Hikaru Genji, known as "the Shining Prince". Elegant natural imagery permeates every aspect of the text, whose achingly poignant chapter titles refer to natural phenomena, such as *matsukaze* (the wind in the pine trees) and *hana chiru satō* (the village of scattered flowers). Plants and celestial bodies like the moon became metaphoric symbols used to convey emotion throughout the book. The character's daily lives, celebrations, partings and reunions are tightly bound to the cycle of the four seasons. Genji communicates his assignations with poetry written on paper dyed with seasonal plants and garlanded with symbolic blossoming branches.

The aristocracy of the period were surrounded by seasonal imagery in infinite variations, notably *shiki-e* (four-season paintings) and *tokonoma* (art alcoves) filled with flower arrangements, calligraphy and incense. They also alluded to the seasons through their clothing. The noblewomen of this period wore the seasons in layer upon gossamer layer of coloured kimonos designed to subtly refer to the season (see Chapter 6). Almost every principal female character in the book is named after a flower and young girls are called *wakana* (young grasses or shoots).

Each flower dwelled in the palace of the Shining Prince, whose grand home, the Rokujou estate, was a palatial residence divided into four quadrants, one for each of the four seasons. The structure, connected by covered corridors, was designed so rooms opened directly onto each of the four seasonally themed gardens. Lady Murasaki (Wisteria), the book's heroine and Genji's great love, was installed in the spring quarter; Lady Hanachirusato (Falling Flowers) dwelled in the summer quarter; Lady Akikonomu, whose name means "loves autumn" (*aki*) was a former *saigu* (a princess who became a priestess of Ise shrine) and lived in the autumn quarter; and Lady Akashi, also known as the Lady of Winter due to her association with snow, resided in the winter quarter.

THE ANCIENT JAPANESE CALENDAR

Long before Japan adopted the Gregorian calendar in 1873, Japanese people relied upon a much older system, a lunar–solar calendar imported from China by way of Korea. It featured a complex system of 72 seasons, including the solstices and equinoxes. They factored in lunation, the period of time it takes for the moon to wax and wane over the course of a lunar month. This calendar was in use from the 6th century till the late 17th century when Japan's feudal government commissioned a new calendar from astronomer Shibukawa Shunkai (1639–1715), who created the Jokyo calendar, an adaptation of China's lunisolar almanac that was unique to Japan's topography and climate. Although Japan now primarily uses the Gregorian solar calendar, you can still find beautiful 72-season calendars in Japan's stationary shops.

Being born into a world of a mere four seasons, I was delighted and intrigued by the concept of ancient Japan's 72 seasons. According to the Japanese almanac, the year was broken down into *shiki*, the four seasons we're familiar with, then into 24 *nijushi sekki* or solar terms and finally into 72 *shichijuni ko* or micro seasons. Each lasts only five days, the equivalent of a modern working week. (You can find a complete list of these in the Resources section at the back of the book.) *Sekki* and *ko* are delicate web-like structures, like the Celtic wheel of the year. These frameworks help break down the year into a comforting, reliable rhythm. Each new *ko* reminds us of the micro-seasonal changes taking place in nature, gently grounding us in the present moment.

The Japanese almanac marks the beginning of each season, and at the heart of each season are the equinoxes and solstices. Together, these make up eight of the 24 solar terms. The remaining 16 are each named for natural phenomena.

How do these divisions sync with the progress of the seasons in your corner of the world?

SEASONAL MARKERS

Risshun – The Beginning of Spring 4 February	*Shunbun* – The Vernal or Spring Equinox 20 March
Rikka – The Beginning of Summer 5 May	*Geshi* – The Summer Solstice 21 June
Risshu – The Beginning of Autumn 8 August	*Shūbun* – The Autumnal Equinox 22 September
Rittō – The Beginning of Winter 7 November	*Tōji* – The Winter Solstice 22 December

SAIJIKI

The Book of the Seasons

Japanese almanacs began as poetic anthologies called *saijiki*, meaning "book of the seasons". They categorize almost all aspects of Japanese daily life within the framework of the seasons, becoming a kind of cultural encyclopedia invaluable to anyone who wishes to understand the relationship between nature and traditional Japanese cultural practices, events and all forms of Japanese art. *Saijiki* became popular from the Edo period (1603–1868) onward. Each season was broken down into six categories: the season, the sky and heavens, the Earth, humanity, observances (such as festivals) and flora and fauna.

The four seasons are fundamental to Japanese poetry, which has always been intimately linked to the natural world. The cycle of the four seasons is punctuated by natural phenomena such as the appearance of the first rainbow, the waxing and waning of the moon, the blooming of flowers, fruit ripening, the departure of geese and the return of swallows, as well as by annual festivals and religious rites. These all play out in the canon of Japanese prose. For almost 400 years, imparting *kisetsu* (seasonal feeling) has been an essential part of haiku, and many poems can be dated down to the month they were written in by the seasonal references included in the poem.

KIGO

Seasonal Words

The Japanese poetry year is broken down by season, and then each season is divided again into early, mid and late. Each stage of the season is alluded to using *kidai* (seasonal topics) and *kigo* (seasonal words). The set phrases form a seasonal vocabulary that refers to a specific season throughout Japanese art, poetry and literature. To speak the language of *kisetsukan*, you need to understand *kigo*.

Traditional Japanese poetry anthologies were organized by theme, the most popular being the four seasons. Over time, a poetic convention developed using terminology made up of thousands of *kigo* (seasonal words) and *kidai* (seasonal topics). *Haijin* (haiku poets) used these essential tools to refer to specific seasons, which became a defining feature of haiku poetry.

Each *kigo* is a Japanese word or phrase associated with a particular season. For example, the recurring motif of *sakura* combined with an *uguisu* (Japanese bush warbler) is an established springtime image. This small dust-coloured bird, also known as the Japanese nightingale, is famous for its mating song, which can often be heard from high up in the cherry trees in early spring, earning it the poetic name *harutsugedori* (spring-announcing bird). There are over 70 seasonal words for cherry blossoms alone and I've included a few of my favourite *kigo* in each chapter.

THE SEASONS OF
JAPANESE POETRY

Spring (Haru)	Summer (Natsu)
Early Spring: 4 February–5 March	Early Summer: 6 May–5 June
Mid-Spring: 6 March–4 April	Mid-Summer: 6 June–6 July
Late Spring: 5 April–5 May	Late Summer: 7 July–7 August

Autumn (Aki)	Winter (Fuyu)
Early Autumn: 8 August–7 September	Early Winter: 7 November–6 December
Mid-Autumn: 8 September–7 October	Mid-Winter: 7 December–4 January
Late Autumn: 8 October–6 November	Late Winter: 5 January–3 February

GOSEKKU
The Five Sacred Festivals

Plants also played an essential ritual role as symbolic talismans in *nenju gyoji* (annual observances). The five plants linked to the *Gosekku* (the Five Sacred Festivals) were initially used as protective charms to ward against malevolent spirits or were consumed for their fabled life-extending properties. Part of these celebrations involved praying for good health and longevity, and a banquet featuring local seasonal foods believed to be full of vital life force. These seasonal celebrations on the auspicious double-odd days of the month have continued to the present day. Artist Kitagawa Utamaro (1754–1806) famously depicted them in his woodblock print series *Yukun Gosekku* (Courtesans of the Five Festivals). Much like Christmas, New Year and Easter in the western world, they are critical points in defining the seasonal year, centred around plants, flowers and trees.

Jinjitsu no Sekku
7 January
Talisman: *Nanakusa* (the seven spring grasses or herbs)
A part of Japan's extended New Year's celebrations when people would go out into the fields to gather seven spring herbs to make a rejuvenating rice porridge called *nanakusa*, which harnessed the power of the spring greens (see Chapter 11).

Joshi no Sekku
3 March
Talisman: *Momo* (peach)
Also known as *Momo no Sekku* (the Peach Festival) or *Hinamatsuri* (the Dolls' Festival). Peaches have an ancient connection to everlasting life, and branches of blossoming peach trees are used as decorations for this spring festival (see Chapter 2).

Tango no Sekku
5 May
Talisman: *Shōbu* (sweet flag iris) and *yomogi* (mugwort)
Known as Children's Day or the Boys' Festival. The aromatic leaves of the *shōbu* are evergreen and represent longevity and everlasting youth. During the festival people bathe with them because their scent is said to guard against misfortune (see Chapter 5).

Shichiseki no Sekku

❋⟶ 7 July ⟶❋

Talisman: *Kaji* (a type of mulberry)

The celebration of a tale of star-crossed lovers is known as *Tanabata* or the Star Festival. The word *kaji* also means "rudder" or "oar", which refers to the oars the lovers, Princess Orihime, the heavenly weaver, and Hikoboshi, the cow herder, used to cross the River of Heaven (see Chapter 5).

Chōyō no Sekku

❋⟶ 9 September ⟶❋

Talisman: *Kiku* (chrysanthemum)

The Chrysanthemum Festival. Chrysanthemums spread to Japan from China, and their longevity mythology was imported with them. They also represent Japan's Imperial family and the season of autumn (see Chapter 8).

YAMA

Mountain

The many faces of Mt Fuji are revealed with the changing seasons, whether garlanded by cherry blossoms, enrobed by mist and a tapestry of inky blue forests or swaddled in snow, they continue to inspire Japan's artists, such as textile artist Itchiku Kubota (see Chapter 6).

Mountain worship is widespread throughout the world's religions, and those in Japan are no exception. Japan is home to several sacred mountains, the most famous being the internationally recognized Mt Fuji, home to Konohana Sakura Hime, the Cherry Tree Blossom Princess (see Chapter 2). Mountains and rivers are vital features of Japan's typographical and mythological landscapes. They are both the sacred homes of gods and the personification of them.

Mountain pilgrimages are an essential part of Buddhism, and almost every mountain in Japan has its own shrine at the foot and summit to the deity who dwells within it. The word for a mountain pass in Japanese is *tōge*, meaning "to offer". Every pilgrim travelling through the pass would make an offering to the spirit of the mountain for a safe pilgrimage. Mountains are also objects of worship for Japan's mountain-dwelling priests or *yamabushi*, who practise *Shugendō*, a blend of shamanism, Taoism, Confucianism and Buddhism. As part of their ascetic training, *yamabushi* undergo a purification ritual called *takigyô* (waterfall meditation), reciting sutras or prayers while standing directly beneath the frigid waters of a flowing waterfall.

The fabled mountain range of Takamagahara or the Plain of High Heaven is the Shintō home of the gods. The Golden Mountain of Buddhism, called Mt Meru or Shumisen in Japanese, is the seat of Buddhist Law and a representation of the universe. Sacred mountains and their imposing forms represent stability, power and eternity. They are a bridge that links Heaven and Earth. The closer to the summit you travel, the further you are from the human world and the closer you are to the Divine.

Yama no Hi
Mountain Day
11 August

Yama no Hi or Mountain Day is one of Japan's more modern national holidays created by the Alpine Association. It celebrates Japan's awe-inspiring mountains, a fitting holiday for a nation whose land is 70 per cent mountainous. People enjoy this holiday by climbing, hiking and appreciating Japan's beautiful mountain scenery.

❀ SEEK OUT BEAUTY ❀ IN EVERY SEASON

Nature is a constant source of inspiration. Every season brings with it new opportunities for beauty, fuelling our spirit and creativity. Author Iwao Matsuhara wrote that one who does not appreciate the beauty in nature, could not be trusted for they surely had a "heart of a stone". He believed that humanity must learn to live and die as beautifully as the flowers do, "so beautiful in their fall as well as their bloom".

Seek out the threads of *kisetsukan* in your own life, gently tug on them and see where they lead. As the writer Elizabeth Gilbert says, the trick is to follow your curiosity. What did you see out of the corner of your eye? Pause and stop for a moment. What has piqued your interest? Ask yourself: is there something here that speaks to me?

- Look for moments of beauty in the everyday – in overgrown gardens, rusting hinges, peeling paint chips and petals in the gutter.

- Experiment with the concept of *mitate* ("to see anew") and look at utilitarian objects with new eyes and a fresh perspective (see Chapter 9).

- Try isolating individual elements, such as one kind of fruit, vegetable or flower. Take time to observe them in detail, so that their uniquely beautiful forms and properties can be better understood and appreciated (see Chapter 3).

- Enjoy moments of anticipation – before the sun rises, the bud opens or the hazy moon is clearly visible in the night sky.

- Recognize the value in beauty obscured, such as an incomplete or obstructed view, hidden by enchanting swirls of mist, fog or diaphanous clouds (see Chapter 8).

- Find beauty not just in the object itself, but in the play of light and dark around it. The long shadows it casts in the sunshine and how it glows illuminated by candlelight.

- If in doubt return to nature. Try going on a nature walk. You will always find something to delight you. If it's the middle of darkest winter or you live in a sprawling city, try an indoor nature walk through your favourite museum or art gallery.

HANAMI

The Ritual of Flower Viewing

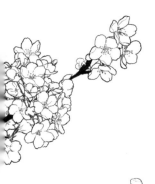

The haze of spring
steaming over
the mountain
cherry blossoms:
I am never sated
of the sight
nor am I of you.

KI NO TOMONORI
TRANSLATED BY DR THOMAS MCAULEY
FROM BOOK FOURTEEN OF
THE *KOKIN WAKASHŪ*

The classical name for March in Japanese is *yayoi*, meaning "new life", and it's often called the month of growth. Spring in Japan is sometimes called the season of farewells and new beginnings because in April, as the trees blossom, the new school year begins for Japanese children. This season is filled with flowers and is synonymous with one of Japan's favourite pastimes, *hanami*, or flower viewing. The most famous flowers of the season are *sakura* or cherry blossoms, the iconic symbol of Japan. The whole country celebrates the arrival of these blooms with daytime picnics and sake-fuelled parties, which continue late into the night.

At its heart, *hanami* is a celebration of spring. People gather together with friends and loved ones to revel in the joy of the long-awaited blossoms. There is an air of anticipation and hope throughout this season. The unfurling spring buds bring with them feelings of hopefulness and a sense of potential for the year ahead. Flowering trees are the artists of spring in Japan. It begins in a pink haze and ends in a flush of neon green as fresh new leaves replace the falling petals that carpet the ground in a brocade of pastels, turning the rivers pink.

THE ROOTS OF *HANAMI*:
A CELEBRATION OF SPRING

Hana means "flower", and *hanami* means "flower viewing", specifically the ritual of enjoying the ephemeral beauty of the cherry blossoms. Long before *hanami* was synonymous with *sakura*, the practice of flower viewing referred to admiring the earliest blooming trees of the year, the *ume* or flowering plum. This tradition began in China and made its way to Japan during the Nara period (710–794). China has venerated the plum blossom (*meihua* or *mei* in Chinese) for centuries. The pastime of reciting poetry and enjoying rice wine under the blossoms originated there. However, it was during the Heian period, when the Japanese capital city moved from Nara to Kyōto (794–1185), that the native cherry blossoms took centre stage. From that point on, *hanami* referred expressly to admiring the cherry blossoms.

Japan's love affair with *sakura* is an ancient one. For centuries *hanami* has been Japan's favourite spring pastime. Each month brings with it numerous annual traditions and rites to observe, but spring is the most cherished of all seasons. *Hanami* is one of the Japanese calendar's most highly anticipated seasonal events because it offers an unparalleled aesthetic experience. Walking through the streets of Kyōto as petals swirl around you, caught on a breeze, is like walking through a dream.

Although the term *hanami* now refers to *sakura* in Japan, globally there are so many beautiful plants and blossoming trees to enjoy in the spring that you can connect with this 1,000-year-old tradition at home by appreciating the beauty of the flowering trees in your own neighbourhood. In England, I love to see the vibrant pinks of blossoming apple trees, the trails of yellow laburnum and the delicate white mist of hawthorn trees. Australia is blessed with royal purple jacarandas, and the almost fluorescent crape myrtle graces the southern United States. Inspired by his collection of Japanese woodblock prints, the artist Vincent van Gogh loved to paint flowering trees, especially the almond blossoms native to his home in the South of France, where they herald the Mediterranean spring.

THE *SAKURA ZENSEN*

The Cherry Blossom Forecast

Each spring, the Japanese Meteorological Corporation (JMC) releases the annual cherry blossom forecast, known as the *sakura zensen*. The JMC uses the iconic *somei yoshino* cherry blossom variety as its guide, which blooms from late March to mid-April. This forecast carefully monitors the cherry blossom front as it moves up the country, beginning in Okinawa and ending in Hokkaido, slowly turning Japan into a pastel-pink wonderland. People all over the country use this forecast to plan their *hanami* parties.

The *somei yoshino* cherry rose in popularity due to its fast-growing nature. These trees are grown from cuttings or grafts from a parent tree, so they all bloom simultaneously because of their identical DNA. Tens of thousands of them were planted all over mainland Japan after the Meji period (1868–1912) and, whenever new cherry trees are planted in public spaces in Japan, they are almost always of the *somei yoshino* variety. When the city of Tōkyō sent 3,000 cherry trees to Washington, DC, in 1912 as a sign of friendship, they gifted twelve different varieties, two-thirds of which were *somei yoshino*. In 1915, President Taft (1857–1930) reciprocated by sending a gift of flowering dogwood trees to Japan. This cultural exchange led to the birth of Washington DC's famous National Cherry Blossom Festival in 1935.

KYOKUSUI NO EN
The Meandering Stream Banquet

At some of the earliest and most lavish *hanami* parties held by the Imperial court, courtiers would gather by a winding stream to celebrate the arrival of spring by writing poetry and drinking sake. As their sake cup floated downstream toward them, the aristocrats would play a game involving composing a brief poem called a *tanka*, the precursor to haiku. The aim was to finish the composition before the cup reached you. This noble pastime is recreated each April at Kamigamo Shrine in Kyōto.

Of course, you don't have to be in Kyōto to enjoy this poetic activity. I love the idea of spending time sitting by a flowing river or garden brook and composing a poem to celebrate spring. To enjoy this tradition for yourself, follow these simple steps.

STEP 1. Leave your devices at home. (This is just a suggestion, of course, but if you do bring them with you put them on silent so you can focus.)

STEP 2. Take your favourite notebook on a walk to a local river or stream. Choose a spot where you can see and hear the water flowing.

STEP 3. Meditate on the theme of spring. What images come to mind? Consider the themes of this chapter – birth, growth, renewal, hope and new beginnings – to help get you started.

STEP 4. Compose your poem. Begin by letting your stream of consciousness flow freely and write down whatever comes to mind. Then look over your notes, choose a word or phrase that speaks to you and develop it further.

If you want to, you can follow the rules of haiku and use the 5–7–5 syllable structure, but most importantly allow the words to flow.

STAGES OF BLOOMING

There are some beautiful Japanese words to describe each stage of development that cherry blossoms go through until they reach full bloom. Most cherry trees bloom long before their leaves appear. So, in early spring, the first thing you'll see is tiny buds forming on their bare branches. These gradually swell and open to reveal clusters of tightly closed flowers, indicating that *sakura* season is not far away.

Tsubomi – At the beginning of the flowering cycle when the cherry trees have started budding but have yet to bloom.

Kaika – The next stage is unfurling buds.

Sakihajime – The flowers have started to bloom.

Mankai –The third stage describes cherry trees that are almost at, or have just reached, full bloom.

Migoro – This is the second-to-last stage, meaning it's the best time to see the flowers; they have reached their peak and are at their most beautiful.

Chirihajime – The final stage of the season, when the petals start to fall from the trees, turning stone paths, rivers and pavements pink.

Hazakura – The cycle begins again; the trees begin to turn a vivid green with the arrival of fresh new leaves.

The colours bloom
And scatter:
In this world
Who lasts forever?

ANONYMOUS[1]

MONO NO AWARE

Sensitivity to the Impermanence of All Things

Every year I patiently await the blooming of the local cherry blossoms and take great pleasure in experiencing as many *sakura*-filled moments as possible. The duality of *sakura* season is that although we ardently await its return each year, the cherry blossoms only flower for a brief period – their peak bloom lasts approximately two weeks. Of course, it's their delicate, transient beauty that makes them so special.

Impermanence is a universal truth, that was revealed to Japan with Buddhism centuries ago. There are several Japanese words and phrases that convey the fleeting nature of existence, which according

---

[1]   Excerpt from the Iroha Poem, attributed to the Heian-era Buddhist priest and scholar Kūkai (774–835).

to journalist and political theorist Nakae Chomin (1847–1901) "never began nor ends; it is eternally abundant and infinite."

One of these terms is *mono no aware*, which describes a sensitivity to the transient, impermanent nature of all things. *Mono* means literally "thing" or "things", and *aware* means "sentiment" or "feeling". An appreciation for the ephemeral nature of life is even more poetic when it is combined with a sense of sadness, which acknowledges and accepts that everything ends. Like autumnal falling leaves, the brief but glorious spectacle of the *sakura* in bloom also evokes *mono no aware*.

While we cherish the precious memories made during *sakura* season, we are also aware of their inherent fleeting nature. They act as a kind of *memento mori*, a gentle reminder that all things must inevitably come to an end, giving us pause to contemplate the cycles of nature, reflecting on the rhythms of birth, death and rebirth. After all, we are as fleeting as the morning dew, vanishing like snowflakes and scattering our petals like spent flowers.

THE FLOWER OF THE SOUL

The worldview of *Mujōkan*, from *mujō* ("impermanent") and *kan*, ("view"), is elegantly explained through the transitions of nature, such as a flowing river, the waning moon and leaves fluttering to the ground each autumn. There is a sense of peace that comes with surrendering to the flow of seasonal time, "the living rhymn of nature", as philosopher Isobe Tadamasa (1909–1995) described it.

In his short story, *Jojoka (Lyric Poem)* Yasunari Kawabata (1899–1972) wrote "I find myself and you in the fauna and flora." And after the loss of his great love, the book's protagonist writes, "you and I will be become flowers of the rose, plum and oleander" as he alludes to how he and his lover will endure as eternal flowers.

And Buddhist philosopher Kaneko Daiei (1881–1976) wrote, "the flower petal falls, but the flower remains" because he believed that although we may perish, our souls live on. Here the *tamashii* or soul is represented as an everlasting flower. Death is not the end but a return to the beginning, to the vast universe from where we came.

SANDAIZAKURA

The Three Great Cherry Trees

Japan is home to a trio of exceptional cherry trees called the Sandaizakura, Japan's three Great Cherry Trees. They comprise the Jindai Zakura, the Neodani Usuzumizakura and the Miharu Takizakura. Each one of these venerable ladies is over 1,000 years old.

The oldest of the three is the Jindai Zakura (the Cherry Blossom from the Age of the Gods), believed to be over 2,000 years old. It grows in the grounds of the Otsuyama Jisso Temple near Hokuto in the Yamanashi Prefecture.

The Usuzumizakura, which stands in Usuzumi Park in the city of Motosu, Gifu Prefecture, was planted by Japan's twenty-sixth Emperor, Keitai, over 1,500 years ago. The name Usuzumi means "light black ink". As this unique *sakura* blooms, its petals transform from pale pink buds into white flowers, but as the tree sheds its blossoms' petals they turn grey.

In the Japanese town of Miharu, Fukushima Prefecture, there are approximately 2,000 *Shidarezakura* or "weeping cherry trees", the most famous of which is the Takizakura. This weeping cherry is estimated to be over 1,000 years old. Takizakura means "waterfall cherry" – the tree was given its name because it resembles a waterfall of blossoms when it's in full bloom. In 1922 the venerable, millennium-old Takizakura became the first cherry tree to be designated as a national monument.

HARU MATSURI

Spring Festivals

Setsubun – The End of Winter
~ 3 February ~

Now that the *ume* or plum blossoms are in bloom, it's time for *Setsubun*, which is one of my favourite Japanese celebrations because it heralds the arrival of spring. *Setsubun* is an annual festival celebrated on the last day of winter before the official beginning of spring in Japan on the fourth of February. According to the old Japanese traditional lunar calendar, it signified the start of the New Year.

Setsubun includes a ritual called *mamemaki*, the scattering of roasted soybeans, which are thrown out of your front door or at someone dressed in an *oni* (demon) mask while shouting, "*Oni wa soto! Fuku wa uchi!*" ("Demons out! Luck in!") This tradition is intended to cleanse away any misfortune or darkness lingering on from the past year and drive away evil spirits for the year to come.

Hinamatsuri – The Dolls' Festival
~ 3 March ~

On 3 March, Japan celebrates Girls' Day, also known as the Dolls' Festival or *Hinamatsuri*. This festival is dedicated to celebrating the growth, happiness and prosperity of young girls in Japan.

From the end of February until 3 March, shops display *tsurushi kazari*, auspicious hanging decorations made from scraps of recycled kimono, and *Hina Ningyō*, dolls dressed in the opulent formal attire of the Heian period (794–1185) on tiered platforms. These elegantly dressed dolls represent members of the Japanese Imperial court, including the Emperor, Empress and their attendants. The Imperial couple is known as Dairibina. The Empress is immediately identifiable by her multiple layers of colourful kimono, called *jūnihitoe*, meaning "twelve layers". This was the formal style of dress worn by the noble women of the Heian period.

The custom of putting *Hina* dolls out on display began in the early 1600s. They were believed to be good luck charms, capable of warding off evil spirits. The dolls are always displayed hierarchically, with the Emperor and Empress at the top and their attendants below. The number of dolls and their size can vary from home to home, but the Imperial couple is a common sight. Elaborate sets of *Hina* dolls are family heirlooms, often passed down from generation to generation.

Haru no Higan – Vernal Equinox Week
18–24 March

During our lives on Earth, we inhabit this "shore". *Higan* is the Japanese term for the other distant shore that Buddhists seek to one day reach – enlightenment or nirvana – and the *Higan* festival is an important holiday for Buddhists throughout Japan. People use this time to pay tribute to the spirits of loved ones. There are two *Higan* seasons in Japan, which correspond to the dates of the spring and autumn equinoxes. So, the traditions and celebrations held during this time mirror each other.

During the week-long celebration people visit their ancestors' graves, make offerings at temples and shrines and enjoy *botan* (peony) *mochi,* a seasonal sweet made from balls of plain *mochi* dough, formed from pounded *mochiko* (glutinous rice) flour. Often called Japanese rice cakes, *mochi* have a delightful soft, chewy exterior and their centres are often filled with sweet ingredients, such as bean paste. *Botan mochi* are covered in red bean paste to celebrate the beginning of *botan* season. This delicacy is served again later in the year to celebrate *Shūbun*, the autumn equinox. Then its name changes and it is called *ohagi mochi,* honouring one of Japan's most beloved autumnal flowers – the bush clover.

Sakura no Hi – *Sakura* Day
27 March

Can you imagine having a designated holiday to celebrate a flower? What a wonderful thing. In Japan, 27 March is *Sakura no Hi* (Cherry Blossom Day). This date was chosen by the Nihon Sakura no Kai (the Japanese Cherry Blossom Association). They aim to protect Japan's cherry trees and raise awareness of the cultural significance of *sakura*. *Hanami* is now a global phenomenon. So, you can celebrate Cherry Blossom Day no matter where you are and connect to the beauty and hopeful anticipation behind this season.

Hanamatsuri – The Flower Festival
8 April

On 8 April Japan celebrates the Buddha's Birthday.[2] According to tradition he was born in a field of flowers, so this celebration is called *Hanamatsuri*, a "festival of flowers" and streets, shops and Buddhist temples are all adorned with spring flowers in Buddha's honour. The festival is also known as *Kanbutsue*, meaning "Buddha Bathing Festival". The celebrations include erecting *hanamido* and making offerings of *amacha*. *Hanamido* are small temple pavilions erected outside the main hall of a Buddhist temple and decorated with seasonal flowers. They house a statue of the Buddha, which sits in a shallow bowl surrounded by floral offerings. The liquid inside the bowl is *amacha*, a naturally sweet tisane made from the leaves of the *ajisai* or hydrangea, which is poured over the Buddha, emulating sweet rainfall.

Midori no Hi – Greenery Day
4 May

Greenery Day is a national holiday that takes place every May in the middle of Golden Week when several Japanese national holidays occur all in one week. *Midori no Hi* is dedicated to honouring nature and giving thanks for its many gifts. The seeds of Greenery Day were sown by the Showa period (1926–1989) Emperor Hirohito, who was known for his great love of nature and excellent knowledge of plants. People habitually visit their favourite botanical gardens or plant trees on this bank holiday in an annual celebration of nature.

---

[2] Vesak is the birthday of Shakyamuni, the historical Buddha. It is traditionally celebrated on the eighth day of the fourth month, according to the lunar calendar. Buddhists around the world usually mark it in May or June. However, since the Japanese adopted the Gregorian calendar, they have celebrated the Buddha's birthday on 8 April, coinciding with sakura season.

Hold Your Own Greenery Day

This is a lovely event you can participate in no matter where you might be. Here are just a few ideas to help get your started. Start your own Greenery Day rituals and please feel free to share them with me (for contact details, see page 84).

- Visit a Japanese garden.

- Go for a walk in the park with a friend.

- Buy some seasonal fresh cut flowers.

- Visit a plant nursery and buy a houseplant for your home or something new for your garden.

- Get your hands dirty, plant something and enjoy watching it grow.

- Prepare a nutritious seasonal salad and garnish it with edible flowers.

- Drink a bowl of matcha or a cup of Japanese green tea.

THE SMALL SEASONS OF SPRING

Risshun – Sekki No.1
The Birth of Spring
⋇ ⁓ *4 February–18 February* ⁓ ⋇

After *Setsubun* comes *Risshun*, marking the official beginning of spring in Japan, according to the ancient lunisolar calendar. *Risshun* means "becoming spring". It is the first of the 24 solar terms or *sekki* that break up the year in traditional East Asian calendars. This way of dividing the year originated in China, spread to Japan in the 6th century and was used until the country adopted the Gregorian calendar in 1873. *Risshun* starts on 4 February and lasts until the next small season, *Usui* (rainwater), begins (19 February, see below). Both *Setsubun* and *Risshun* are also part of *Haru Matsuri* — the Spring Festival.

    Risshun takes place just a couple of days after Imbolc, the pagan holiday that according to Celtic tradition marks the start of spring. The arrival of *Risshun* means that the worst of the winter is over, and my beloved *sakura* season is not far away. You may already be able to spot some early blooming cherry blossoms in your area. These always lift my spirits and remind me just how close we are to the most beautiful time of the year.

Usui – Sekki No.2
Snows Melt
⋇ ⁓ *19 February–5 March* ⁓ ⋇

Usui means "rainwater", and at this time of the year around 19 or 20 February, winter's snows begin to slowly thaw and melt away. As it becomes warmer, these snow drifts give way to spring rains, although in the northernmost parts of Japan the snow remains on the ground. Around this time exquisite *hanami*-themed sweets begin to appear in the windows of Japan's *wagashi* shops, in anticipation of the upcoming cherry blossom season.

Keichitsu – *Sekki* No.3
Insects Awaken
6–20 March

Around 5 or 6 March, insects and other small creatures such as frogs awaken from their winter slumber and the first spring herbs begin to sprout. This time of year is also sometimes called *kinomedoki*, (trees budding). Japanese peach trees bloom around this time.

Shunbun – *Sekki* No.4
The Spring Equinox
21 March–4 April

Shunbun no Hi is the Japanese celebration of the spring equinox, the moment when the sun is positioned directly above the centre of the equator. As a result, the hours of light and dark are perfectly balanced and equal. At this time of the year, the veil between our world and the spirit world is said to be at its thinnest. In Japan, this is celebrated on 20 or 21 March. This national holiday takes place in the middle of a seven-day Buddhist celebration called *Haru no Higan*, the vernal equinox week (see page 49).

Seimei – *Sekki* No.5
Clear and Bright
5–19 April

By this time flowering trees such as the cherry, dogwood and magnolias have all begun to bloom. The skies are clear and full of fragrant flowers and birdsong. According to the *Koyomi Binran* (*Handbook of the Japanese Calendar*), an almanac from 1787, the name for this season is an abbreviation of *seijo meiketsu*, an ancient idiom meaning everything is clean, bright and lively.

Kokuu – Sekki No.6
Grain Rains
⫸⁓ *20 April–4 May* ⁓⫷

Kokuu takes place around 20 or 21 April. This is late spring in Japan and characterized by *harusame* or gentle spring rains, which are essential for the growth of grains and cereals such as rice. Soon Japanese farmers will flood their rice paddies and plant their precious seedlings.

SAKURA KIGO

Seasonal Words for *Sakura* Season

Traditional Japanese poetry anthologies were organized by theme, the most popular being the four seasons. Over time a unique poetic vocabulary developed made up of *kigo* (seasonal words) and *kidai* (seasonal topics). These essential tools were used by haiku poets to allude to specific seasons, and this became a defining feature of haiku poetry. *Kigo* are divided into six categories: the season; the sky and heavens; the Earth; humanity; observances (such as festivals); and flora and fauna.

Each *kigo* is a Japanese word or phrase associated with a certain season. For example, the recurring motif of *sakura* in combination with an *uguisu* (Japanese bush warbler) is an iconic image of springtime. This small dust-coloured bird, known as the Japanese nightingale, is famous for its mating song, which can often be heard from its perch high up in the cherry trees in early spring, earning it the poetic name *harutsugedori* (spring-announcing bird). There are over 70 seasonal words for cherry blossoms in Japanese. These are just a few of my favourites.

Hatsuzakura – *hatsu* means "first", so these are the very first *sakura* to bloom each year, sometimes called early-blooming *sakura*, meaning cherry blossom.

Hanagasumi – literally meaning "a flower haze" or "mist", when numerous cherry trees are in full bloom all at once; it creates a cherry blossom haze, like clouds or mists of flowers.

Hanafubuki – *fubuki* means "snowstorm" and *hana* means "flower", a veritable flurry of petals, a phenomenon that only occurs at the end of cherry blossom season. As the trees shed their delicate blooms the breeze carries them away, creating a snowstorm of petals that flutter to the ground like snow, carpeting the earth in flowers.

Yozakura – cherry blossoms viewed at night, often illuminated by lanterns.

Hazakura – meaning "cherry tree leaves". Once the flowers have faded and *hanami* season is over, the cherry trees are full of newly sprouted leaves.

Ame no sakura – *ame* means "rain"; this is the poetic sight of gentle spring raindrops falling on cherry blossoms.

Yukizakura – the sight of cherry blossoms in bloom combined with freshly fallen snow. This rare and poetic sight is a combination of the word *yuki*, meaning "snow", and *sakura*, meaning "cherry blossom". This phenomenon often occurs in Nagano Prefecture.

KONOHANA SAKUYA HIME

The Cherry Blossom Princess

The *Kojiki*, written in the 6th century, is Japan's earliest mythological and semi-historical record. It includes the story of a mythical goddess Konohana Sakuya Hime, the Cherry blossom Princess, the spirit of *sakura* and guardian of Mt Fuji. She is also the youngest daughter of the mountain god Oyamatsumi.

According to legend, when Ninigi no Mikoto, the celestial grandson of the Sun Goddess Amaterasu Ōmikami, was sent down to govern Earth, he descended to the foot of Mt Takachio. It was there he saw Konohana Sakuya Hime walking along the seashore. Overwhelmed by her beauty, he instantly fell in love with her and declared his intention to marry her. So, Ninigi sent word to her father, Oyamatsumi. In return, he sent both his daughters, Sakura Hime and her elder sister Iwanaga Hime, the Eternal Rock Princess. The mountain god had hoped that by marrying both sisters, the prince's life would flourish like the cherry blossoms and he would live a life as eternal as the rocks.

However, Ninigi only wished to marry Sakura Hime. So, he sent Princess Iwanaga back to her father and did not heed his warnings that his union with Sakura Hime would shorten his life. Soon after their marriage, he became mortal. According to legend, the mortal Ninigi no Mikoto eventually became great-grandfather to Emperor Jimmu, the first Emperor of Japan. It is said that this is why the lives of Japan's Emperors – and indeed all humanity – are brief and then fall and scatter like cherry blossoms.

SPRING RECIPE
Preserved Cherry Blossoms
Sakura Shiozuke

Food is one of the main ways we can connect to the seasons. Japanese cooking uses several parts of the beloved cherry tree, not just its prized blossoms. The young green leaves are pickled and powdered to use in spring sweets, and its much-admired bark is made into elegant tea caddies.

Preserved cherry blossoms are one of the key seasonal ingredients in Japanese spring dishes and the essential element you'll need to create your own *hanami* at home. I make them every year and use them to make my *sakura* shortbread, madeleines and *inari* sushi. They are very versatile and can be used in both savoury and sweet recipes. Each April, I carefully harvest the flowers just before they reach full bloom and then pickle them using plum vinegar and salt. The preferred variety for making pickled cherry blossoms is *yaezakura*. These later-blooming flowers are multi-layered, with large, perfectly pink petals.

Usually, when you incorporate edible flowers into your cooking or baking, you'll be working with dried flowers or petals. However, because Japanese cherry blossoms are pickled in salt, so you'll need to soak them for 15 minutes to remove most of the salt before you can add them to your dishes. If you attend a Japanese wedding, you might be offered *sakurayu* – cherry blossom tea. This tisane is made from salt-pickled cherry blossoms steeped in hot water and is often served on festive occasions.

Ingredients

You only need three ingredients to make salted cherry blossoms.

* **One cup or handful of cherry blossoms, enough to loosely fill a jam jar** (be careful not to crush them or pack them in too tightly).

* **2 tsp salt (you can use fine table salt or a flakier variety – the choice is yours.** This is an approximate measurement, so adjust it based on the quantity of flowers you are using and keep adding it till they are completely covered).

* **2 tsp *Ume Su*** – an *ume* and *shiso* vinegar (optional, but the red *shiso* gives the vinegar a wonderful deep fuchsia colour that helps maintain the delicate pink of the blossoms).

Method

Gather your cherry blossoms. Look for clusters of blossoms that have not yet fully opened, as these are ideal for pickling. Its best to pick your flowers first thing in the morning, if possible. If you are not lucky enough to have a cherry tree in your garden, try to forage your flowers away from main roads. When foraging for any plant or flower, remember the honourable harvest.[3] Ask for permission, take only what you need, use whatever you take and give thanks.

Carefully wash the cherry blossoms and gently pat them dry.

Sprinkle some salt in the base of a clean and sterilized jar.
Place some cherry blossoms in the jar, sprinkle with another layer of salt and continue to layer them until all the flowers are coated with salt. Then you can season them using *ume* and *shiso* vinegar, which will aid the pickling process and help them retain their pink colour.

Make sure all the blossoms are covered with salt and vinegar, then place a weight over them – I use a sterilized pebble. Seal the jar and keep it in the fridge for three days.

After three days, take the blossoms out of the jar and place them on a sheet of baking parchment or in a flat tray to air dry, which takes approximately 1–2 days.

Once they are dry on both sides, they're ready to store. Place the salted petals in a jar and layer them with salt. Then you can keep them in the fridge until you're ready to use them.

---

[3] You can learn more about this important concept in Robin Wall Kimmerer's fantastic book *Braiding Sweetgrass*.

IPPON ZAKURA

Solo *Hanami*

All you really need to celebrate *hanami* is yourself and *ippon zakura,* a single cherry tree. There are certain trees in my neighbourhood that I like to visit each spring. I pack my tea things into a basket, fold up a picnic blanket and head out to check on them. After greeting my old friends and taking pictures of the blossoms, I spend some time beneath the trees. I whisk a bowl of tea and sit quietly, enjoying their company and looking up at the canopy above me, watching the light filter through their rosy lens. Sometimes a gust of wind will catch the flowers at just the right angle, sending a shower of petals down on me, landing in my tea and in my hair. It's these solo encounters with the *sakura* that are so precious. I look forward to them every year. You can do this in London, Paris or Tōkyō. Thanks to the enduring popularity of *sakura*, there are now cherry trees all over Europe, the USA and East Asia that you can make a pilgrimage to and experience your own cherry blossom moment.

JAPANESE MICRO SEASON NO.11

SAKURA HAJIMETE SAKU

The First Cherry Blossoms Bloom
26–30 March

According to the classical Japanese calendar, the year is divided into 72 *ko* or micro seasons, each lasting only five days. This traditional Japanese calendar marks the passing of the seasons by observing the changes that occur in the natural world throughout the year. For example, the eleventh of the Japanese micro seasons is *sakura hajimete saku*, meaning "the first cherry blossoms bloom". I love the concept of a calendar based on observing the micro-changes that take place in nature against the wider backdrop of the changing seasons. Don't you?

VARIETIES OF CHERRY BLOSSOM

There are more than 600 varieties of wild cherry trees and *satō zakura*, domesticated garden cherry trees, in Japan, with blooms varying from bone white to vivid scarlet. (There are even rare lime-green and canary-yellow varieties.) These are just some of the more common kinds you might encounter:

1. ***Somei Yoshino* – Japan's most prolific sakura (*Prunus yedoensis*)**
    The *somei yoshino* is Japan's most common variety of cherry tree, used to predict the *sakura zensen*, Japan's annual cherry blossom forecast. It has almost pure-white flowers with a hint of pink at the centre.

2. ***Yaezakura* – Multi-layered cherry blossoms (such as *Prunus serrulata sekiyama*)**
    These are my favourite kind of *sakura*. *Yaezakura*, meaning "multi-layered cherry blossom", is an umbrella term for all *sakura* with more than five petals. Some types can have up to 200 petals. This includes exquisite late-blooming varieties such as the *kanzan* (*Prunus serrulata sekiyama*). These fluffy pink beauties are also the kind that is pickled and preserved for tea (see page 57) and used in a variety of Japanese spring dishes.

3. ***Yamazakura* – Mountain or Hill Cherry (*Prunus serrulata spontanea*)**
    These are the wild and untamed ancestors of the domesticated Japanese cherry tree. They grow wild in forests and on the Japanese mountainside.

4. ***Tai Haku* – The Great White Cherry (*Prunus serrulata taihaku*)**
    This variety is renowned for its large snowy-white flowers and young copper-coloured leaves.[4] I have a particular fondness for

---

[4]   This variety had become extinct in Japan until Englishman Collingwood "Cherry" Ingram (1880–1981) came across one growing in an English garden in Sussex. After several attempts, he managed to help it get re-established in Japan in c.1932.

this cherry tree because once the flowers reach *mankai* or full bloom, the fluffy white clouds of blossom will be full of bees.

5. ***Shidarezakura* – Weeping Cherry Tree *(Prunus shidarezakura)***
   Like weeping willow trees, these weeping cherry trees have long, trailing branches that cascade towards the ground creating a waterfall effect.

6. ***Shikizakura* – Four Season Sakura**
   (Prunus subhirtella autumnalis)
   This is a rare variety of cherry tree that flowers in the spring and then again in the autumn, just as the Japanese maples turn red. In 2019, I made the pilgrimage to Obara, a small town in Nagoya where you can see 10,000 of these trees bloom each November.

UTAMAKURA

Poetic Places

Utamakura means "poetic places". This beautiful Japanese literary convention originated from a classical form of Japanese poetry called *waka*. The poetic places are a combination of sacred sites and historic locations and they became a kind of shorthand used by Japanese poets to represent the seasons and evoke certain emotions. The concept spread throughout traditional Japanese art forms and can be seen in both literature and fine art, which is replete with recurring seasonal motifs.

In the land of cherry blossoms, it's no surprise that *sakura* are the subject of thousands of poems and works of art throughout Japanese history. The *Kokinshū* (*Collection of Ancient and Modern Poems*), Japan's first Imperial collection of *waka* (classical poetry), contains more than 60 *sakura*-themed poems and several references to Mt Yoshino in Nara, one of Japan's most sacred mountains and famous *hanami* locations, enshrined in both literature and art. This UNESCO World Heritage Site is home to more than 30,000 cherry trees stretching as far as the eye can see. Mt Yoshino is one example of *utamakura*. Whenever Yoshino appears in Japanese art or poetry it is always a reference to spring, because of its long association with *hanami* and cherry blossoms. This connection is so strong that merely mentioning Yoshino conjures up images of *sakura* for the reader.

Do you have any poetic places in your life? Perhaps somewhere you visited often as a child, which holds a special place in your heart or where a special seasonal event took place?

HARU WAGASHI

Sweets for Springtime

Wagashi is the umbrella term for all traditional Japanese sweets. *Wagashi* are a signifier of the seasons unique to Japan. These edible works of art gently remind us to pause and celebrate the beauty of the season. In the spring, Kyōto's confectionary shops showcase imagery of young green shoots, butterflies and cherry blossoms.

Toraya, one of Japan's most celebrated *wagashi* makers, was established in Kyōto more than 500 years ago and still makes approximately 70 varieties of *sakura*-themed sweets. Each sweet has a poetic name, and certain sweets are only available for brief periods throughout the year. Traditional Japanese *wagashi* are shaped like fruits, flowers, nuts and leaves, harking back to the earliest Japanese sweets served during the tea ceremony, which were natural delicacies such as dried persimmon and roasted chestnuts. Here are some of my favourite spring *wagashi*.

Hanaikada – A "cherry blossom petal raft" – the poetic name of this sweet – is the Japanese name for a mass of fallen petals floating down a stream, turning the water pink at the end of *sakura* season. This sweet mourns the passing of spring while encapsulating one of the most beautiful phenomena of the season.

Sakura Mochi – The iconic sweet of spring. There are several regional variations of *sakura mochi*. Kansai-style *sakura mochi* are pale pink and filled with *anko* (red bean paste). They are wrapped in a pickled cherry blossom leaf, which gives the treat its unique salty-sweet flavour. The Kanto version is called *Chomeiji sakura mochi*. It's easy to distinguish from the Kansai-style *mochi* because it looks like a crêpe. The flat disc of pink *mochi* is rolled, filled with *anko* and wrapped in an edible cherry blossom leaf. This delicate sweet makes its first appearance of the year on 3 March for *Hinamatsuri*. It continues to be served from then onwards throughout the *hanami* season.

Hanami Dango – *Dango* are small, sticky, sweet rice dumplings made from a combination of *joshinko*, rice flour, and *shiratamako*, glutinous or sweet rice flour. Skewers of *dango* are enjoyed in Japan all year round, but there are certain varieties that are traditionally eaten according to the season. *Hanami dango* is the famous *sakura* season version of this classic treat. Each colour of these tricolour dumpling skewers represents a seasonal element. For example, pink represents the blossoming cherry trees, white symbolizes the snow of the previous winter and green, which is traditionally achieved by incorporating *yomogi* (mugwort), represents the colour of young spring grass.

HANAMI AT HOME

How to Throw Your Own *Hanami* Party

Create your own spring traditions by hosting a *hanami* party. If you attend a *hanami* party in Japan, there are certain elements that add to the experience, which you can also recreate at home, wherever that might be. During my first spring in Japan, I attended three very different *hanami* parties, which were some of the highlights of my trip.

STEP 1. Find a spot under a cherry tree where you can hold your party. Explore your neighbourhood, get to know your local cherry trees and nearby parks to find the perfect *hanami* picnic spot.

STEP 2. Make a bentō. A bentō filled with the traditional dishes of the season is a great place to start and will help get you in the mood for *sakura* season. I love making a bentō to take with me on *hanami* picnics with friends. Don't worry if you don't have the time or skills of the bentō artists you see on Instagram. Simple dishes like *inari* sushi – sweet tofu skin pockets filled with seasoned sushi rice and shredded pickled plums garnished with salted *sakura* blossoms – are the perfect snack and can be enjoyed by everyone.

STEP 3. What will you drink beneath the blossoms? Sake or Japanese green tea are both great options. If you like sake, you could scatter a few petals across the surface of your cups and create *hanamizake*. Sake is always a popular drink to consume under clouds of blossom at the many *hanami* picnics and parties that go on late into the night each spring in Japan as the *sakura* are illuminated overhead. Often, whole cherry blossom flowers or petals are added to the sake.

STEP 4. Remember to bring some seasonal *wagashi*. The most popular traditional sweets of the season are *sakura mochi* and *hanami dango*. Don't worry if you can't access *wagashi* or *wagashi*-making ingredients where you live. Western sweets infused with *sakura* are a great alternative. My personal favourites are *sakura* shortbread and *sakura* madeleines, both baked with salted cherry blossoms mixed into the dough to achieve that addictive salty sweetness – just another suggestion for something you could make for your own picnic (see #hanamiathome for more ideas).

STEP 5. Take photos of your friends beneath the trees, enjoying the feast and making lovely *hanami* memories!

An optional extra idea for *yozakura*, nighttime cherry blossom viewing, is to add some small solar-powered lights and/or lanterns to the cherry tree in your garden.

PS. When you make your own #hanamiathome celebration or take yourself for a little solo *hanami* picnic, please feel free to tag me @_natalie_leon when you share your photos. I can't wait to share virtual *hanami* with you all through your #hanamiathome posts.

Chirashi Sushi – Scattered Sushi

If you're feeling a little braver, *chirashi* sushi is a popular dish you can make for a *hanami* party. *Chirashi* or "scattered" sushi, is a dish of deconstructed sushi ingredients served on a bed of seasoned rice. You can customize it to your taste, use a mixture of cooked and raw ingredients, and make it purely vegetarian or vegan if you wish.

This dish is often served during happy celebrations like *Hinamatsuri* (the Dolls' Festival, see page 48) and is perfect for *hanami* picnics. I enjoy spending some time cutting all the vegetables into *sakura* petals and flowers, which is very relaxing but purely optional. You can simply chop your ingredients and scatter them over freshly cooked rice to make a simple *chirashi donburi* or rice bowl.

I like to use a combination of fresh, crisp vegetables such as sugar snap peas, carrots, cucumber and zucchini (courgettes), as well as pieces of shredded *tamagoyaki*, a Japanese-style omelette. I also add edible cherry blossoms and *nori* (seaweed) flowers for my special *sakura*-season version.

OUBAITŌRI

Bloom in Your Own Time

The four kanji which make up the word *oubaitōri* represent each of Japan's spring flowering trees, the plum, cherry, peach and apricot. This four-character idiom is a reminder that, as Theodore Roosevelt once said, comparison is the thief of joy, and just like seasonal flowers each of us possesses our own unique beauty. The cherry, plum, peach and apricot all possess their own gifts, whether it be their eye-catching blooms, delicious fruits, elegant bark or delicately perfumed flowers. We enjoy the gifts of each tree because they all have their own merits and people are no different.

- **Avoid comparisons** – we each grow, bloom and flourish at our own pace, in our own time.

- **These things cannot be rushed** – nature operates on her own schedule.

- **Treat yourself** with the same kindness you show others.

- **Instead of dwelling on what you feel is lacking** – try shifting your focus and celebrating your unique strengths and abilities.

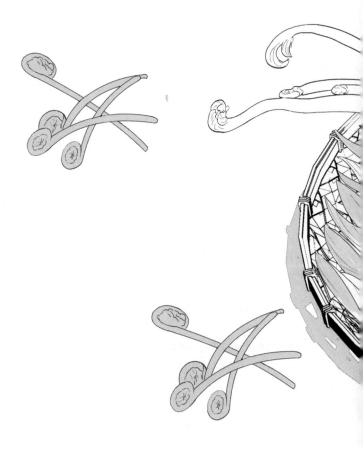

SHUN

Savouring the Seasons

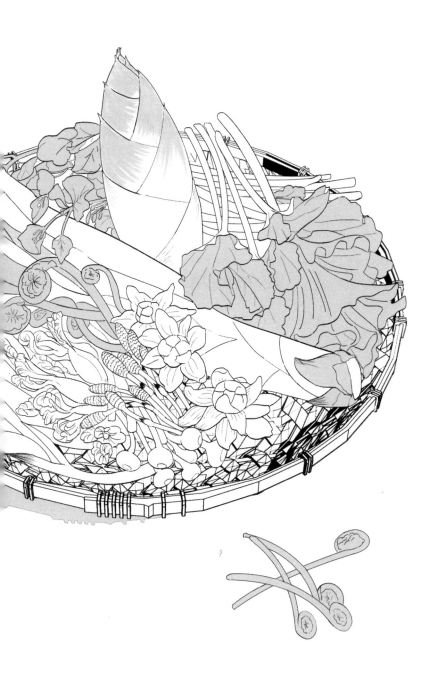

Japanese cuisine is a year-round celebration of the seasons. Chefs and diners alike highly anticipate the return of beloved seasonal ingredients each year, such as *sansai* (wild mountain vegetables) in the spring and *matsutake* mushrooms in autumn, taking great delight in preparing and enjoying them. The final dishes are edible tableaux, often garnished with the seasons' most celebrated plants and flowers.

WASHOKU

Traditional Japanese Cuisine

The Italian anthropologist Fosco Maraini once described Japan's food as a "delicate communion with the fields and leaves or a wood by moonlight". I couldn't have put it more perfectly, except to say that it is also a communion with both land and sea. *Washoku* is a compound word that includes two characters. The first character, *wa* refers to Japan as a nation, or something Japanese. It also represents harmony, a crucial element of any Japanese meal. The second character, *shoku*, means "food", "to eat" or the "culture of eating". But traditional Japanese food or *washoku* is more than just a type of cuisine – it's a whole food system, the basis of which is called *ichiju sansai*, meaning "one soup and three dishes".

UNESCO officially recognized the importance of *washoku* in 2013 and inscribed it into the Representative List of the Intangible Cultural Heritage of Humanity, noting its association "with an essential spirit of respect for nature that is closely related to the sustainable use of natural resources". *Washoku* encompasses several types of *ryōri* or cuisines. Each one of these has its own history and unique style, but seasonality is a core component in all three. *Kaiseki ryōri* is the exquisite formal cuisine, which began as an accompaniment to the tea ceremony. *Shōjin ryōri* is the modest vegetarian meal eaten by Buddhist monks since the Kamakura period (1185–1333) and *obanzai* is Kyōto-style home cooking.

ICHIJU SANSAI

One Soup, Three Dishes

A traditional Japanese meal of *ichiju sansai* ("one soup and three dishes") is served alongside pickles, a bowl of rice and a cup of tea. The three dishes are usually varied to include something grilled (*yakimono*), something simmered (*nimono*) and something raw (*namasu*). Rice always occupies the lower left quadrant of the table or tray; this is a position of honour and respect called the *kami za*. Opposite it on the right-hand side is the soup bowl. The third dish sits behind them, at the point of an imaginary triangle.

ITADAKIMASU

I Humbly Receive

Itadakimasu, meaning "I humbly receive", is a phrase linked to Buddhism taught to school children from a young age. You might overhear it in a Japanese restaurant as people begin their meal. Although it's been likened to saying *bon appetit* (good appetite), it's much more like a meditation or a prayer, like the custom of saying grace before meals. When you say *itadakimasu* before a meal, you are acknowledging not only the wonderful person who cooked this delicious meal for you but also the farmer you may never meet, who grew the vegetables you're about to eat, the gifts of plants, animals and even the universe itself for sustaining and nourishing you. This daily practice of showing sincere appreciation and gratitude can transform your relationship with food. Instead of being something that we take for granted, every meal becomes a gift. As a result, we become more acutely aware of what we're eating. What goes into our meals, and every grain of rice, becomes a precious commodity not to be wasted.

OHASHI

Chopsticks

In a Japanese restaurant, you will almost always find your chopsticks placed together horizontally in front of your meal, resting on a chopstick rest (*hashioki*). Their fine tips will be pointing to the left, creating a bridge or boundary between you and the meal you are about to receive. The Japanese word for chopsticks (*hashi*) also means "bridge" or "edge".

These humble tapered utensils are much more than just cutlery. They act as the bridge between us and the gods of the natural world. Your food is a gift from the gods, the bounty of nature. So, when you pick up your chopsticks, you cross this bridge in the same way you cross the threshold of red *torii* gates into the sacred space of a temple. Early examples of Japanese chopsticks that were used to make ritual offerings were tapered at both ends, allowing humans and gods to share a meal, each eating from one side.

Each family member in a Japanese household will have their own chopsticks, which are not used interchangeably. Spare pairs of chopsticks are kept specially for guests and ritual offerings to the gods. This is because traditionally people believed that part of your soul was imbued into the chopsticks through daily use and because your lips touched them. Chopsticks are also often given as a symbolic gift of friendship because they represent a bridge between two people. For the same reason they're a popular wedding present – the matched pair represents the couple's bridge to happiness.

GOHAN

The Importance of Rice

A grain of rice is the heart of Japanese food culture. It is the foundation on which Japanese society was built.

Rice farming in Japan began over three millennia ago and rice has been the nation's primary crop ever since. Rice was Japan's currency until the 12th century when they started using coins imported from

China. Without rice, you cannot make sake, miso or mirin, all essential components of Japanese cuisine, let alone sweets like *mochi* or *dango*.

The word *gohan* means both "rice" and "meal" because, in some households, a bowl of rice accompanied by a few pickles and a bowl of miso soup was a complete meal.

The rice life cycle is the rhythm of daily life in the Japanese countryside, and its beauty is a timeless story that transforms the rural landscape each year. It starts with freshly planted rows of green seedlings in the spring that grow tall in the summer, swaying in the wind, and are finally harvested once the fields turn gold in the autumn. The result is the glistening white pearls we use in our rice cookers.

Sacred Flowers and Grains

In ancient Japan, flowers were associated with grains – especially rice, the primary grain in Japan. A proliferation of spring flowers meant there would be an abundant autumn harvest. The ritual of *hanami* or flower viewing, came about as a way of heralding that harvest. The inextricable link between *gohan*, Japan's most iconic grain, and *sakura*, its most iconic flower, dates back thousands of years to ancient Japan. Each grain was considered precious because it was believed to be the vessel for a god's sacred spirit. Cultivating rice meant invoking *inadama*, the spirit of the rice plant.

According to ancient Japanese cosmology, each spring *Yama no Kami*, the God of the Mountain, would leave his mountain home and descend to dwell in the cherry trees planted at the edge of the rice paddies. There he became *Ta no Kami*, the God of the Rice Paddies. The mountain deity would give a part of his soul in the form of grains of rice to enable the farmers to grow a new crop and feed their village, remaining there until the autumnal harvest feast. When the cycle was completed, the villagers offered pearls of *shinmai*, freshly harvested rice, to the god in thanks. Then in spring, the cycle began anew.

In the late Edo period (1603–1868), farmer Kinase Tsunenosuke wrote an almanac stating that rice seedlings should be planted when the cherry blossom petals began to fall and the *yamabuki* (yellow *Kerria Japonica*) began to bloom. The blooming cherry blossoms signalled the god's arrival and that it was time to plant the next rice crop.

A Rice Dish for Every Season

Rice planting season in Japan begins in late April and ends in June, depending on the region. As you travel through the countryside in May, you'll see the freshly planted seedlings emerging from flooded rice paddies, which become like watery mirrors reflecting the landscape of the sky above. Japan has a rice dish (*gohan mono*) for every season and special occasion, many of which you can make at home as part of a Japanese-inspired seasonal meal.

Here are some seasonal favourites. Why not try one?

Haru (Spring)
Takenoko gohan, bamboo shoot rice, is cooked with finely sliced young bamboo shoots, one of the iconic foods of spring in Japan. You can also celebrate springtime at home with *mame gohan*, rice studded with fresh green spring peas.

Natsu (Summer)
Ume gohan, made with shredded *umeboshi* (salted Japanese plums) and *shiso*, is perfect for the summer because of its salty, tart flavour. *Shōga gohan* (ginger rice) is a dish enjoyed between June and August when *shinshōga*, young, pink-tipped ginger, is in season.

Aki (Autumn)
Shinmai (new rice), the first rice harvest of the year and prized for its softness, is one of the representative tastes of autumn. *Kuri gohan* (chestnut rice) is made with autumn's golden chestnuts cut into quarters and cooked with rice, another *aki* delicacy.

Fuyu (Winter)
Yaki imo gohan, rice made with Japanese sweet potatoes, is a real late autumn/winter treat. Purple-skinned *yaki imo* are much sweeter than their European equivalents, so much so that they're a popular ingredient for desserts in Japan. You can find them stone baked and wrapped in newspaper, still warm, in local greengrocers. If you're lucky, you might even hear the song of the local *yaki imo* truck as it makes its neighbourhood rounds, just like the ice cream vans of my

childhood. *Seikan* (red rice), served at festivals and celebrations such as weddings and birthdays, is made with *adzuki* beans and *mochi gome* (glutinous rice).

KAISEKI RYŌRI

Eating the Seasons

Historian Isao Kumakura once described Japanese food as "a canvas for the beauty of nature". It's difficult to articulate quite how ethereal and exceptional your first experience of a *kaiseki* meal is. This visually captivating feast of bite-size delicacies, which takes you on a journey through the flavours of the season, is one of the highlights of staying at any traditional Japanese inn or *ryokan*. *Kai* means "bosom", and *seki* means "stone". This is because young monks used to keep a warmed stone concealed within their robes to help stave off hunger between their morning and evening meals. Over time this term evolved to mean a "light meal".

The exquisite multicourse dining experience we now associate with the term *kaiseki* began as a simple meal to accompany the tea ceremony so that guests were not consuming strongly caffeinated tea on an empty stomach. This has evolved into one of Japan's greatest culinary traditions. Since then, the tradition has diverged into the modest *cha kaiseki* served at formal tea gatherings, and the more lavish *kaiseki* served in restaurants and *ryokan*.

Kaiseki elevates food to an edible form of art. Each menu celebrates the season's best ingredients, with each exquisitely plated, intricate dish balancing and complementing the others. Modern *kaiseki* takes inspiration from several different Japanese culinary traditions, including *yusoku ryōri*, the elaborate food of the Heian period court, *honzen ryōri*, the dishes enjoyed by samurai households during the Muromachi period (1336–1573) and s*hōjin ryōri*, the humble vegetarian fair eaten by Buddhist monks ever since the Kamakura period (1185–1333).

Each elegant *kaiseki* experience is made up of several small plates and numerous courses. A *kaiseki* meal includes *sashimi*, something simmered, something grilled, something with vinegar as a palate cleanser, something fried such as tempura, a soup and, of course, a rice dish. It ends with the *mizumono* ("a matter of water"), a seasonal Japanese sweet or dessert. A *kaiseki* lunch or dinner can include as many as 14 dishes, which constantly change and evolve throughout the year to reflect each new season.

The Three *Ki* of *Kaiseki*

Three concepts underpin the art of *kaiseki*:

1. *Kisetsu*, meaning "season".

2. *Ki*, meaning "vessel" or "dish".

3. *Kikai*, the Japanese word for "occasion" or "chance".

1. **Kisetsu – Season**
    According to chef Nobuhito Yoshida, seasonality is one of the most essential elements in Japanese cuisine. *Kaiseki* restaurants change their menus monthly to reflect the changing season and Japan's many traditional festivals and annual events. For example, in January, the theme is the New Year and in April, the *sakura* season. In July, celebrations such as Gion *Matsuri* or *Tanabata* are celebrated. And in September, *tsukimi* (moon viewing) and December, winter-flowering camellias are the inspiration.

2. **Ki – Vessel or dish**
    Japanese serving dishes include a stunning variety of vessels. Depending on the season, courses are presented in a combination of lacquer, porcelain, chilled glass, earthenware, bamboo or even seashells. I can vividly remember a little sunshine-yellow *kiku-* (chrysanthemum-) shaped dish, an elegant blue-and-white Arita porcelain butterfly and the rustic warmth of a Karatsuware plate used to serve previous *kaiseki* meals.

3. *Kikai* – **Occasion, opportunity or chance**
   Timing is everything. Each occasion is a unique opportunity to
   be treasured – a chance to create something beautiful, seasonal
   and of the moment.

Hassun

The second course of a *kaiseki* meal is called the *hassun*. It is traditionally
presented on a cedar tray, which is where its name comes from, and
represents the bounty of the season. It always contains something from
the land and something from the sea. This appetiser is the dish I most look
forward to because it sets the scene for the whole meal. It's an exquisitely
plated seasonal tableau comprised of one type of sushi and several small
side dishes. As chef Yoshihiro Murata describes it, the *hassun* "occupies
the same place in a *kaiseki* meal as an overture holds in a symphony".
This is not an understatement. In the past, I've enjoyed an April *hassun*
garnished with cherry blossoms consisting of a butterfly made of sweet
potato, slithers of carrot shaped like petals and thinly sliced lotus root
dyed pale pink – all served nestled together with wild greens and the first
broad beans of spring.

HASHIRI, SAKARI AND NAGORI

Eating in Season

As chef and author Nancy Singleton Hachisu says, "eating seasonally
just makes sense" because you're eating something at the peak
of its flavour and texture, not to mention when it's least expensive.
Seasonality is a fundamental precept of Japanese cuisine, which
celebrates the passage of time by utilizing the best regional ingredients
of the changing seasons. Japanese chefs excel at making the most
of what's in season, and each season can be broken down into three
stages, the *hashiri*, *sakari* and *nagori*.

Hashiri – The Beginning

The first appearance of a particular ingredient or the first harvest of the year. That first bite and taste of your favourite fruit or vegetable that you look forward to all year.

Sakari or Shun – The Peak

Shun is often described as "what's in season", but it's more than this. It is the ripest or best of what's in season, when an ingredient is at its peak, perfectly ripe and at its finest in terms of flavour and nutritional value.

Nagori – The End

The last remnants of the harvest and the last opportunity to enjoy particular herbs, fruit or vegetables until next year. It also signals the end of one season and the beginning of the next.

OBANZAI RYŌRI

Home Cooking in Kyōto

Often described as Kyōto home-style cooking, *obanzai* was born in Kyōto, passed down the generations and is an integral part of the cultural heritage of the ancient capital. The term *obanzai* was coined by Shige Omura in 1964 to describe how Kyōto people eat at home. What makes it so unique is the focus on seasonality, the use of locally grown produce called *kyo yasai* (Kyōto vegetables), which should make up 50 per cent of the dish, and the five philosophies behind the physical act of cooking outlined below (see page 80).

A typical *obanzai* meal consists of several small vegetable-based dishes, one soup, one main dish and a bowl of rice. These are made using various cooking methods, such as grilling, steaming, frying, boiling and sautéing. They are often seasoned with *shiro-miso* (white miso), a fermented condiment made from soybeans, and *usukuchi shoyu* (light-coloured soy sauce). Both are prized by Kyōto chefs for their delicate colour and flavour.

Three Types of *Obanzai*

1. ***Shunsai* – Shades of Spring**
   This phrase refers to the fresh vegetables of the current season, the best of now. *Shunsai* is made up of *shun*, meaning "season" or "period" and refers to what ingredients are in season, and *sai*, meaning "vivid colours". These dishes are designed to be prepared and eaten on the same day.

2. ***Jobisai* – Stored Food**
   These Japanese cooking staples are side dishes that should be eaten within the next two to three weeks. They are often batch-cooked in advance and kept in the fridge or frozen, and usually contain salt, vinegar, honey or sugar so they last.

3. ***Hozonsai* – Preserved Foods**
   Honzon means "to preserve certain elements of an *obanzai* meal" that often last for an extended period. This way, parts of the meal can be prepared in advance. These dishes can keep for even longer than *jobisai*, making it much easier to make a bentō or a multi-dish meal such as *obanzai*.

According to *obanzai* researcher and head of the Japan Foodist Association, Susumu Fujikake, *obanzai* dishes are "conditioned according to seasonality, ceremonial events and customs". In each *obanzai* dish, you can feel the changing seasons. They are reflected in the meal through careful choice of ingredients, cooking methods, plating and decoration. *Obanzai* dishes may appear deceptively simple, but they are created based on several fundamental principles about balance, zero-waste living and hospitality, which capture the spirit of *obanzai*.

The Five Core Concepts of *Obanzai*

Shimatsu – From Beginning to End
Shimatsu means both "the beginning" and "the end" of something. This concept encourages the chef to use every element of the ingredients they have available, wasting nothing. *Shimatsu* could be called the culinary version of *mottainai* (zero-waste living – see Chapter 4). It's an important reminder not to waste valuable resources.

Honmamon – The Genuine Article
In *Kansai Ben* (the Kansai dialect), *honmamon* means "genuine" or "authentic". In terms of cooking, it applies to using well-made tools and utensils and sourcing high-quality whole fruits and vegetables, which can be expensive, so keeping in mind the philosophy of *shimatsu* (wasting nothing) is even more important. One of the rules of *obanzai* is that the chef should know the origin of 50 per cent or more of their ingredients – a reminder to all of us to pay closer attention to the sources of our food.

Deaimon – The Marriage
Deaimon means "marriage" or "encounter". It is the coming together of two different elements to create something new. In Japanese cooking, it's traditional to use one component from the land and one from the sea in the same dish – for example, *wakame* (seaweed) and *takenoko* (bamboo shoots).

Anbai – Finding Balance
Anbai, meaning "seasoning", "flavour" or "taste", is about finding a balance between ingredients – just enough salt and just enough sugar – without throwing off the balance of the dish.

Kokorodzukai – Consideration of Others

Hospitality or *omotenashi* is an essential part of Japanese culture and this is especially evident in the preparation and serving of food, whether in an upscale *kaiseki* (see page 75) restaurant or the cosy kitchen of a local farmer. *Kokorodzukai* is a word made up of *kokoro*, meaning "heart" and *zugai*, meaning "using". This word is rooted in compassion and care for others – in this case, for those you are cooking for.

What Can We Learn from *Obanzai*?

- Focus on eating in season.

- Eat a balanced diet.

- Prioritize local produce.

- Aim to cook with minimum waste, using every part of the vegetable, fruit, etc.

- Incorporate more pickled and preserved foods into our menus.

- Batch-cook dishes in advance so we can enjoy a healthy and delicious meal later.

- Eat whole fruits and vegetables.

- Pay attention to the origins of our food and its ingredients.

- Cook with love and care for our friends and family.

MORITSUKE

The Art of Japanese Food Arrangement

Accomplished ceramicist and restaurateur Kitaoji Rosajin (1883–1959) famously declared that "dishes are clothing for food". Traditional Japanese meals usually consist of several exquisitely presented small plates designed to be a feast for the eyes as well as the palette. Dishes are garnished with seasonal plants and flowers and presented in vessels whose colours and design complement their contents perfectly.

Rosajin suggested we should plate food as we would arrange flowers. One of the things that makes a meal in Japan such an enjoyable and memorable experience beyond the food itself is the gorgeous plating or *moritsuke*, the artistic way dishes are presented both individually and as a group. Chefs spend a great deal of time and energy selecting the dishes, cups and glasses for every meal they create, often sourcing these elements from local craftspeople.

Each small plate must complement the dish's colours to showcase the food to its best advantage while referencing the season. There should be a harmony of colour, flavour and ingredients. In one restaurant, I remember being served a simple fruit salad on a flat celadon green dish lined with translucent iridescent paper, making each piece of fruit placed upon it shine like a precious jewel.

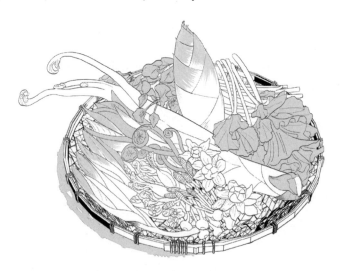

The Principles of *Moritsuke*

Ma – The Beauty of Empty Space. Vessels should not be filled to the brim. Instead, think of the dish as a canvas or gallery for your food. Just as you would when hanging a painting, leave a healthy amount of space between the food and the rim of the dish to allow both the visual aspects of the food and the receptacle to be enjoyed.

Contrast – Contrast is a critical element of Japanese aesthetics. It features in various art forms, including *kitsuke*, the art of dressing in a kimono. In terms of cuisine, it means that circular foods are presented in square dishes, and vice versa. This rule also applies to the use of colour: dishes and their vessels are paired to create a harmonious contrast.

Asymmetry – The Japanese aesthetic preference for odd numbers over even ones means that food is served in groupings of three, five and seven.

Seasonality – Decorative elements from nature, such as leaves, buds and edible flowers, can all be used to reinforce a seasonal theme. In the spring, your plate might be garnished with a sprig of cherry blossom, in the summer with fresh green maple leaves, and in the autumn with golden chrysanthemums. Natural elements can also serve as vessels that will delight guests, such as the hollowed-out shell of a ripe *yuzu* or a fiery orange persimmon.

Serving ware – Just like the menu, tableware should also change with the seasons. In the summer, vessels might include bamboo baskets and chilled glass bowls. In the winter, warm rustic earthenware, which retains heat, is a welcome change.

GOSHIKI

The Rule of Five

The rule of five is one of the principles that underpins Japanese cooking. There are five colours (*goshiki*), five cooking methods (*goho*), five tastes (*gomi*) and five senses (*gokan*).

Goshiki – The Five Colours
Aka (red), *shiro* (white), *ao* (blue/green), *ki* (yellow) and *kuro* (black). Red and yellow are warming and stimulate the appetite; blue/green are cooling and refreshing; white is clean; and black accents everything.

Goho – The Five Cooking Methods
These comprise *niru* (simmered), *musu* (steamed), *ageru* (fried), *yaku* (grilled) and *nama* (raw). The word *nama* can describe raw food as well as refer to the knife skills involved in slicing *sashimi* and the decorative cutting techniques used in Japanese food.

Gomi – The Five Tastes
These are *kan* (sweet), *ka* (bitter), *kan* (salty), *san* (sour) and *shin* (spicy).

Gokan – The Five Senses
Gokan means when we eat, we engage all our senses. First, we take in the food with the feast before our eyes. Then, when we lift the lid of a dish and the steam wafts toward us, we enjoy its aroma through smell. Next, we sip our soup or take a bite of tempura and hear it crunch. Japanese food has lots of wonderful textures. This is where we engage touch – enjoying the slight chewy bounce of a bowl of perfectly cooked *udon* noodles. Finally, the sensation of taste comes last at the end of our multi-sensory journey.

Applying the Rule of Five
in Your Kitchen

- Using the rule of five, we can create more balanced meals.

- A wide variation of colour on our plates means we consume a wide range of vitamins and nutrients.

- A meal containing each of the five methods of cooking will keep us feeling satisfied and full.

- Eating is more than just a matter of taste. A meal should activate all five senses.

- A variety of colours and forms delights our eyes as well as our palette.

- A refreshing raw element, such as a salad or something lightly pickled, is the perfect foil for fried or roasted foods.

SHŌJIN RYŌRI

Buddhist Temple Cuisine

More and more vegan and vegetarian restaurants are opening in Japan every year. However, Japan already has a rich tradition of vegetarian food in the form of *shōjin ryōri*, which dates back to the Kamakura period (1185–1333). *Shōjin* means "earnest commitment" and *ryōri* means "cooking" or "cuisine". Buddhist monks and priests brought this type of food back when they returned to Japan after completing their training in Song Dynasty China (1127–1279). What began as a very modest meal designed to sustain monks during long periods of meditation gradually became more elaborate over time. This style of meat-free cuisine gained popularity in the 13th century and coincided with the spread of Zen Buddhism. Its prevalence was attributed primarily to the efforts of the monks Eisai (1141–1215) and Dōgen (1200–53) and it can still be enjoyed at restaurants and temples across the country. A *shōjin ryōri* meal often includes plant-based protein such as *fu* (wheat gluten), tofu and *yuba* (soymilk skin).

The Three Pillars of *Shōjin*

1. The first is *shun* – eating the best of what's in season.

2. The second is *shindofuji*, a Buddhist phrase meaning "body and soil are one and the same". It means so much more than "you are what you eat". We have become so disconnected from where our food comes from. *Shindofuji* is a reminder that what we eat becomes a part of us, that we are a part of the earth from which it came – reinforcing our connection to the land and grounding us in nature instead of being distinct from it.

3. The third is *ichimotsu zentai*, which means "using the whole thing". This practice is parallel to the *obanzai* tradition of *shimatsu* (see page 80), ensuring nothing goes to waste.

FORAGING IN JAPAN

Like most British children, my first foraging experience involved picking blackberries from hedgerows at the end of the summer holidays. Now I make cordials, jams and infused honeys as part of my own seasonal foraging rituals. Foraging is a great way to familiarize yourself with the local landscape and connect with nature's calendar. Depending on the season, you'll be rewarded with an embarrassment of riches, from spring greens and edible flowers to nuts, berries and stone fruit.

Foraging has been practised in Japan since the Jomon period (c.8000–400 BCE), Japan's Neolithic age, when tribes of hunter-gatherers called the Japanese archipelago their home.

The tradition of gathering wild greens in the spring, which came to Japan from China in the 8th century, remains in the form of *nanakusa gayu*. *Nana* means "seven", *kusa* means "herbs" or "grasses" and *gayu* "rice porridge". *Nanakusa gayu* or seven-herb rice porridge is eaten, as a kind of detox after families have indulged over the festive winter season (see page 88). As chef Kunio Tokuoka explained, bears do something similar, "participating in nature's detox program" when they emerge from hibernation in the spring, intentionally seeking out bitter leaves and grasses, such as dandelions, to cleanse their system after months of hibernating.

During my research for this book, in one of many antiquarian second-hand book shops I visited in Kyōto, I was ecstatic to unearth an Edo period (1603–1868) woodblock print by the artist Teisai Hokuba (1771–1844), who was a student of Katsushika Hokusai (1760–1849). It features two beautiful kimono-clad women foraging for dandelions, showing just how popular this spring tradition was by the Edo period. There is even a dedicated Japanese micro-season referencing this tradition and reminding us to follow nature's example.

JAPANESE MICRO SEASON NO.67
SERI SUNAWACHI SAKAU

Parsley Flourishes
❧ 5–9 January ❧

Seri, often called Japanese parsley, is a peppery spring herb that grows wild near mountain streams. *Nanakusa no Sekku* (the Feast of Seven Herbs) takes place on 7 January, which used to be called *Jinjitsu*, the day of spring herbs. *Jinjitsu* was originally one of the *Gosekku* – the five seasonal festive days in the ancient calendar. This is when, following tradition, people enjoy *nanakusa gayu* or seven-herb rice porridge to officially mark the end of the New Year festivities. The savoury porridge contains seven wild spring herbs and is traditionally eaten for breakfast on the morning of 7 January. This gentle, nourishing dish of rice and leafy greens is believed to ward off evil spirits and bring good health for the year ahead.

The Seven Herbs Used in *Nanakusa Gayu*

1. **Seri** – Japanese parsley/water dropwort

2. **Nazuna** – Shepherds Purse

3. **Gogyo** – Cudweed

4. **Hakobera** – Chickweed

5. **Hotokenoza** – Niplewort

6. **Suzuna** – Turnip

7. **Suzushiro** – Daikon radish

Sansai – Wild Mountain Vegetables

Only after I began to immerse myself in Japan's seasonal culture did I discover its rich foraging tradition and learn about the joys of *sansai* – the wild mountain vegetables that are indigenous to Japan, such as *takenoko* (young bamboo shoots), *fuki* (butterbur) and *warabi* (bracken). *Sansai* is a word made up of the characters for mountain and vegetable. The older generations are the guardians of Japan's foraging wisdom, and they are disappearing just as the natural habitat of *sansai* is disappearing. As author Winifred Bird wrote in her book *Eating Wild Japan*, "by eating *sansai* – by taking them into our bodies – these places become part of us." These words direct us back to *shindofuji*, one of the three pillars of *shōjin* (see page 86). By consuming wild mountain vegetables like these, we become a part of their world, and they become a part of ours. Whenever I eat *sansai*, it feels like a privileged experience to indulge in something so wild that was gathered with such care. Eating them is to take part in an ancient *washoku* tradition. I hope that the renewed interest in foraging I've witnessed in the UK and abroad since the Covid epidemic will lead to the conservation of their mountain and forest habitats and that more people will endeavour to care for and protect the *sansai* so that future generations can enjoy them.

For a brief period in the spring, from February to May, chefs and cooks all over Japan prepare to make the most of *sansai* season. *Nigai*, or a slight bitterness, is part of the distinctive taste of *sansai* and is therefore associated with the arrival of spring itself. It's also one of Japanese cuisine's five essential flavours. As a result, *sansai* are considered the pinnacle of *shun* and the most sought-after of Japan's spring ingredients.

Spring Bitterness

Sansai can be difficult to find outside Japan, but if you'd like to add a little *nigai* or bitterness to your spring rituals, you can add the following plants to your salads. You could even try making your own *nanakusa gayu*. Simply make a plain rice porridge on the hob or in your rice cooker and then add the blanched and chopped bitter spring greens of your choice. Here are some substitute suggestions:

- Dandelion leaves

- Arugula (rocket)

- Kale

- Mustard greens

- Watercress

- Turnip greens

- Sprouting seeds such as mung beans.

The closest European equivalent of this tradition is Swedish bitters, a tincture of bitter herbs taken as a digestive, named after the 18th-century Swedish physician and Rector of Medicine, Dr Claus Samst.

Warabi En – Bracken Park

At the foot of Mt Iide in Yamagata, where the snows can last until August, there's a thriving community of foragers. Yamagata *sansai* is considered especially delicious because of the heavy snowfall and the clear water that runs down the mountain into the free-flowing rivers and streams, which nourish these plants. *Warabi*, or young bracken, is a particular kind of *sansai* that grows abundantly in the area. The locals know this part of Nakatsugawa as Shirakawa Warabi En or Warabi Park.

On a late spring day in early May, I visited the home of Yoshi and Mitchi san, who took me foraging at the base of the mountain. There was still snow on the ground as we climbed into the back of Yoshi san's white pickup truck and held on tight as we ascended the mountainside. Our treacherous ride was rewarded almost instantly. As soon as we disembarked, I saw butterbur flowers peeking out of the sloping undergrowth. After gathering the pale green leafy stems, I spotted a small cluster of my favourite comma-shaped *sansai*, called *kogomi*. These are fiddleheads, the tightly curled fronds of young ostrich ferns. Although they were covered with a soft downy protective layer, when I gently peeled them back, I was spellbound by the delicate coiled fronds I found inside them.

After filling our baskets and being careful not to pick too much from any one patch to ensure the plants would return next spring, we went back to the house where we washed, blanched and prepared the *sansai*. Less than two hours later, we were enjoying heaving baskets of freshly made wild tempura, *sukiyaki* (hot pot) and my favourite dish of the night, blanched fiddlehead ferns dressed with *ponzu*, a simple dressing made from soy sauce and citrus fruits.

Five Types of *Sansai*

If you're lucky, you might encounter *sansai* soba or *sansai* tempura on the menu when you visit Japanese restaurants in the spring. Regrettably, *sansai* season is short, so these beautiful leafy greens and delicate fronds are a true seasonal delicacy.

Takenoko – Young Shoots of Moso Bamboo (*Phyllostachys edulis*)
The word *takenoko* includes the kanji for *take* (bamboo) and *shun*, meaning "season". The new bamboo shoots are the children (*ko*) of the bamboo groves that encircle temples and grow wild throughout Japan. *Takenoko* are the tender young bamboo shoots that should ideally be harvested before they break through the soil and are exposed to sunlight. *Takenonko* requires a lot of preparation, including being boiled with *nuka* (rice bran) for an hour to remove any bitterness. They are one of the most commonly found *sansai*, often prepared as *takenoko gohan* (bamboo shoot rice). Their peak season is from March to May, coinciding with cherry blossom season.

This is the only time of the year you can enjoy fresh creamy white *takenoko*, which is cherished just as much as the first asparagus spears to appear each spring in Europe.

Warabi – Bracken *(Pteridium aquilinum)*
Young bracken shoots are described as the "young fruits of the hill" in the Heian-period novel *The Tale of Genji*. *Warabi* are used to make a gelatinous starch, the main ingredient in one of Kyōto's oldest traditional desserts, *warabi mochi*, which was enjoyed over 1,000 years ago in Genji's time. Historically *warabi* has also been enjoyed in various forms in Korea, China, Russia and by the indigenous peoples of North America.

Fuki – Butterbur *(Petasites japonicus)*
The butterbur and its buds *(fukinotou)* ideally need to be harvested before the buds fully open. Then, the stalks are cooked down with soy sauce and sugar until they're almost candied, and the buds are finely chopped and mixed with miso.

Taranome – Angelica *(Aralia elata)*
As I found out first-hand, the young shoots of the angelica tree can be especially tricky to harvest because each branch is covered in fine thorns.

Kogomi – Ostrich Fern *(Matteuccia struthiopteris)*
These are vibrant green fiddleheads, the tightly coiled heads of young ostrich ferns. Their English name is based on their visual similarity to the finial of a violin.

If you're curious to find out what edible plants can be foraged in your neighbourhood this spring, why not consult a foraging guide or join a local foraging workshop.

Mitaki-en

I had eaten *sansai* several times before, once in a beautiful minimalist soba restaurant in Tōkyō and another surrounded by deer and luminous green forests in Nara. However, nothing could prepare me for the joyful experience of Mitaki-en.

Tucked away in Tottori Prefecture in the mountain village of Ashizu is a haven for *sansai* lovers. Entering the forest glade of Mitaki-en is like entering a Studio Ghibli film. You cross the threshold by passing through a thatched gate and immediately you feel you have been transported to another world of deep green, home to giant rocks and ancient trees covered with velvety-soft mosses. A flock of white chickens wander across your path, alighting on a nearby tree stump. The sunlight softens as it filters down through the trees and illuminates the young green maple leaves. Small winding paths lead you around a cluster of traditional Japanese buildings and rustic farmhouses whose thatched roofs have become gardens, teeming with foliage and wildflowers.

As I sat sipping my *hōjicha* (roasted green tea), eating the last bite of my *sakura yokan* and watching the shadows cast by the foliage play across the rocks, I wanted to stay in that moment forever. This restaurant opens each spring on 1 April. The seasons define the menu – the staff forage daily for fresh ingredients collected before the morning dew dries. Here you can dine on a slow feast of bamboo shoot *sashimi*, *sanshō* miso and freshly pressed *warabi* tofu. It is the ultimate *sansai* experience.

NAORAI

Eating with the Gods

When you eat a Japanese meal, you are never alone. You are taking part in an ancient tradition of eating with the gods. As part of Japanese *matsuri* (festivals), a Shintō offering called *shinsen* is made to the gods. It is made of local seasonal produce, a mountain of rice and rice-based foods such as *mochi* (rice cakes), and drinks such as sake. At the end of the festival, the offering is removed from the altar and enjoyed by those present, laypeople and clergy alike, in a feast called the *naorai*. Partaking in this sacred meal was designed to strengthen the connection to the *kami* (gods), to absorb their power and receive their protection.

LESSONS WE CAN
LEARN FROM *WASHOKU*

Eating with Intention

Any meal can be elevated to a more pleasurable and memorable experience by practising gratitude and appreciation.

- Practise gratitude for a meal to remind yourself that it's a gift from the person who made it and nature's endless generosity.

- Eat mindfully, taking your time not to rush through a meal by chewing slowly and savouring every bite.

- Choose to focus solely on the meal in front of you, putting down your smartphone and avoiding trying to do several other things simultaneously.

- Eat with your eyes. Notice all the colours of the rainbow on your plate.

- Take a moment to appreciate the character of each bowl or dish, whether it's the elegant simplicity of a clean white plate or the intricate details of a vintage bowl.

Growing a Japanese Kitchen Garden

If you love to cook Japanese food at home, then there are several fresh ingredients you might like to add to your kitchen garden that will enrich your cooking. It used to be impossible to find these plants outside Japan but that's no longer the case. Happily, they're now much more widely available and can be grown in pots on a balcony or windowsill and don't need much space to thrive. One of my small spring pleasures is stepping out of the back door to snip a couple of fragrant leaves of *kinome*, my hands scented with its peppery aroma.

Myoga (Zingiber mioga)
Myoga (Japanese ginger) is a late-spring ingredient. The young buds of this ginger plant are eaten raw, thinly sliced and added to dishes such as dressed tofu. These hardy plants die back over the winter and return in the spring.

Shiso (Perilla frutescens)
Shiso (Perilla or Beefsteak plant) is the perfect addition to any herb garden. There are three varieties of this plant: red, green and bicoloured. An iconic early summer ingredient from the mint family, all three are great in salads. *Aka jiso* (red *shiso*) is an essential ingredient used to make *umeboshi* (pickled plums). *Shiso* is an annual, non-hardy plant that won't survive the first frost, so make the most of it during the spring/summer.

Yuzu (Citrus junos)
One of Japan's many indigenous citrus fruits, what sets *yuzu* apart is its incredible fragrance, which dwells in its glorious yellow rind. Growing one is a lot like caring for a lemon tree. *Yuzu* plants need to come indoors or go into a greenhouse during cold, wet winters but are happy outside in a sunny spot

during the summertime. Their golden fruits are in season from November till January and are the highlight of autumn/winter cuisine in Japan. Watch out for their impressive thorns when tending to your precious *yuzu*!

Mizuna *(Brassica rapa var. nipposinica)*
Mizuna (Japanese mustard greens or potherb mustard) is part of the cabbage or brassica family. This annual herb has lovely, serrated leaves that are often used raw in soups and salads. These leafy greens are compact and easy to grow in pots; they like sun or light shade and are quite hardy. If you cut them regularly, they will reward you with repeat salad harvests.

Sanshō *(Zanthoxylum piperitum)*
Sanshō (Prickly ash) is prized for its fragrant young leaves in the spring called *kinome*. *Sanshō* is sometimes called Japanese pepper because it produces aromatic pods that resemble peppercorns in the autumn. Like peppercorns these are dried and then ground. *Sanshō* is one of Japan's oldest seasonings. *Sanshō* plants are hardy and sun-loving, they also like to be fed the same food as citrus trees, so if you have a *yuzu*, you can use the same feed for both trees. The trees lose their leaves in the autumn, but they return the following spring.

Edamame *(Glycine max)*
Edamame (Soybeans) make a perfect instant snack or side dish. These podded beans are easy to grow and can be plucked straight from the vine to eat or grilled with a pinch of salt or chilli. The plants can grow up to a metre tall, so make sure to give them some support and a nice sunny position.

Shishitō *(Capsicum annuum)*
Shishitō (Lion peppers) are generally mild and sweet. They're easy to grow and will keep on giving until the first frost. They're happiest in a warm environment. *Shishitō* are perfect picked while they're still green and simply grilled with a little sea salt – just how you would enjoy them in a local *yakitori* restaurant.

Sustainable Travel Tips for Eating and Shopping in Japan

People often ask me what to pack for their first trip to Japan. There are three things I always travel with, especially in Japan. They can help make your adventures in Japan (and anywhere else) much more sustainable.

1. Your own set of travel chopsticks. This cuts down on the use of *waribashi*, the disposable chopsticks that have become ubiquitous in Japan and abroad. This in turn helps prevent deforestation.

2. A refillable water bottle. Japanese water is safe to drink, and carrying a water bottle with you is a sustainable alternative to buying multiple plastic water bottles.

3. A reusable shopping bag. Always pack a compact reusable bag to avoid coming home from the supermarket with excess plastic bags.

MOTTAINAI

Zero-waste Living

The Japanese expression *mottainai*, meaning "what a waste!" or "don't be wasteful", is based on a centuries-old ethos that embraces the idea of respecting resources and their value while also reducing waste. Its origins derive from two words – *mottai* (importance or sanctity) and *nai* (lack of something). Japanese folk crafts like *boro boro* (visible mending) and practices like *kintsugi* (golden joinery) perfectly embody the *mottainai* spirit, which incorporates elements of Japanese Buddhism, Daoism, Confucianism and Shintoism. For example, a unique type of vengeful spirit from Japanese folklore known as *tsukumogami* perfectly expresses the ideals of *mottainai*.

This worldview reflects a desire to live harmoniously with nature, conserving resources and minimizing waste. No country has a perfect track record when it comes to sustainability. However, many traditions, practices and concepts from Japan have inspired me on my journey to living a slower, more seasonal, greener way of life. I'd like to share some of them with you in the hope that they might inspire you to live more seasonally and sustainably too.

I've been wearing vintage clothes and buying second-hand pieces for my home since I was a teenager because it has always just made sense to me. So, the concepts of reuse, reduce and recycle have always aligned with my core values and how I live my life, especially after spending more than a decade buying and selling vintage items in London. These beautiful old things were often better made, built to last and more affordable. They had great character and soul and were, of course, more eco-friendly than the mass-produced products we encounter today.

KAMIKATSU

Japan's First Zero-waste Town

The first place in Japan to make a zero-waste pledge was Kamikatsu – a small town hidden in the remote mountains of Shikoku Island in Tokushima Prefecture. The town is home to a ride-sharing system and a recycling centre, which acts as a community hub and includes a zero-waste craft brewery made from architectural salvage, and a sustainable hotel built using recycled materials donated by the residents. The hotel's restaurant, Café Polestar, serves dishes made from local, seasonal produce. All designed to help the community reach its ultimate carbon-neutral goal.

Their volunteer-run *Kuru Kuru* emporium is full of second-hand items donated by locals that other residents can use for free. The shop also sells the sustainable artwork of local artisans who upcycle old kimono and fabrics to create homewares and fashion accessories. The residents of Kamikatsu separate their recycling into an impressive 45 categories and currently recycle more than 80 per cent of their rubbish, making the town an incredible model for the future of sustainable living in both Japan and abroad.

Kuru Kuru
Round and Round

As an island, Japan has fewer natural resources than other countries, so they have had to learn to conserve what they have.

The Japanese phrase *kuru kuru* means round and round. It's a good reminder to respect our planet's valuable and finite resources by repairing or repurposing things instead of discarding them, or donating goods that no longer serve us so that others can enjoy them. Used goods gain a new lease of life when they are recycled, reused and repurposed by someone else.

The *mottainai* worldview has never been more relevant. As Kenyan environmentalist and Nobel Prize laureate Wangari Maathai (1940 –2011) said when advocating for the *mottainai* philosophy, "Even on a personal level, we can all reduce, reuse and recycle." She referred to *mottainai* as the fourth R of a sustainable circular economy: recycle, reduce, reuse and respect.

Lessons We Can Learn from *Mottainai*

How can we embrace the spirit of *mottainai*? Before buying something new, ask yourself the following questions:

- Do I really need this?

- Will I use it?

- Does it add value to my life?

- Does it bring me joy?

- Does it serve a purpose?

- Is there an alternative, something I already own that I could reuse or repurpose?

- Do I already own something similar?

- Can I buy it second-hand?

- Was it made ethically?

- How long will it last?

FASHIONED FROM NATURE

Home to some incredible renewable natural fabric fibres, Japan has a rich textile history beyond Kyōto and the opulent silk kimono originally worn by the samurai class. In fact, Japan's farmers, fisherfolk and indigenous people have their own rich textile traditions. These exceptional garments and homewares – made from natural fibres such as hemp, linden, elm, wisteria and banana – are woven into the fabric of Japan.

Shina Fu

Shina fu (linden fibre) is a coarse fabric made from the inner bark of the linden tree, a deciduous tree found in Northern Japan. Before the use of cotton and hemp fabrics spread, linden was commonly used to make *noragi*, hardwearing workwear. It's still produced in some remote mountain villages bordering Yamagata and Niigata.

Nibutani Attushi

The Ainu, the first people of Japan, created robes made of *nibutani attushi* (elm bark). The word *nibutani* comes from the Ainu language; it means "a land where trees grow thickly".

Fuji Fu

Fuji fu, or wisteria vine fibre, is one of Japan's oldest fabrics, dating back to the Jomon period (14,000–300 BCE). The luxury versions of this textile were woven with silk threads, and less opulent versions were interwoven with *washi* (paper). Over time, wisteria fabric becomes softer and warmer as it ages.

Bashō Fu

Bashō fu (banana fibre) comes from the *itobashō* (*Musa liukiuensis*), a type of wild banana found on the tropical islands of Okinawa. These plants produce delicate but resilient fibres that are very permeable, making them ideal for life in the sub-tropical climate of the whole chain of Ryukyu islands. *Bashō fu* is designated as an Important Tangible Cultural Asset and was once worn by the royal family of the Ryukyu Kingdom.

Consider the clothes in your own wardrobe and the items in your home. You may be surprised by the amount of items made from natural fibres you own. For example, you may have clothes made from linen, the world's oldest known woven fabric, which is spun from a blue flowering plant called flax or linseed. Coir, which you might find in your brushes and mats, is made from the outer fibres of a coconut husk. And check your reusable bags – the jute plant produces extremely long fibres that are often used as twine and fashioned into bags.

Boro Boro
Visible Mending

Boro boro, meaning "rags" or "tattered", is a practice born out of the necessity to repair textiles using scraps of fabric, often attached with a simple running stitch. In rural communities, cherished garments would be passed down from one generation to the next. Each would mend and patch them as necessary, adding to the previous generation's work and creating an intricate patchwork made of layers and layers of visible mending, much like a treasured family quilt handed down the generations.

Sashiko
Tiny Stabs

Sashiko ("little stabs") stitching is a decorative way of reinforcing a garment to make it thicker, warmer and more durable, ultimately lengthening the life of the garment. This functional form of geometrical Japanese embroidery involves using pure white thread on a deep indigo-blue background, reminiscent of footprints in the snow. Doing *sashiko* is one of the ways the women in Japan's snow country passed the time during the long winter months.

Tsutsumi
Wrapping

Tsutsumi is the concept and process of wrapping and packaging. The word means "package" or "present" and it plays a vital role in Japan's culture of gift-giving or *omiyage*. In Japan, gift-giving is an art form and gifts are always exquisitely wrapped. The kanji or character for *tsutsumi* is a pictograph symbolizing a baby inside the womb. Author Kunio Ekiguchi once said that in Japan, giving a gift is like wrapping one's own heart.

Japan is a nation wrapped in the delicate natural fibres of the plants and trees it uses to create handmade paper and silken textiles. The Japanese practice of wrapping objects in fabric spans over 1,000 years, beginning during the Nara period (710–794). The Shosoin treasure house at Todaiji Temple in Nara is home to the oldest piece of Japanese wrapping cloth.

Furoshiki
Wrapping with Fabric

Furoshiki are squares of printed cloth such as cotton, hemp or silk, traditionally used to wrap gifts and precious possessions in Japan. These multipurpose cloths can carry, store and cover almost anything. The word *furoshiki* is a combination of the kanji for *furo*, meaning "bath", and *shiki*, meaning "to spread". This is because bathers traditionally brought their toiletries and clothing to the local *sentō* or bathhouse wrapped in *furoshiki*.

Coming in endless colours and designs, *furoshiki* are very versatile and my personal favourite is seasonal motifs. I've used them for years to wrap presents and take my bentō and fragile tea wares on picnic adventures at home and abroad. Using and displaying them is one of the many simple ways to celebrate the changing seasons.

Furoshiki are not only a beautiful art form but have the potential to be so much more. They are an eco-friendly and more sustainable alternative to wrapping paper, which often isn't biodegradable. These chic and versatile textiles can also be transformed into reusable, spacing-saving fabric bags to replace unnecessary single-use plastic bags by making strategically placed knots or attaching handles to them. A 1,000-year-old tradition, *furoshiki* are a beautiful way to bring a little more Japanese seasonal feeling into your home and simultaneously reduce your use of plastics.

Furoshiki at Home

You can use *furoshiki* at home to:

- Store linens and bedding.

- Wrap Christmas or Chanukah gifts.

- Protect delicate items such as teaware when travelling.

- Use as a picnic blanket.

- Make into an extra bag to take to the farmer's market or go foraging.

- Use as a place mat.

- Organize things for storage.

- Use as a handkerchief.

- Wear as a scarf.

- Carry your yoga mat.

- Protect a bottle of wine or sake.

- Wrap a bunch of flowers.

Tenugui

Tenugui are long, thin, rectangular pieces of cotton fabric that double as a multipurpose accessory. Edo-period bathers used *tenugui* to dry the body after a soak in the local *sentō* (bathhouse). Much like handkerchiefs, *tenugui* are also used to wipe away sweat and dust and protect the head from the elements. *Tenugui* are a household essential, but they're also great to take with you on the go because they're lightweight, absorbent and they air-dry quickly. Use them in the kitchen as tea towels, drying cloths, placemats or seasonal decorative artwork. Just like *furoshiki, tenugui* are affordable and available in a vast variety of colours and seasonal designs.

Have nothing in your homes that you do not know to be useful or believe to be beautiful.

WILLIAM MORRIS

MINGEI

The People's Art

Champion of the *Mingei* movement, Sōetsu Yanagi (1889–1961) was a lifelong collector of folk craft who saw "everyday beauty" in the humble utilitarian objects made by the anonymous craftspeople of the Japanese countryside. Yanagi was heavily influenced by British artist William Morris (1834–1896), one of the inspirations of the Arts and Crafts movement. In many respects the *Mingei* movement of the 1920s, which celebrates traditional Japanese folk crafts, bears similarities to the Art and Crafts movement, which began in England in the 1880s in reaction to the Industrial Revolution.

Japan's *Mingei* movement was also a reaction to the mass-produced and machine-made. In our disposable modern world of mass consumption, both movements have a great deal to offer when we consider the issues of sustainability and overconsumption we currently face. Yanagi saw in *minki* (utensils of the people) the seeds of a new philosophy of aesthetics, which he called "forgotten beauty". He created the word *mingei* to describe these honest and simple handmade objects made with respect for their natural materials of bamboo, wood, paper, straw and stone. *Mingei* is an abbreviation of the phrase *minshūteki na kōgei* or "the people's art". These asymmetrical, irregular and imperfect folk-art pieces, such as *kintsugi* (repairing ceramics with gold), *boro boro* (visible mending or patchwork) and *sashiko* (Japanese country stitching) were born in Japan's snow country. In regions such as Tohoku, Aomori and Yamagata, where these textiles were made during long frostbitten winters, they set a new standard for beauty.

What Makes an Object *Mingei*?

According to Sōetsu Yanagi, an object must meet these criteria to be considered a piece of *mingei*:

- The work itself is your best signature. So, the piece must be unsigned and made by nameless artisans.

- It must be a functional item designed for daily use, such as a plate or a bowl.

- It should be simple and unsophisticated, without excess ornamentation.

- It should be one of many similar pieces.

- It should be inexpensive.

KINTSUGI

A Vein of Gold

Kintsugi, meaning "to join with gold", is a 15th-century practice of repairing ceramics with lacquer (*urushi*) made from tree sap, and highlighting the flaws by gilding them with powdered gold. The word *kin* means "gold" in Japanese, and *tsugi* means "stitching" or "joining together". The liquid used to repair the ceramics is the tree's lifeblood; it's a precious commodity because extracting it shortens the tree's life. The philosophy of *kintsugi* touches on several Japanese concepts, such as *mottainai* and *sabi* (beautiful imperfections that demonstrate the passage of time – see Chapter 9). Instead of immediately discarding something simply because it is chipped or cracked, it can be repaired, reused or repurposed. *Kintsugi* can be the birth of something new, or a new phase of life. By embracing our broken pieces, we can begin to heal and put ourselves back together, giving ourselves a new lease of life.

Musician and Zen Buddhist Leonard Cohen famously wrote about the "brokenness of things". Ultimately, everything is broken and cracked; we are all flawed, imperfect beings. We carry our literal and metaphorical scars with us always, but they need not define us. *Kintsugi* repairs forever change the topography of an object, adding value to it and making it a work of art, just as scars and the passage of time change the landscape of our bodies. Our scars are reminders of everything we have endured. They are proof of life, of our survival. Instead of hiding them, what would happen if we allowed ourselves to cherish our imperfections like veins of gold?

What Can We Learn from the Art of *Kintsugi*?

- To accept what is.

- To embrace our vulnerabilities.

- To cherish our possessions and treat them with care and respect.

- To challenge our disposable mindset.

- To place value on our history.

- To embrace impermanence and imperfection.

- To celebrate our flaws.

- To be resourceful.

- Cracks add value; scars add character.

- It is a reminder of our strength and fragility.

- It is proof of our resilience.

THE SUSTAINABLE JAPANESE HOME

Shizenbi (natural beauty) lies at the heart of Japanese aesthetics and traditional Japanese structures. Traditional Japanese *machiya* (townhouses) are built using a palette of natural elements, which wrap around a *tsuboniwa* (pocket garden), a small internal courtyard garden, in layers of mulberry paper, bamboo, stone, grasses and native woods.

Natural elements, materials and textures are woven through the fabric of Japanese homes. Try bringing natural materials and textures into your home – wood, bamboo, rattan, willow and rushes all make beautiful homewares. These can be in the form of furniture, mats, baskets or even a simple turned wooden bowl to place some fruit in. Then when you begin to introduce seasonal elements like a basket of flowers or a few grasses collected on a walk, you will have the perfect space to showcase them. There's something about a room with wooden or stone floors, exposed bricks or beams, that lets you hear their seasonal songs better. The more you surround yourself with nature, the more calming and inspiring your living space will be.

Surround yourself with natural fibres and textures. Straw mats, wooden floors, bamboo baskets, rattan furniture and earthenware – these pieces mark the passage of time, ageing slowly and gracefully with gentle use. Using natural elements and materials like wood, bamboo and rattan in our homes softens and diffuses the harsh line between inside and outside. Instead of reminding us that we are separate from nature, it helps us to feel a part of it. Just as teahouses are designed to be a part of the natural landscape, their humble natural forms blend into their surroundings.

Takezaiku
Bamboo Work

This fast-growing, strong but flexible grass is a mainstay of East Asian art and design. Gently swaying bamboo groves are an iconic part of Japan's natural and cultural landscape and bamboo is used endlessly as a building material, as a food source and to make everything from tea utensils and baskets to architectural elements in the Japanese home. Basketry is a traditional Japanese craft demonstrating bamboo's natural beauty and versatility. These baskets can be sculptural works of art or practical vessels for fruit, flowers, tea utensils or charcoal for the tea ceremony.

Kago
Baskets

Baskets or *kago* made from woven strips of bamboo are a ubiquitous item in the Japanese home, the perfect synthesis of form and function. These versatile vessels are used for everything from displaying flowers, to serving dishes, as shopping baskets and elegant storage solutions. Japanese basketry is a sustainable art form that brings natural warmth and texture into your home as well as acting as a wonderful green alternative to cold, hard and unsustainable plastics.

I collect handwoven baskets from all over the world – whether they're made in France, Indonesia or Japan doesn't matter, only that they speak to me. Baskets are a utilitarian household item made the world over, often by unknown craftspeople. Take them to the farmers market, use them to store your blankets and kindling, organize your cleaning supplies or keep your fruits and vegetables in them. William Morris and Sōetsu Yanagi would have approved of these pieces because they are both beautiful and functional.

Bonzaru
Serving Plates

Bonzaru or *zaru* (serving plates) are multipurpose kitchen staples used as sieves, plates, trays and serving dishes. They're made from finely woven bamboo that is naturally biodegradable, antibacterial and water absorbent, which makes them great for rinsing, draining, serving and drying food. If you visit Japan during the summer months and order *zaru soba* (chilled soba), your buckwheat noodles will be served on one of these beautiful natural dishes.

Washi
Japanese Handmade Paper

Japanese stationery has captivated the world, and for good reason. Japan has been making its own unique kind of paper or *washi* for over 1,000 years. Japan produces more varieties of handmade paper than any other country in the world. It is used in countless ways to protect precious kimonos, wrap gifts, write calligraphy, cover lanterns, folding screens and sliding doors and to make fans. *Washi* is made from the inner bark of living trees, using the long fibres of native shrubs, such as *kōzo* (paper mulberry) and *mitsumata* (paper bush). This naturally soft, off-white-coloured, and lightly textured paper is strong, versatile and beautiful. It also has a rich history of being repurposed and recycled – for example, libraries often use it for conservation. Paper clothing or *kamiko* is made from recycled fibres of old ledgers woven into paper fabrics (*shifu*).

Ikkanbari
Lacquered Paper

Ikkanbari is a traditional Japanese lacquered paper craft. It is made by laminating several sheets of thin *washi* together by pasting them onto bamboo or wood frames and then lacquering them with layer upon layer of amber-coloured *kakishibu* (persimmon tannin dye), a deep amber liquid made from the aged, fermented juice of unripe persimmons. *Kakishibu* is an ancient Japanese method of waterproofing, stiffening and strengthening the paper while also acting as a natural antibacterial and insect repellent. These sheets of paper can be made into baskets, boxes and umbrellas. They're also used as *katagami* (stencil papers) to create the stencils used in *katazome* (resist dyeing) of fabrics for kimono.

Shōji
Paper Screens

Shōji are the elegant sliding doors, windows and room dividers used in traditional Japanese architecture. This iconic element of Japanese design is a partition made from a wooden or bamboo lattice frame covered in delicate translucent *washi* paper. These doors divide the inside from the outside. The beauty of *shōji* is that they soften this barrier, gently allowing air, sunlight and shadows to diffuse through them. Once drawn back, they create perfectly framed views of the gardens beyond. Throughout the year, you can see the silhouettes of trees swaying in the breeze and hear the chorus of birds and insects through the *shōji*.

The Japanese home changes with the seasons. In the humid Japanese summers, the *washi* paper covering the room dividers absorbs moisture and releases it later in drier weather. *Shōji* are living, breathing walls made of natural fibres. They can also be removed completely, opening the house up to the outside and breaking down the barrier between the inside and the outside even further. In the summer, they are sometimes replaced with *sudare*, natural bamboo blinds designed to provide ventilation and give protection from the sun at the same time.

Your Seasonal Home

Nature is never very far away when you live in Japan. Traditional homes and restaurants are made from natural materials and seasonal flowers hang from baskets on the walls or sit in alcoves. You can reflect the changing seasons throughout the year in your own home by changing your interior landscape to reflect the changes in scenery that are taking place outside your window.

Enjoy the season you're in – don't rush to embrace summer before spring ends. Savour the last honeyed drops of summer before autumn deepens. Each season has so much beauty and poetry to offer. Decorate for the upcoming season with fresh or dried flowers, leaves, berries, pine cones and branches that can be composted later. Build up a little collection of treasured seasonal objects that you can bring out and display each year. Mine includes postcards, woodblock prints, pebbles, *furoshiki*, *tenugui* (see page 107) and pieces of folk art.

- Wrapping small items like a tissue box or a plant pot in a *furoshiki* can give your home an instant seasonal update.

- Replace heavy darker autumn/winter furnishings like blankets, throws and cushion covers for lighter, airier options in the spring/summer.

- Arrange a vase or basket with seasonal flowers and place them near the entrance of your home to greet you and your guests when you come home.

- Hang a *tenugui* that celebrates the delights of the upcoming season.

- Curate a few small objects that immediately evoke the season and place them around your living space.

- Use a selection of scents in the form of oils, candles or incense to evoke the changing seasons.

Japanese-Inspired Sustainable Swaps

- Exchange cling film for beautiful beeswax wraps made with Japanese printed fabrics.

- Try using a *konjac* facial sponge.

- Switch single-use plastic cutlery for a set of reusable bamboo cutlery.

- Swap plastic sponges for biodegradable *tawashi* – traditional Japanese scrubbing brushes made of palm fibres.

- Switch teabags for loose-leaf teas. The used tea leaves make excellent fertilizer.

- Wrap gifts in *furoshiki* instead of wrapping paper that can't be recycled.

- Switch your plastic toothbrush for a bamboo one.

- Use *tenugui* as a tea towel instead of kitchen paper.

Tatami

It's difficult to describe the understated beauty of tatami and the quiet pleasure of a *washitsu*, a traditional Japanese-style room made using *shōji* (sliding doors) and covered in tatami mats. Writer John Herrick eloquently compared it "to carpeting your living room with an early autumn evening". When you move from a western room to the outside or into a garden to feel the grass beneath your feet, you immediately feel the difference; you are instantly rooted in nature. In a tatami room, you are already grounded in nature because you have a meadow beneath your feet. This is because tatami mats are made of a thick rice straw core, covered in a layer of soft woven *igusa* (rushes), bordered by a narrow strip of fabric. Some western homes and spaces have natural hardwood floors, polished and softened like pebbles on the beach by waves of footsteps over the decades; the warmth of the wood makes these rooms immediately more appealing. The same can be said of tatami rooms.

Tawashi Brushes

A small, easily overlooked household staple you'll find by the sink in almost every Japanese home is *tawashi* or traditional Japanese scrubbing brushes traditionally made of palm fibres. These hardwearing, compostable brushes are used to scrub vegetables like burdock and lotus root, but they work just as well on carrots and potatoes. You can also use them to clean your pots and pans. Others are made from coir, the biodegradable fibres of a coconut husk. The coarser bristles are best for cleaning vegetables, while the softer variety made from hemp is best for cleaning more delicate items like fruit.

KOKORO

The Heart of the Craftsperson and Spirit of Their Tools

Contemporary master carpenter Toshio Odate wrote in his article "The Soul of the Tool", "For a *shokunin*, a craftsperson with skill, speed and

professional responsibility, tools aren't just things; they have a soul."
Handmade objects possess something that is lacking in mechanized
production; this is what the potter Bernard Leach (1887–1979), a
contemporary of Sōetsu Yanagi, called "the heartbeat in the work".
The artist/craftsperson imparts something of themselves – their life
force – into the work. He perceived handcraftsmanship as the "intimate
expression of the spirit of man". Over time our tools also become
an extension of ourselves. Through daily contact with their tools or
machinery such as a loom, something of the artisan – their essence
– is transmitted, leaving a residue that impacts both the tools and the
finished item.

In Japan, it's not unusual for objects and beloved tools to have
names, just as people and pets do. In the world of tea, each utensil has
its own poetic name – see Chapter 9. Tools are considered an extension
of the craftsperson who uses them. They receive their names when
they are created or used for the first time. Naming them is a mark of
respect and a show of gratitude for their service. Tools are treated with
great care, and each New Year they are carefully cleaned, oiled and
sharpened, and gifted offerings of *mochi*. This was the traditional way
of thanking the tools for their hard work on our behalf and for their
crucial role in the s*hokunin's* life.

Hari Kuyō
The Festival of Broken Needles
8 December in the Kanto region
8 February in the Kansai region

When tools reach the end of their useful life, they are thanked in
ceremonies such as the *Hari Kuyō*, known as the Festival of Broken
Needles or Needle Mass. This Buddhist and Shintō service dates back
400 years. Each winter it is held for expired and broken sewing needles,
which are blessed and laid to rest in a pillowy soft block of tofu. Folklorist
Tanaka Senichi suggests "memorial services for inanimate things hark
back to ancient folk beliefs about the animate nature of things", such
as the belief in *tsukumogami* (tool spectres).

In the animist tradition, inanimate objects, plants and animals are
believed to possess a spark of spiritual essence called *anima*, meaning

"life", "breath" or "spirit" in Latin. These memorial services are an opportunity to say farewell to these small, often overlooked household objects and show gratitude to them for their valued life of service. When things have reached the natural end of their useful life, Japanese people say *"Otsukaresama deshita"* or "Thank you for your hard work".

Tsukumogami
The Disgruntled Spirits of the Things We Discard

Images of Japanese *tsukumogami* (tool spectres), a uniquely Japanese form of spirit or *yōkai* (supernatural creatures), have existed for at least 400 years; their popularity has increased through the recent boom in Japanese pop culture, such as in manga and anime. According to a scroll from the 14th century, called the *Tsukumogami ki* (*Record of Tool Spectres*), after 100 years of service everyday household objects such as umbrellas, mirrors and lanterns were imbued with a *kami* (spirit). Like all things with individual souls, they also developed their own unique wills and personalities. They became prone to playing tricks on people and, although often harmless, they could become resentful if abandoned by the human masters whom they had so faithfully served. According to legend, these tools and utensils became vengeful spectres who terrorized the local community until a benign *tsukumogami* in the form of a set of animated Buddhist prayer beads eventually pacified them. Ultimately, the story of the *tsukumogamiki* is a cautionary tale about the dangers of consumer culture, which in the spirit of *mottainai* warns us not to be wasteful, while reminding us to treat our belongings with more care and respect.

The *In'yo zakki* (*Miscellaneous Records of Yin and Yang*) explains people are especially vulnerable to *tsukumogami* at the end of the year, during the annual spring-cleaning tradition of *susuharai* (soot sweeping), when families would clean their homes from top to bottom, sweeping away any bad fortune in preparation for the New Year. Then, they would often discard old, damaged furniture and utensils, piling them up at the side of the road.

ŌRYŌKI

Just Enough

There are several mindful and sustainable Japanese eating traditions we can take inspiration from; one is called *ōryōki*, a Buddhist term that originally comes from the Sanskrit word *patra*, meaning "a vessel that contains just enough". This is the name of the set of lacquered bowls used by Soto Zen Buddhist monks and the meditative practice of eating using them, which requires precise movements and focuses on mindful awareness and appreciation. The portion of food served is just enough – no more, no less. The meal is carefully balanced so that it is not too salty nor too sweet but still flavourful. This tradition continues today. When a monk is ordained, they receive a set of *jihatsu*, three nested bowls, a pair of chopsticks, a wooden spoon, a cloth napkin and a *setsu* (spatula-shaped utensil) used to clean the bowls with tea or water. The *Zuhastu*, or Buddha Bowl, is the largest bowl of the set, symbolizing the Buddha's wisdom. This is all contained within a cloth bundle, tied with a knot that represents a lotus. The set is used for formal meals during monastic training.

There is a ritual that governs the proper use of these bowls through a series of controlled and precise movements that embody the philosophy of *ōryōki*, of not taking more than we need to sustain us. In his book *Celebrating Everyday Life*, John Daido Loori Roshi (1931– 2009), Abbot of the Zen Mountain Monastery in New York's Catskill Mountains and founder of the Mountains and Rivers Order, wrote that *ōryōki* is more than ritual, it's a state of mind. In his words, "It's a state of consciousness. Because food is life, it is of utmost importance that we receive it with deepest gratitude. When we eat, we consume life. Whether it's cabbage or cows, it's life."

In the modern world, a sense of abundance is achieved through constant expansion. We are always concerned with amassing more: more wealth and more stuff. What if, instead, we focused on cultivating an abundant richness of heart and mind (*kokoro no yutakasa*) through giving, receiving and practising gratitude, instead of accumulating more material riches (*mono no yutakasa*)?

KAKINOHA

Wrapping with Leaves

Japan is known for its elaborate, eye-catching packaging (sometimes over-packaging). However, my favourite type of Japanese packaging is the natural kind. Japan has several types of edible and biodegradable natural food wrappers and a long tradition of *kakinoha*, wrapping with persimmon leaves.

Kakinoha Zushi

Kakinoha zushi or persimmon leaf sushi is made with seasoned rice and *saba* (mackerel), which is then neatly wrapped in a persimmon leaf known to have antibacterial properties. The leaves also impart a sweet, earthy aroma whose natural tannins help to preserve the fish. You can enjoy this local delicacy all year round during a trip to Nara.

Sakura Mochi

These iconic spring sweets are served wrapped in a pickled cherry-tree leaf. This traditional form of Japanese confectionery is said to have originated 300 years ago in a shop near Chomeiji Temple, an area in Tōkyō known for its rows of cherry blossom trees, which line the Sumida River. The temple's groundskeeper, who would sweep up the fallen leaves each autumn, lamented their waste. So, instead of discarding the leaves, he started preserving them in salt and they are used to wrap the *sakura mochi* we know and love.

Some Lesser-known Naturally Wrapped Japanese Sweets

Depending on the season, there is always a naturally wrapped sweet on offer, taking advantage of the leaf's natural antibacterial properties. These are some of the ones I've encountered.

Chimaki – A sticky rice dumpling wrapped in green bamboo leaves and then steamed. They can be filled with sweet red bean paste or savoury fillings of meat and vegetables.

Kashiwa Mochi – Oak-leaf *mochi* enjoyed during the Children's Festival (see page 146).

Mizu Yokan – A summer sweet served in a piece of green bamboo.

Sasa Mochi – This can be plain or covered in either a chunky or fine *anko* (red bean paste) and then folded into a neat triangle shape using a *sasa* bamboo leaf and steamed, which gives the *mochi* a delicate bamboo flavour.

Sasa Dango – This is the cousin of *sasa mochi*, also called *yomogi dango*. A dark green sweet, this gets its natural colour and flavour from *yomogi* or mugwort. It's filled with sweet red bean paste and beautifully wrapped into a parcel using *sasa* bamboo leaves. The leaves keep the sweet fresher for longer.

Tsubaki Mochi – A rice cake sandwiched between two glossy green camellia leaves.

KAISŌ

Sustainable Superfoods

A staple of the Japanese diet, sea vegetables such as *nori, wakame* and *kombu* grow in abundance along the Japanese coast, which is home to over 1,000 kinds of *kaisō* or seaweed. These sustainable future foods are fast growing, don't require fertilizer and much like trees they release oxygen and absorb carbon dioxide. They are also nutritionally dense superfoods, packed with vitamins, minerals and multiple health benefits.[5,6] Seaweeds and algae are a sustainable food source popular in East Asia and are also used in cooking throughout China, Korea and

---

[5] Fitzgerald, C *et al.* (2011) "Heart health peptides from macroalgae and their potential use in functional foods", *Journal of Agricultural and Food Chemistry*, 59(13), pp. 6829–36.

[6] Rajapakse, N and Kim, S-K (2011) "Nutritional and digestive health benefits of seaweed"', *Marine Medicinal Foods – Implications and Applications, Macro and Microalgae*, pp. 17–28.

Taiwan. Closer to home you can find edible seaweeds in Scotland, Ireland and Wales in the UK and in Alaska and California in the US.

Nori – A red algae that looks almost black, with a subtle green sheen when dried. If you've ever eaten sushi, then you'll instantly recognize *nori*. Sold in roasted sheets it's a versatile seaweed that you can shred and use as a garnish for rice or noodle dishes, or to make your own homemade *onigiri* (rice balls) and, of course, sushi.

Wakame – A type of tender slightly sweet dark green sea kelp. Experiment by adding it to soups, salads and pickles.

Hikari – A black seaweed that looks like dried tea leaves. Try adding it to rice dishes or salads.

Kombu – Another kind of sea kelp used to make soup stocks like *dashi* broth, one of the building blocks of Japanese food. If you save the simmered *kombu* from your homemade *dashi* broth, you can turn it into a delicious side dish called *tsukudani,* a relish made from sliced *kombu* simmered in soy sauce, mirin and sugar.

Umibudō – Also known as "sea grapes". They are a popular salty seaweed delicacy from Okinawa that look like a cluster of green grapes in miniature.

Kanten – Agar agar or *kanten* in Japanese. Used in both savoury and sweet dishes, this can be used to make elegant clear jellies from a kind of red algae called *tengusa*. It's a wonderful vegan alternative to gelatine.

TSUKEMONO

The Japanese Art of Preserving

Japanese pickles are an essential part of any authentic Japanese meal. Much like other aspects of Japanese food, they change with the seasons and there are countless regional variations. Japan's dedicated pickle shops offer a veritable rainbow of options. The most common ingredient for *tsukemono* is *daikon* radish. In the spring, you might be served a dish garnished with a flower made of petal-pink translucent slithers of radish; in the winter, that same radish will be pickled a brilliant yellow with *yuzu* juice.

Evidence of pickling both wild and cultivated vegetables in Japan dates back to the 8th century, and preserved food is at the core of *washoku* (traditional Japanese cuisine – see Chapter 3). This tradition originated in Hokkaido, Tohoku and Hokuriku, Japan's northernmost territories, where pickling was an essential way to preserve food for the long, harsh winters, especially in Japan's snow country. Pickling is also a great way to use up a glut of summer vegetables and minimize waste by using food scraps to make watermelon rind pickles.

Seven Types of Japanese Pickles to Try

We now know how beneficial fermented foods such as kimchi, sauerkraut, miso and kombucha are for our health.[7,8] Why not try some of the endless variety of Japanese pickles to add some more fermented foods to your diet? You could even make your own.

Shiozuke – Salted pickles, such as salted cherry blossoms.

Misozuke – Pickles made with miso.

---

[7]   Taylor, B C *et al.* (2020) "Consumption of fermented foods is associated with systematic differences in the gut microbiome and metabolome", *mSystems*, 5(2).

[8]   Dimidi, E *et al.* (2019) "Fermented foods: Definitions and characteristics, impact on the gut microbiota and effects on gastrointestinal health and disease", *Nutrients*, 11(8), p. 1806.

Katsuzuke – Pickles made with sake lees, the discard from the sake-making process.

Nukazuke – Pickles made with *nuka* or fermented rice bran.

Kōjizuke – Pickles made with *kōji*, the essential mould used to make sake, miso, mirin and soy sauce.

Suzuke – Pickles made with vinegar.

Shoyuzuke – Pickles made with soy sauce.

Why Drink Loose Leaf Tea?

Another thing that connects Britain to Japan is our deep love of tea. In the UK, we use 61 billion tea bags each year. That's enough to cover the equivalent of almost 31,000 football or soccer pitches, meaning that we throw away 167 million tea bags every day.[9] Unfortunately, there is no such thing as a completely sustainable tea bag. Sadly, they all contain microplastics to a greater or lesser extent. As I began my tea journey, I replaced black tea with green tea and teabags with tea leaves, and I have never looked back. I drink loose-leaf tea every day. There are so many benefits, both for you personally and for the environment, and there's never been a better time to make the switch.

Loose-leaf tea is:

- Better value for money because you're not paying for unnecessary excess packaging.

- More sustainable, far less wasteful and better for the environment overall.

- More aromatic and contains more antioxidants and flavour.

---

[9] Mirreh, M. (2021) https://www.independent.co.uk/life-style/food-and-drink/uk-tea-football-pitch-poll-b1785356.html, *"Britons get through enough tea bags a year to cover almost 31,000 football pitches, survey claims"*, 11 January.

- More flexible – you can experiment with your own unique blends.

- Adaptable, as it allows you to control the strength of your brew depending on your personal preference.

- Easy to reinfuse multiple times.

You can also try making cold brew versions of your favourite teas and adding garden herbs and fresh fruit in the summertime.

CHAGRA – SPENT LEAVES

Chagra is the Japanese word for spent tea leaves, which can be used throughout your home in various ways once you've enjoyed every last drop of tea they have to offer! First, ensure your tea leaves are completely dry. The best way to do this is to leave them out in the sun or to bake them.

Ways to use them include:

- Adding them to your house plants as fertilizer or to the garden as compost.

- Putting them in a sachet and placing them in the bath water for a relaxing soak.

- Switching dried lavender for dried tea and filling small drawstring bags with the leaves, which are natural deodorizers for wardrobes and drawers.

- Eating them! You can enjoy eating high-quality tea leaves like *gyokuro* seasoned with a little *ponzu* sauce – they're delicious!

- Making homemade soap or a face mask with them.

- Burning them as a natural insect repellent.

DŌTOKU

The Virtues of the Land

The custodians of Rakudo-An, an incredible 120-year-old *azumadachi* (east-facing) farmhouse in rural Toyama, introduced me to the concept of *dōtoku*, which means the virtues of the land or soil. It's said that the term was coined by Sōetsu Yanagi (1889-1961), founder of Japan's folk-art movement who spent time in Toyama in the 1940s. *Dōtoku* is a compound word which includes *toku,* meaning "virtue, benevolence, morality or ethics", and the word *do* or "earth" – the third of the five elements. According to the Chinese five-element system that Japan adopted, each element possesses a virtue; earth's virtue is integrity.

Rakudo-An sits on the Tonami Plain, surrounded by rice paddies and a unique landscape called *sankyoson* (scattered settlement). Homes are surrounded by their own private forest, dispersed between rice fields. Rakudo-An is a *kominka* (traditional folk house) which embodies the principles of regenerative tourism and the virtues of the soil of Japan. Built from natural materials, it was designed to exist in harmony with its rural setting. The hotel focuses on using local, seasonal produce and championing the plentiful artwork of regional artisans and craftspeople, thanks to Toyama's long-established connection to *Mingei*. Places like Rakudo-An are a great source of inspiration for a more sustainable way of living and travelling. Through them, we can experience the benevolence of the Earth. What are the virtues of the land you live on?

❀ Sustainable Travel Ideas for ❀ Your Trip to Japan

Accommodation

- Travel the less-beaten path; get off the golden route.

- Do a farm stay in the Japanese countryside.

- Stay at family-run *minshuku* (guest houses) and *ryokans* (inns).

- Book a *shukubo* (Buddhist temple lodging).

- Support recovering regions such as Tohoku, which is still rebuilding after an earthquake and tsunami devastated the region in 2011.

Getting Around

- Take public transport. Use Japan's fast and efficient transport network of high-speed trains, buses and, of course, the Tōkyō metro.

- Go hiking.

- Hire a bike.

Sustainable Activities for Every Season

❀　Spring　❀

- Go foraging.

- Attend a *hanami* (flower-viewing) party (see Chapter 2).

- Visit a tea farm.

- Try forest bathing.

- Visit Mt Yoshino.

- See the wisteria at Ashikaga Flower Park.

- Attend the *Miyako Odori* (spring dance performance by apprentice geishas – see page 190) in the Gion district of Kyōto.

- Celebrate peony season at Yuushien in Matsue.

- Witness living history at the Hirano Jinja Cherry Blossom Festival.

- See the azaleas at Mifuneyama Rakuen (see page 203).

❀ Summer ❀

- Go white water rafting.

- Make a wish for *Tanabata*, the Star Festival.

- Climb Mt Fuji.

- Swim in Lake Biwa.

- Enjoy a fireworks display.

- Take part in a summer purification ritual.

- Attend Gion *Matsuri* (see page 237).

- Go to the beach.

- Take part in a *bon odori* dance.

- Visit the lavender fields in Hokkaido.

- Try *kakigōri*, a shaved ice dessert.

- Hunt for fireflies.

- Join an indigo dyeing workshop.

❀ Autumn ❀

- Go maple leaf hunting.

- See the fields of cosmos flowers at Showa Kinen Park.

- Try maple leaf tempura in Minoh.

- Attend a moon viewing party.

- Wander through fields of pampas grass in Hakone.

- Visit a chrysanthemum festival.

- Eat Japanese sweet potatoes.

- Harvest *yuzu* in Kochi.

- See the ginkgos turn gold.

- Pick grapes, peaches and plums in Yamanashi or apples in Aomori.

- Enjoy a temple light-up event and see the autumnal landscape illuminated.

❀ Winter ❀

- Soak in an *onsen* (hot springs) surrounded by a snow-covered landscape.

- Learn about the Ainu, Japan's indigenous people at the Upopoy National Ainu Museum in Hokkaido.

- Eat *nabe* (Japanese hotpot).

- Visit the snow monkeys in Nagano.

- Explore a *kamakura* (igloo) village.

- Go skiing or snowboarding.

- See UNESCO World Heritage site Shirakawa village covered in snow.

- Cook on an *irori* (traditional sunken hearth).

- Marvel at the ice sculptures at the Sapporo Snow Festival.

❁ All Seasons ❁

- Take a cookery class.

- Visit local temples and shrines.

- Eat in small family-run restaurants.

- Attend a tea ceremony.

- Support local tourism and book a tour with a local guide.

- Learn how to make traditional Japanese sweets.

- Take a public bath at the local *sentō* (bathhouse).

- Buy your gifts and souvenirs from local craftspeople.

MIZU NO MICHI

The Way of Water

The world of dew
is the world of dew
And yet, and yet ...

KOBAYASHI ISSA

TRANSLATED BY ROBERT HASS

One of Japan's most ancient names is *Mizuhonokuni* (the Land of Abundant Rice), an abbreviation of the phrase, *Toyoashihara no Mizuho no Kuni*, which describes a land of abundant water, full of ripening ears of rice. *Mizuho* is a poetic way of saying that Japan is a bountiful and fertile nation because it receives enough rainfall during the rainy season to produce a plentiful rice crop and maintain its lush green landscape, much like William Blake described my homeland England as a green and pleasant land.

June in Japan is characterized by the beginning of *tsuyu*, the rainy season. Just as the *ume* (plums) are beginning to ripen, the country is covered in water-loving *ajisai* (hydrangeas), blooming in luminescent shades of hot pink, inky blue and lilac. The rainy season gives way to the long hot, humid summer, defined by the search for coolness and accompanied by imagery of stars and the River of Heaven (the Milky Way); these represent the month of *Suzuki* (July). The stars refer to *Tanabata*, the Star Festival, one of Japan's five most ancient and sacred festivals.

JAPAN'S CREATION MYTH

Japan is embraced by the ocean on all sides, so it's no wonder that water permeates the veins of its traditional art and culture, a lasting reflection of Shintō-Buddhist mythology. Powerful aquatic imagery remains everywhere throughout Japan, from its preservation in everyday speech in the Japanese words for a tornado, *tatsumaki* (dragon coils) and a water faucet, *jaguchi* (snake mouth), to the country's cultural practices and architectural details. Ancient water purification rites are still observed daily. Dedicated festivals take place yearly among statues that are still visible throughout present-day Japan and embody the Shintō-Buddhist goddesses Benzaiten, Kannon and Mizu no Kamisama, who still act as conduits for the enduring power of water.

The Japanese archipelago is made up of almost 7,000 islands. Of these, approximately only 416 are inhabited. According to legend, Japan was borne out of fragrant moisture when two siblings from the seventh generation of gods – Izanagi (he who beckons) and Izanami (she who beckons) – stood on the Floating Bridge of Heaven and thrust a jewelled celestial spear called *Ama no Nuboko* into the swirling mass of sea below. They watched as Izanagi drew back the spear and the droplets that fell from its tip became land, forming the islands of Japan.

KIYOMIZUDERA

The Temple of Pure Water

Kiyomizudera, home to Kannon (the Goddess of Mercy), is one of Kyōto's most iconic Buddhist temples. Seated in the foothills of Mt Otowa, it was built 1,200 years ago on the site of the Otowa no Taki waterfall, whose famed healing waters still flow below the temple's main hall. There they are divided into three streams. One represents health, the second, love and the third, wealth. You can only drink from one of the three, so choose wisely!

TEMIZU

Hand Water

Shintō personifies natural elements such as rivers, and ritual purification through water is one of the four vital elements of Shintō. This cleansing of the body of all pollutants, whether physical or spiritual, was first practised by one of Japan's mythic creators, Izanagi (see page 135), when he embarked upon *misogi*, or purification through bathing, after he returned from a failed attempt to rescue his sister Izanami from the underworld. To purify himself, he bathed in the waters of a nearby stream, which resulted in the birth of the *kami* of pollution and the *kami* of purification. Japan's snow-capped mountains and waterways are sacred and their waters are used for making offerings, for cleansing ourselves and for irrigating the fields.

Before entering a sacred space in Japan, such as a Shintō shrine, it's essential to purify yourself literally and metaphorically. This practice is called *temizu* (hand water) and is still observed daily in modern-day Japan. At the entrance to every Shintō shrine, you will encounter a *temizuya* or *mizuya* (purification fountain), often decorated with a dragon who watches over you as you wash your hands to cleanse both mind and body before entering.

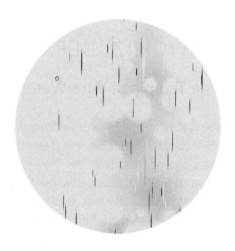

How to Purify Yourself Before
Entering a Shintō Shrine

1. Look for the *hishaku* or bamboo water ladle.

2. Pick the ladle up with your right hand.

3. Fill the *hishaku* with a scoop of water from the fountain and pour some onto your left hand.

4. Then switch the ladle to your left hand and pour the water over your right hand.

5. Pour a little water into your left hand and take a drink from it.

6. Next, tilt the handle of the ladle until it is in the vertical upright position and allow the remaining water to flow down over the handle of the water dipper.

7. Finally, replace the ladle with the pouring side facing downward, ready for the next person to use.

NAGOSHI NO HARAE

Summer Purification Rituals
30 June

Twice a year, in the summer toward the end of June and again at the end of December, you might come across giant rings made from long wild grasses called *chinowa*, outside the entrance to Shintō shrines. When people pass through these wreaths, they create a figure of eight, by first circling around the left side of the hoop, then entering it again and circling the right-hand side; and finally they complete the figure of eight by passing through it once more and turning to the left. After this act they are cleansed of any bad luck that might have been following them throughout the year. This ritual is called *chinowa kuguri*.

Circles have appeared in art forms around the world, from every culture, from the Celts to the Mayans. They can represent the wheel of the year, eternity, a ring-shaped Chinese moon gate,[10] a purification ritual or the Japanese *ensō* (circular form). It's interesting to meditate on the circle as a symbol of the turning wheel of the year, the flow of time and the cyclical nature of the seasons.

In the mindful practice of Japanese *sumi-e* (ink painting) or *shodō* (calligraphy), the deceptively simple *ensō* symbol represents absolute enlightenment, strength, elegance, *mu* (the void) and the universe itself. Calligraphy students practise making an unbroken circle on a page, uninhibited and in a single stroke, without lifting the brush from the page. The pressure you apply to the brush dictates the width and character of your circle.

BENZAITEN

The Goddess of Everything That Flows

Japanese mythology draws from both the Shintō and Buddhist traditions. This combined pantheon contains several aquatic gods, including three female deities intimately linked with water: Benzaiten (the most famous of the three), Kannon and Mizu no Kamisama. Benzaiten, the pre-eminent Goddess of Water in contemporary Japan, is both river *kami* (deity), ocean goddess and the adopted daughter of the Dragon King of Munetsuchi. She was first introduced to Japan with Mahayana Buddhism in the 6th century CE through Chinese translations of the *Sutra of Golden Light*.

---

[10] Traditionally, a moon gate is a circular opening in a garden wall made of brick or stone, that provides an auspicious welcome to those who enter through it. This unique feature originates from Chinese architectural design.

In Japanese myth, rivers are often anthropomorphized. Benzaiten is the legendary personification of the river that flows down from Mt Meru, the sacred mountain home of Chakrasamvara, a tantric form of Shakyamuni, the historical Buddha. In Japanese art, she is often depicted descending from the clouds while riding a dragon and playing the *biwa* (lute). Her headdress is adorned with a *torii* gate and the figure of Unajin, a *kami* (deity) with the body of a snake and the face of an elderly, grey-haired man. In another form, she might appear as a woman with the coiling tail of a snake who possesses a jewel that grants wishes, like that of the Dragon God Ryūjin, who rules the oceans. Since the 10th century CE, people have prayed to Benzaiten to end droughts due to her relationship with dragons, the bringers of rain.

Like her Hindu equivalent, Saraswathi, she is the goddess of everything that flows, including rivers, knowledge, music and the arts. Benzaiten is the only female member of the *Shichi Fukujin*, Japan's Seven Lucky Gods, who have sailed the seas together for over 1,000 years in their *takarabune*, a wooden ship laden with treasure. Her close association with water links her with agriculture and those seeking prosperity. Her principal island sanctuaries are the "Five Great Benten" sites, where it is said that she can grant all manner of wishes. The most famous of these is the shrine of Itsukushima Jinja, recognizable for its "floating" *torii* gate emerging from the sea, off the coast of Miyajima.

KANNON

The Goddess of Mercy

Benzaiten bears many similarities to Kannon (the Bodhisattva of Mercy), who is worshipped throughout East Asia. Kannon hears the cries of all those in peril at sea over the din of raging storms, and rescues shipwrecked sailors. As a nation of fishers and anglers, Japanese people have always survived on the bounty of the ocean, watched over by Kannon, whose statues can be found in watery grottos and shrines dotted along the coastline throughout Japan.

As the Japanese form of the Pure Land Buddhist deity Guanyin (China) or Avalokiteshvara (India), Kannon arrived in Japan with

Buddhism via the Silk Road in the late 6th century CE. Kannon is a Bodhisattva, a Sanskrit term for one who has achieved enlightenment according to Mahayana Buddhism but has chosen instead to remain on the earthly plane to help humanity reach nirvana (enlightenment). This benevolent goddess has over 30 incarnations, allowing her to appear in any form to alleviate suffering and give salvation to those in need. In her female form, Kannon represents the divine feminine, rising to popularity through the cloistered women of the Heian (794–1185) court, empowering them by offering universal enlightenment to all through the *Lotus Sutra*. Previously, women had been excluded from attaining Buddhahood because femininity was seen as something that had to be overcome to reach nirvana; this is when her close association with women and mothers began.

MIZU NO KAMISAMA

The Shintō Goddess of Water

Mizu no Kamisama, the Shintō Goddess of Water and one of the *Shi no Ōkami* – the Four Great Gods and elementals of wind, water, earth and fire – is also a patron of fertility and motherhood, worshipped by women praying for safe and easy childbirth. Throughout Japan, in private gardens, near mountain springs and at the edges of verdant rice paddies, you'll find small rocks dedicated to her, inscribed with the characters for *suijin* (water god), an ancient form of water deity still worshipped by farmers and fisherfolk today. Mizu no Kamisama is the apex of the term *suijin,* which encompasses all heavenly and earthly manifestations of water, including dragons, snakes and turtles. In Tōkyō's famous Tsukiji fish market, supplicants visit Suitengu Shrine (the Palace of Suiten, another name for *suijin*) to offer prayers to these goddesses of water, who oversee the fish market and its traders. Several annual *matsuri* (festivals) are held throughout the summer at holy sites dedicated to the Shintō deity of water; they ask for bountiful harvests, the banishing of disease and protection from water-related disasters.

RYŪ

Dragons

Belief in such creatures predates written history; dragons have always occupied a central role in East Asian art and mythology, encompassed by the Sanskrit term *naga,* the serpent-like guardians of Buddhism. *Ryūjin Shinko,* meaning "dragon god faith", is a Shintō belief that venerates dragons as water deities capable of shape-shifting and using their transformational magic to take human form.

Representations of *ryū* or dragons are another constant at Japanese temples and shrines across the nation. Dragons are members of the *Hachi Bushū* (Eight Legions), classes of spirits charged with protecting the *Dharma* (Buddhist law). They are a group of celestials and supernatural beings also said to be present when the historical Buddha first laid out the *Flower Sutra.*

RYŪJIN

The Dragon God

The lush tropical islands of Ryukyu (modern-day Okinawa) have become famous tourist destinations. However, beneath the ocean waves and hidden between the isles lies the fabled coral palace of Ryūjin, the Dragon God. Legend has it that his coffers are filled with treasures, such as jewels that can control the ebb and flow of the tides. According to myth, dragons dwell in expanses of water and the caves near Benzaiten's shrines. The larger the body of water, the more influential the dragon inhabiting it. In the pages of the *Enoshima Engi,* an 11th-century mythical-historical work, Benzaiten placates and eventually marries the dragon that terrorized Enoshima. According to Chinese philosophy, dragons possess male yang energy, which complements Benzaiten's female yin energy: the two halves of order and chaos demonstrating the duality of the universe. Dragons are often depicted carrying Benzaiten through the heavens and are linked to her aquatic symbology; they control rain, tempests and the tides, with their breath transforming into clouds that can become rain or fire.

SHIKI NO NIWA

The Four Seasons Garden

Several Japanese fairytales from the Muromachi period (1336–1573) mention the "garden of four seasons in four directions". My personal favourite is the tale of Urashima Taro, the fisherman who saved a sea turtle and was rewarded with a visit to the home of the Dragon King, where he fell in love with Otohime, the Dragon Princess. F Hadland Davis retold the story in *The Myths and Legends of Japan*, describing the fairytale palace of the Dragon King. *Ryūgū* is the Dragon King's residence beneath the waves, another world not bound by nature's natural laws, where time moves differently to the surface world.

The Dragon King's domain is home to the utopian garden of the four seasons in four directions, where according to Davis, "all the seasons lingered together", displaying nature's "infinite variety of beauty". Here there are blossoms all year round and the flowers never fade. In the east, butterflies flit through cherry blossoms representing an eternal spring. In the south, crickets sing under the tree's lush summer canopy. In the west, the trees are aflame in a never-ending autumnal scene. Lastly, in the north lies a frozen pond surrounded by fresh snow drifts trapped in winter's perpetual icy embrace.

ONSEN

Bathing in Nature

Japan is a volcanic island home to 27,000 hot springs scattered across the shoreline, beneath waterfalls and deep in the mountains. The proliferation of *onsen* (hot spring baths) across large swathes of the country is a testament to the continued cultural significance and importance of bathing rituals in contemporary Japan. My favourites are called *rotenburo* – open-air hot-spring baths that allow us to literally bathe in nature. Every element of the experience, from the baths we sit in made from rocks in the natural landscape or hinoki cypress tubs and the clean mineral-rich water we soak in, to the stunning natural views surrounding us, immerses us in nature literally and figuratively.

Do you live somewhere with natural geothermal hot springs, like Japan, Iceland or the USA? If not, why not try wild swimming instead?

KYŌKAI

Liminal Spaces

The pre-modern Japanese playwright Chikamatsu Monzaemon (1653–1725) described water as the place where man meets woman, life crosses over into death and the known world merges with the world beyond. As an island nation, Japan has a symbiotic relationship with water, which can be traced back to its creation myth (see page 135) and is continuously reflected through its classical art and literature. Water represents femininity, purification and metamorphosis in Japanese mythological and folkloric traditions. It can even act as a portal to another realm.

Kyōkai, or liminal spaces, exist on the edges of a boundary. They are transitional places or times such as bridges, tunnels, crossroads, twilight or the threshold of a traditional *tatami* room (see page 117). They are also spaces between worlds. For many cultures, including Japan, bridges and bodies of water are symbolic of transition. For example, Japanese noh theatres occupy two worlds: the stage represents the mortal realm, while backstage is the *ikai*, home to the supernatural. The theatres are traditionally built over water to cleanse the space, so the gods may enter and take up residence in the *matsu* (pine) painted on the back wall of the main stage. To reach the stage actors must cross a bridge, allowing them to transition from the *ikai* into the world of the living, traversing literally and metaphorically into another realm.

Plum rain
Young leaves illuminated
Neon green

NATALIE LEON

TSUYU

The Rainy Season

The end of May and the beginning of June marks the start of the rainy season. *Tsuyu* or *baiu* is the name for the Japanese rainy season, but it literally translates to "plum rain". This alludes to the heavy raindrops that fall as the *ume* (plums) ripen, turning from vivid green to warm yellow. The *ume* or plum season is short, so you have to act quickly. The best time to make *umeshu*, Japanese plum wine, is when the plums are still green.

Finding Beauty in the Rain

The world reveals itself anew when it rains. As author Iwao Matsuhara wrote, the unsurpassable beauty of the land is revealed when "Nature broods and sobs in the drizzling rain." Japanese has a myriad of poetic words and phrases to describe different types of rainfall.

- Look for the raindrops glistening on every leaf.

- See how the mosses have become almost luminous after the rain.

- Observe the hidden colours of pebbles and bark revealed by water.

- Find reflections in every puddle.

- Watch how the fallen flowers and damp petals become beautiful evanescent compositions.

 *NATSU MATSURI*

Summer Festivals

Hachijū Hachiya – The 88th Night

2 May

This special event in the tea farmer's calendar takes place on the 88th night after *Risshun*, the official beginning of spring in Japan. This is when the first tea of the year is harvested. This tea is called *shincha* (new tea), sometimes called the "first flush". *Shincha* is only available for a brief period in the late sping and early summer.

Kodomo no Hi – Children's Day

In Japan, 5 May is *Kodomo no Hi*, Children's Day, also known as *Tango No Sekku* (Boys' Day). The final national holiday in Golden Week, Children's Day is another of Japan's more ancient festivals, one of the *Gosekku* (Five Sacred Festivals), the five feast days held at the Imperial court during the Nara period (710–794). *Koinobori* (colourful carp-shaped streamers) are the emblems of Children's Day. You can see them swimming through the sky during the month of May.

Ajisai Matsuri – The Hydrangea Festival
Mid-June

The wild mountain *ajisai* (hydrangea) is native to Japan and is the ancestor of the *Hydrangea serrata*, the iconic flower of the Japanese rainy season. The name *ajisai* means water-drinker. Hydrangea season is celebrated yearly with *Ajisai Matsuri* (hydrangea festivals) held all over Japan. In Kyōto, you can visit Mimurotoji, the so-called Temple of Flowers, famous for the 20,000 hydrangeas that bloom there each June.

An alternative name for the hydrangea is the "tea of Heaven". In Japan, the leaves of the *Hydrangea serrata* are used to make *amacha*, a naturally sweet tisane. This herbal tea is poured over statues of the Buddha during *Kanbutsue* (the Buddha bathing ceremony), a celebration of his birthday, and enjoyed as part of the annual festivities. *Amacha* (sweet tea) is used as a substitute for *amrita*, the elixir of immortality. According to legend, upon his birth, the Buddha was "baptized" with *amrita* by nine dragons.

Tanabata – The Star Festival
7 July[11]

In July, bamboo branches waving in the breeze covered in brightly coloured decorations grace almost every temple and shrine in Japan to celebrate *Tanabata* (Evening of the Seventh), Japan's most romantic

---

[11] *Tanabata* celebrations in Sendai, one of the biggest *Tanabata* festivals in Japan, begin on 7 August.

matsuri. Tanabata, also known as the Star Festival, celebrates the story of two star-crossed lovers: the heavenly weaver Princess Orihime, daughter of Tentei the Sky King, and her love, Hikoboshi the cow herd. According to the original Chinese legend, Orihime was a weaver for the celestial deities. While visiting Earth, she fell in love with Hikoboshi. They married and started a family. However, the Sky King grew angry with Orihime for neglecting her loom, turning her into the star Vega and her husband into the star Altair. The two stars are forever separated by *Amanogawa* or the River of Heaven (the Milky Way). They wait for each other on opposite sides of the river but can only reunite once a year on 7 July, the seventh day of the seventh month of the lunisolar calendar, when all the *kasasagi* (magpies) in the world flock to them, spreading their wings to form a bridge over the celestial river for them to meet. In Japan, it is said that if the sky is cloudy on the seventh of the seventh, they will be unable to meet, and the resulting raindrops are their tears of frustration.

The most common form of *Tanabata* decorations are *tanzaku* (paper or poem strips). These colourful slips of paper are used to write wishes on, then tied to freshly-cut bamboo branches at local temples and shrines. In the Edo period (1603–1868), the wishes took the form of poems. Originally people wrote their poems on *kaji* (mulberry leaves). The fibres of the mulberry plant are still used to make Japanese *washi* paper.

❀ MAKE YOUR OWN ❀
WISHING TREE

Try making your own miniature wishing tree at home. Write your wishes on slips of paper and hang them from the tree. Then you can invite your friends, family and any guests who visit to add their wishes to your wishing tree and enjoy the tree as part of your seasonal summer altar or festive decor.

Materials

White/coloured paper or origami paper

Scissors or a guillotine

A hole punch

A pen

Ribbon or some string

A bamboo branch or a small bamboo potted plant

STEP 1. First, select the colours you'd like to use to make your *tanzaku.* These are the coloured slips of paper you'll write your wishes on. They can be plain white or any colour of your choice. I like to use a selection of pastel origami paper to make my wishing tree.

STEP 2. Next, use the scissors or guillotine to cut them into long thin strips. Ideally, the *tanzaku* should be rectangles of approximately 7x15cm (3x6in).

STEP 3. Use your hole punch to make a hole at the top of each slip of paper, approximately 1cm (⅓ in) of the way down.

STEP 4. Now you can write your wishes on the slips of paper and thread the ribbon or string through the holes.

STEP 5. Finally, tie your *tanzaku* onto the bamboo.

UMI NO HI

Umi no Hi or Marine Day coincides with the end of the rainy season (*tsuyu*) and takes place on the third Monday in July. People in Japan traditionally celebrate by going to the beach. Perhaps we could adopt this worldwide and take one day a year to give thanks to our oceans and seas. Why not embrace this aquatic holiday and make it your own?

Ideas for Celebrating Marine Day

You can take part in this celebration of our oceans and seas, no matter where you might be. Here are just a few ideas to help get you started. Start your own Marine Day rituals, and please feel free to share them with me.

- Go on a day trip to the seaside with friends or family.

- Take your dog for a walk along the coastline.

- Pick up litter on your local beach.

- Go for a swim in the ocean.

- Take your sketchbook to the pier and draw or paint the waves as they come crashing in.

- Prepare a meal of responsibly sourced fish and give thanks for the ocean's bounty.

OBON

The Festival of Returning Spirits
15 August

In Japan, August brings with it the hottest period of the year. The month is marked by the many traditions surrounding the three-day celebration of *Bon* or *Obon*. This Buddhist festival is over 500 years old and celebrates the return of ancestral spirits. First, bonfires and *chōchin* (lanterns) are lit to beckon the spirits home in a ritual called *mukaebon*. Then at the end of the festival, they are burned again to help guide the ancestors back to the spiritual plane; these are called *okuri* (send-off fires). One of Japan's most famous *Obon* celebrations is the Daimonji Festival in Kyōto, during which a series of enormous 200m-long (220yd) *gozan okuribi* (ritual fires) are lit on five mountainsides. They burn throughout the night and are visible from a great distance, helping the ancestors to find their way home.

This Buddhist celebration and its use of light is similar to the practice of *yahrzeit* (anniversary), during which members of the Jewish faith mark the anniversary of a loved one's death by keeping a memorial candle burning for 24 hours.

RYOO O MITSUKERU

Finding Coolness

There are many traditional ways to keep cool during *natsubate*, meaning the "dog days of the humid Japanese summer". Shades of blue and green evoke bodies of water, the sky and the ocean, so stylized images of *suihen* (water-related things) are printed in blue and white on floor cushions and *yūkata*, casual cotton kimonos designed to be worn in the summer. The confectionery shops in Kyōto are full of translucent water-themed *wagashi* (sweets), all aiming to emulate feelings of refreshing breezes and cooling waters to help provide a little respite from the summer's intense heat.

How to Create Feelings of Coolness in the Summer

In the summer months, I like to pack up my tea things and take them to a shady spot near a river or a lake. I make cold brewed tea and coffee daily and serve matcha in a glass *natsu chawan* (summer tea bowl). These shallow tea bowls are rarely seen outside of Japan. This type of glass teaware is a Japanese summer staple because the glass allows the matcha to stay cooler for longer. If you go out for sushi, you might also receive a beautifully plated glass dish of fresh *sashimi* on top of a bed of ice, designed to keep the fresh fish cool.

There are lots of ways to try and cope with the extreme heat of Japanese summers. One of them is finding a sense of coolness through aquatic imagery and the sound of water *(mizu no oto)*. In Japan, it is believed that if you think of cold water and surround yourself with its colours, images and sounds, it will help to cool you down. So here are a few Japanese-inspired suggestions.

- Make *kanten* jellies using agar agar and fresh summer fruits.

- Sprinkle a little pinch of flaky sea salt on slices of ripe watermelon – it will help to replenish your electrolytes and it tastes fantastic!

- Eat delicious *kakigōri*, Japanese-style shaved ice.

- Try making some *hanagōri* (flower ice) by freezing edible seasonal flowers, such as pansies, violas and nasturtiums, in ice cubes and adding them to your drinks.

- Drink cold brewed tea. Why not experiment with adding garden herbs such as mint for freshness or lemon verbena for a hint of citrus?

- Enjoy *zaru* soba; these cold soba noodles are one of Japan's iconic summer dishes. I like to garnish mine with edible flowers from the garden.

- Carry a fan with you at all times. The *uchiwa* (flat summer fan) and *sensu* (folding fan) are essential summer accessories in Japan.

- Hang a *fūrin* (wind chime) and enjoy the tinkling sound as it flutters in the breeze.

- Take a walk down by the river.

- Cool off by dipping your feet in a flowing stream.

THE SMALL SEASONS OF SUMMER

Rikka – Sekki No.7
The Start of Summer
⁂⁓ *5 May* ⁓⁂

Rikka, which takes place on 5 or 6 May, is the seventh of the twenty-four *sekki*, the divisions of the solar year. This marks the official beginning of summer in Japan. *Rikka* takes place between the Vernal Equinox and the Summer Solstice. The forest's canopy and grasses are becoming lusher and greener every day.

Shōman – Sekki No.8
Lesser Ripening
⁂⁓ *21 May* ⁓⁂

Shōman (the lesser ripening) begins on 21 or 22 May. The first fireflies of the season begin to appear, and white and purple wisteria drapes languidly from arbours, creating a dreamlike display.

Bōshu – Sekki No.9
Grains on Ears
꙳⁓ 6 June ⁓꙳

Bōshu (grain beards or seeds) follows on 6 or 7 June. After that, the rice transplanting season begins, which coincides with the rainy season. Japan is full of summer flowers, including azaleas and irises.

Geshi – Sekki No.10
The Summer Solstice
꙳⁓ 21 June ⁓꙳

Geshi (the Summer Solstice) takes place on 21 or 22 June. It's the longest day of the year, which occurs during the middle of Japan's *tsuyu* or rainy season, the peak of the rice-planting season.

Shōsho – Sekki No.11
Lesser Heat
꙳⁓ 7 July ⁓꙳

Shōsho (lesser heat) begins on 7 or 9 July, just as the lotus flowers start to bloom but wither by the afternoon. The seventh of the seventh is the start of *Tanabata* (the Star Festival), see page 146.

Taisho – Sekki No.12
Greater Heat
꙳⁓ 22 July ⁓꙳

During *taisho* (greater heat), the hottest part of the summer, people begin the practice of *uchimizu*, sprinkling water in front of their homes and businesses. Originally this was an offering to the gods, now it's to prevent dust and help keep cool.

NATSU KIGO

Seasonal Words for Summer

Kunpu – A fragrant summer breeze that carries the scent of seasonal flowers.

Ryūsui – Flowing or running water, especially the sound of a stream, which is a respite from the heat of the summer.

Hashi-i – Sitting on a veranda or cooling off on the porch in the summertime.

Amanogawa – The Japanese name for the Milky Way, which means the River of Heaven.

Yūyake – This means a "burned evening", but it suggests the red afterglow of a sunset.

Hotarugari – *Hotaru* (fireflies) hunting. Across Japan, electric fireflies are briefly visible at dusk during the summer months.

Koinobori
Carp Streamers

Japanese *koi* (carp), sometimes called *nishikigoi*, originally arrived in Japan from China. The first recorded mention of them in Japan was in c.71 CE. According to a Han Dynasty myth, a carp that successfully swam upstream, surviving the rapids of the Yellow River and the Dragon Gate Waterfall, would then transform into a dragon. In Japan, *koi* are symbols of strength, determination and courage. *Koinobori* (carp streamer kites) reference that myth. This ancient story was given a new lease of life in the form of the Pokemon Magikarp – now you know the legend behind them!

NATSU WAGASHI

Sweets for Summertime

Summer is the season of confections that celebrate water, such as *minazuki*, which means "water month". The name of this sweet refers to the farming custom of flooding freshly transplanted seedlings in the rice paddies each summer. In the past, to beat the intense heat of Japanese summers, the ice stored in the Imperial icehouses (*himuro*) over the winter would be sliced and served to the members of the Imperial court on the first day of the sixth lunar month. Then, adzuki beans and a syrup made from the vine of the amakazura plant were poured over the ice before it was served to the Emperor and the Imperial court to alleviate the stifling summer's heat.

Minazuki – *Wagashi* artisan Hajime Nakamura explains that *minazuki* was originally created for those who could not access ice, which was a luxury. This triangular-shaped sweet is made of *kudzu* (a naturally starchy plant) or glutinous rice flour and the surface is topped with sweet adzuki beans. It's designed to suggest a sheet of ice to drive away the summer heat.

Kashiwamochi – Oak-leaf *mochi* is a plain rice cake stuffed with red bean paste, which is served wrapped in an oak leaf. The tradition of oak-leaf *mochi* eaten on Children's Day began in the Kamakura period with the rise of the samurai class. The oak leaves represent unbroken family lineages, making them a type of edible good luck charm.

Ajisai Kinton – This hydrangea-inspired *wagashi* is made from bean paste passed through a strainer. The shreds are coloured in shades of blue and purple.

Mizu Shingen Mochi – More commonly known as a water-drop cake or raindrop cake, this crystal-clear and translucent confection resembling a drop of dew is actually a jelly made from water and agar agar.

JAPANESE MICRO SEASON NO.29
AYAME HANA SAKU

Irises Bloom
꙰ *27 June – 1 July* ꙰

Japan is home to several varieties of iris: the *ayame*, the taller *hanashōbu* and the wild rabbit-eared *kakitsubata,* which all bloom in June. These elegant flowers have been immortalized in Japanese poetry, art and literature since the Heian period (794–1185). The *hanashōbu* (Japanese iris) is the floral emblem of Children's Day, and you'll often see these beautiful flowers on display at this time of the year.

Shōbuyu
Bathing with Irises

Shōbu (Acorus) also known as sweet flag, is named for its fragrant leaves and visual similarity to the leaves of irises, often called flags in English. This strongly scented, wild-water-loving plant is prized in both China and Japan for its medicinal properties. Chopped sweet flag was added to sake and sipped by nobles at the Imperial court and people placed *shōbu* leaves beneath their pillows as a talisman. In the Japanese Heian-period classic, *The Pillow Book,* Sei Shōnagon (966–1017) describes the elegant beauty of the Sweet Flag Chamberlains – young women dressed in white, who wore garlands of irises in their hair and distributed long stems of sweet flag to courtiers during the Sweet Flag Festival, now known as Children's Day or Boys' Festival.

Japan has a history of seasonal bathing rituals. For example, the tradition of bathing with *shōbu* leaves in May is an ancient practice dating back to the Nara (710–794) or Heian era (794–1185). At this time of the year, you might see bundles of these long sword-like leaves on sale in the local supermarket. Over time *shōbu,* which is also an ancient word for "sword", became associated with heroism and the warrior spirit due to the shape of their leaves. The phrase *shōbu zukuri,* which means "iris leaf", refers to the graceful, curved tip of this style of Japanese *katana* or sword.

ONOMATOPOEIA

The Sounds of Nature

The Japanese language has infinitely more onomatopoeic words than English. When I spoke with author Naoko Abe, she explained that many of these onomatopoeic phrases are used to describe the myriad sounds of nature, giving voices to the birds, the insects and even the rain. She added that one of the ways she feels the richness of the seasons is through such Japanese onomatopoeia. In English, we have lots of whimsical phrases to describe the volume of rainfall, but Japanese engages different senses to describe the sounds of nature, the unique music that only nature can create. Do you have any onomatopoeic words or phrases that are personal favourites?

Mushi no Ne
The Insects' Song

Toward the end of summer until early autumn, on hot, humid evenings, the iconic chirping sounds of *mushi* (insects) that can be heard coming from the fields and grasses is a "symphony" presented by the *suzumushi* (crickets) and *semi* (cicadas). Each insect has a distinctive voice or *koe*, and in Japanese they have their own unique onomatopoeic phrases. Do you ever hear the insects singing in the summer?

Onomatopoeia for the Four Seasons

Spring – The sound of light rain falling is *shito shito, para para* or *potsu potsu*.

Summer – The summer song of the *suzumushi* (crickets) is *rii-n rii-n. Mushi* means insect, and *suzu* means bell.

Autumn – The rustle of autumn leaves underfoot is called *kasa kasa.*

Winter – In the winter, when you walk on freshly fallen snow, the crunching sound it makes underfoot is *saku saku*. As you watch the snowflakes gently falling from the sky, they are known as *shin shin*. Although the snow falls silently, in Japanese the word *shin* or "deep" is repeated to suggest the silence deepening as the snow blankets the ground.

SHINSHŌ FŪKEI

Recollected Vistas

For author Naoko Abe, the insect's annual summer concert evokes a concept called *shinshō fukei*. The word *fukei* means "landscape" or "scenery". *Shinshō fukei* is a recollected image in your mind's eye. The four characters that make up the phrase mean heart, image, wind and shadow, which can also be translated as the scene within your heart. Abe describes it as something deeply embedded in your memory; it could be an image or sound you grew up with. It's a cultural touchstone that's unique to the climate where you grew up and is a part of you, though you may not even realize it.

KIBUNE

May–September

Kibune in Kyōto Prefecture is famous for *kawadoko ryōri* – food served on a riverbed veranda. Each summer restaurants nestled in the forest alongside the Kibune River set up *kawadoko* (dining platforms erected over the river). On these verandas, guests can dine over the river. There you can enjoy a delicious meal of locally caught freshwater fish and edible wild plants while you listen to the sound of the water rushing beneath you and enjoy the cool breeze of the river.

SHINROKU

New Green

After the last cherry blossoms have fallen Japan transforms into a deep green wonderland. This is the season of *shinroku* ("new green"). After the spring rains and a long winter, the first flush of spring foliage that emerges at the end of cherry blossom season is almost supercharged. A vivid neon green in colour, these prized young leaves have a translucent quality. In the early morning light, they become like panes of glass – the sunlight filters through them creating a prismatic green mosaic. In Japan, leaves are treated much like flowers, enjoyed throughout the country and immortalized in art and design – especially the new green leaves of late spring and the golden ginkgo and fiery *momiji* of autumn.

The stars of this time between late spring and early summer are the *aoi kaede*, the blue leaves. *Aoi* means "blue" and *kaede* means "frogs' hands", and the term refers specifically to green maple leaves. Although the words *kaede* and *momiji* are often used interchangeably to talk about spring foliage, *momiji* refers specifically to Japan's spectacular autumn leaves. Young *momiji* look like green five-pointed stars. When you go into the mountains of Ohara in Northern Kyōto and look up, layer upon layer of delicate green lace washes over you like green waves, turning the sky into a sea of green stars. This fresh, new green is pulsing with life. In Japan the colour green not only represents nature, but also health and vitality. And as evergreen trees are considered to be immortal, green also represents immortality itself.

FINDING BEAUTY
IN THE DARKNESS

Japan appreciates the play of shadows more than any other nation I've encountered. Writer Jun'ichirō Tanizaki (1886–1965) illuminates the beauty of shadows perfectly in his seminal text on Japanese aesthetics, *In Praise of Shadows*: "were it not for shadows, there would be no beauty."

In the summer, shade becomes a precious commodity. *Aoi momiji*, the fresh new blue maple leaves, are a lush, bright green. As you walk beneath them enjoying *ryokuin* (green shadows), you can seek respite from the heat in their shade; this is called *konoshitayami*.

Have you ever lit a candle beneath a vase of flowers in a dark room? When there is no other source of light, the candle illuminates the details of the flowers in a completely different way. This is something the Dutch Masters understood – the power of shadow and the magic of candlelight.

In Edo-period Japan, members of the Imperial court lived with decorative *byōbu* (free-standing folding screens) covered in gold leaf, which created a soft glow, diffusing the light in rooms illuminated only by candlelight or *andon* (oil-burning lanterns). The details of the artwork in the room were accented and accentuated in entirely new ways when lit in this way, in sharp contrast to being flooded with light as we often are in modern city living.

While natural light is a beautiful gift, why not take a moment to enjoy the dark side? Light a candle near a vase of flowers or in front of one of your favourite works of art and you will see it in a whole new light.

KIMONO

Wearing the Seasons

The "Thing to Wear"

The term "kimono" comes from the Japanese words *mono* meaning "thing" and *kiru* meaning "to wear". It came into use in the Meiji period (1868–1912) when the craze for all things western led to a need to distinguish between western and Japanese clothing. *Kimono* – literally "a thing to wear" – is derived from its precursor, the *kosode* (*ko* meaning "small" and *sode* meaning "sleeves"). As Anna Jackson, Keeper of the Asian Department at the Victoria and Albert Museum, explains, *kosode* is an umbrella term encompassing all garments "with sleeves that swing". In traditional forms of Japanese dress, there is less emphasis on the body of the wearer and more focus on the garment itself. The T-shaped cut of the *kosode* is a blank canvas for designers; they are, in effect, wearable pieces of art, not just two-dimensional but three, moving with the wearer.

Instead of emphasizing the bust or the waist, greater focus is placed on the surface design of pieces like the kimono, rather than the cut. The combination of colour, fabric and decorative elements indicate the owner's gender, age and status. For example, black kimono are worn by both men and women for formal occasions and *furisode*, brightly coloured kimono known for their long flowing sleeves, are traditionally worn by unmarried women to celebrate their coming of age. The colours and designs of kimono also reflect the changing seasons of the year.

My love affair with kimono began at a young age when my mother took a large, brightly coloured bundle of fabric out of a polished, black, lacquered cabinet. As she slowly unfurled it, I realized that it was, in fact, not just a piece of fabric but a kimono, and not just any kimono but a heavily embroidered and lavishly decorated one with metallic threads and a weighty, padded hem. I later learned that it was an *uchikake*, a special type of kimono worn as an overcoat layered over a white bridal kimono. I was hooked. My love of kimono has never wavered; it burns brightly to this day and has taken me to the temple markets of Kyōto, the flea markets of Paris and countless art exhibitions, workshops and talks to learn more about this incredible T-shaped garment.

The Global Impact of Kimono

The kimono is arguably one of the most iconic articles of clothing in the world. Its ongoing impact on global fashion cannot be overstated. Ever since the first kimono arrived in Europe, they have captured the hearts and minds of the western world. When kimono debuted on the global stage at the Great Exhibition in 1851 fashion lovers swiftly adopted them, and the rest is history. Since then, the kimono has continued to inspire and delight the art and fashion worlds, serving as a source of innovation and imagination to countless artists, such as Camille Monet, Vincent van Gogh and James McNeill Whistler, as well as designers like Paul Poiret, Madeleine Violet, Alexander McQueen and Yves Saint Laurent.

Types of Kimono

Yūkata are unlined cotton kimono designed to be worn for summer festivals, fireworks displays and relaxing inside *ryokan* (traditional Japanese inns) after visiting the *onsen* (hot spring baths). You'll often see them in either classic indigo-dyed designs or bold, colourful motifs of iconic Japanese summer staples such as watermelons, fireworks and sunflowers.

Iromuji are modest, single-coloured kimono, often worn for tea ceremonies.

Komon is a type of casual kimono that is completely covered in small, finely detailed patterns.

Furisode literally means "swinging sleeves". This elegant variety of kimono is iconic and instantly recognizable because of its long, flowing sleeves. Young women wear these traditionally brightly-coloured kimono with bold designs on their Coming of Age Day or at graduation.

Tomesode (fastened sleeves) are formal kimono worn by married women. The pattern on the cloth only extends below the waist on this type of kimono. The black version is the most formal version and is called a *kuro tomesode,* which bears five family crests. It's traditionally worn for formal occasions, such as weddings, by the mother of the bride or groom.

Uchikake are heavily embroidered silk kimono with a padded hem; these are only worn on formal occasions, such as weddings, as an outer layer.

IRO

The Traditional Colours of Japan

Throughout history, in Japanese society, social status has been expressed through colour. The government used sumptuary laws restricting the use of *kinjiki* (specifically forbidden colours such as deep purple), which could only be worn by priests and the nobility. Most people could only wear shades of brown, grey or indigo blue. Vibrant colours that required vast amounts of dye to create were reserved for members of the court.

Kokoro no Iro
Colours of the Heart

Japan's fundamental or primary colours are black, red, white and blue-green. They appear on kimono and throughout daily life in Japan; each one represents one of Japan's *Gogyo Setsu* or five elements, which gave colours additional significance. They all relate to the changing nature of the sky as the sun moves through the day. The Japanese word for red (*aka*) comes from the word *akashi* or "to brighten", referencing the break of dawn. Once daylight has dawned, objects become clearly visible. *Shiro* (white) is derived from the word *shiroshi*, meaning "to appear". At dusk, things become obscured once more; *ao* (blue) is derived from the word *aoshi*, meaning "vague" or "obscure". Finally, as the night draws in, the Japanese word for black (*kuro*) comes from the word *kurashi*, meaning "darkness".

Japan's paintbox may be the most beautiful I have ever seen. In autumn, how many shades of red can you identify? In the spring, how many different pinks? How many shades of cool blues and lush greens can you pick out in the summer? What about in the winter, under the snow? How many variations of white do you see?

GOGYO SETSU

The Five Elements

Gogyo Setsu (the theory of the Five Elements) is the Japanese name for the ancient Chinese concept of *Wuxing*, meaning the Five Phases or Five Agents. *Wu Xing* came to Japan alongside *onmyodo*, the theory of yin and yang, and both originated from Taoist cosmology. According to agronomist Ninomiya Sontoku (1787–1856), "Yang makes things grow, and yin makes things quiet down." As yin and yang ebb and flow throughout the year, everything emerges, recedes, eventually declines and is reborn in a never-ending cycle.

According to Taoism, there are five elements: wood, fire, earth, metal and water. Each phase or agent has its own corresponding season, colour, cardinal direction and a mythical guardian protecting it. Everything in nature is comprised of these essential elements, and all the transformations that take place in nature occur due to the interactions of these five dynamic agents of change. References to the Five Elements can be found throughout everyday life in Japan, such as the five-coloured banners and the coloured threads of amulets and talismans sold at Shintō shrines. This system is still used in Japanese garden design. These elements also correspond to human life's five phases or stages: birth, growth, maturation, death and rebirth.

Colours and Their Associations

AKA – RED

Element: Fire (*Ka*)
Season: Summer, characterized by the sun's warmth and nature's swelling and flowering.
Direction: South
Planet: Mars
Guardian: Scarlet Bird
Virtue: Politeness

Japan's iconic red lacquerware has become one of the nation's representative art forms. In Japan, red is a sacred colour – the colour of rituals, festivals and ceremonies – believed to ward off evil and help prevent natural disasters. Shintō shrine maidens (*miko*) wear red pleated trousers called *hakama* as part of their ceremonial robes, and red *torii* gates stand at the entrance to Shintō shrines.

Akebono iro is a shade of red called "dawn". The unofficial national colour of Japan, red, also represents the red rising sun that dawns each day. It is depicted on Japan's national flag, linking Japan back to its ancestors, the descendants of the legendary Sun Goddess Amaterasu.

Shuiro, a shade of vermilion made from cinnabar, is one of Japan's oldest colours. It dates back to the Jomon period (4,000–300 BCE). It has been used for official seals since ancient times and is still used for inking personal seals (*hanko*) in Japan today.

Japan's most famous shade of red, *akabeni,* is a vivid shade of pure crimson red used since the early Edo period (1603–1868). *Akabeni* (sometimes called *beni*-red) could only be worn by those of the samurai class; young women from samurai families who wore kimono completely dyed in this particular shade of red were called *akahime,* meaning "red princess". *Beni*-red dye comes from the petals of the safflower, *Carthamus tinctorius,* also known as *benihana,* which has been used to create shades of red since the Middle Ages. The flowers grow in Yamagata in Northern Japan. The red petals are harvested in the summer and made into patties (*beni-mochi*) that historically were transported to Kyōto to be made into rouge or used for dyeing textiles.

AO – BLUE-GREEN

Element: Wood (*Ki*), which represents the vital essence of trees.
Season: Spring, a period of growth, abundant vitality and expansion.
Direction: East
Planet: Jupiter
Guardian: Blue Dragon
Virtues: Patience, forgiveness and kindness

Ao (blue-green) is one of Japan's oldest colours and has become one of its most iconic, primarily due to its connection to *aizome* (indigo-dyed textiles), *aizuri* (indigo-tinted woodblock prints) and blue and white ceramics such as Imari porcelain, which are emblematic of Japanese design.

One of the oldest dyes in the world, indigo has been cultivated and used as a natural dye for more than 6,000 years, appearing in textiles throughout South America, West Africa, Southeast Asia and East Asia. These iconic shades of blue are achieved using fermented dye extracted from the leaves of the indigo plant. The darkly dyed fabrics are called *kon* (dark blue), and the lighter ones *ai* (indigo blue). Japan's unique relationship with the colour blue resulted in the term "Japan Blue", coined in the Meji era (1868–1912) by British chemist Robert Atkinson (1850–1929). The plants used to dye kimono were often also used medicinally, and people believed wearing them would alleviate illness. Indigo, a natural pesticide, was thought to be good for stomach ailments, fever and warding off insects. Hard-wearing work clothes and homewares were often dyed with indigo.

In many languages, including ancient Japanese, the colours we define as blue and green in English were colexified – both expressed using a single word – as *ao* or *aoi*. In Japanese, the word *ao* can refer to either blue or green, depending on the situation. The colour *ao* covers a broad spectrum ranging from deep blue to a yellowish green. Modern Japanese does have a word for green, specifically *midori*. Still, it's a relatively recent addition compared to the ancient blue-green.

Green is one of the colours I strongly associate with Japan because of its endless lush gardens, mossy rocks, bonsai, bamboo groves, tea fields and, of course, liquid jade or green tea drinking culture – the colour of nature, young shoots, leaves and grasses. *Yanagi iro* is the colour of the weeping willow, a hue designed to be worn in the springtime when the new willow tree buds begin to appear.

Midori, the colour green, pulses with life; in Japan, green represents nature but also youth, health and vitality. Evergreens such as *matsu* (pine trees) are thought to be immortal, so the colour green is also the colour of immortality (see Chapter 11). *Moegi* (shoot or sprout green) is a vibrant shade of yellow-tinted green, like the fresh new foliage of spring. It is one of Japan's oldest recorded colours and has been a symbol of youth since the Heian period (794–1185). The Japanese word for a newborn is *midorigo* (green child).

SHIRO – WHITE

Element: Metal (*Kinzoku*), which comes from *kin* the Japanese word for gold.
Season: Autumn, a period of gathering, harvesting and collecting.
Direction: West
Planet: Venus
Guardian: White Tiger
Virtue: The innate ability to know right from wrong.

Pure white is not a colour but the absence of colour and, therefore, the absence of impurity. As such, *shiro* (white) is the colour of the gods and all things sacred in Japan. Shintō priests dress in pure white robes, white sand indicates sacred spaces and white paper marks sacred trees. Meanwhile, white rice and *mochi* (rice cakes) are offerings made to the gods.

White is the colour of snow-covered landscapes and cracked ice. It represents purity and new beginnings and is a key component in the significant events of Japanese life: births, deaths and marriages are all accompanied by the colour white. Brides wear an all-white ensemble of white kimono called *shiromuku* for a traditional wedding ceremony held at a Shintō shrine, completed by a *wataboshi*, a white bridal hood that acts like a western veil, concealing the bride's face from everyone except the groom till the end of the ceremony. When paired with its polar opposite, *kuro* (black), it represents the highest level of formality. In a similar way to western weddings, the bride wears white, and her equal and opposite, the groom, wears a formal black kimono bearing his family crests, called *montsuki*.

KURO – BLACK

Element: Water (*Mizu*, or *sui*).
Season: Winter, a period of quiet contemplation, stillness and retreat; as the Earth cools we move inwards both literally and figuratively.
Direction: North
Planet: Mercury
Guardian: Black Tortoise
Virtue: Wisdom and inner peace

If white represents day and daylight, then its partner, black, must represent darkness and night. Specific colours also had spiritual associations. Black, for example, provided protection against evil.

Black is a dignified colour representing high formality. During the Heian period (794–1185), the *mofuku* (Japanese mourning dress) was similar to that of the Victorians, moving from the darkest to the lightest shades of black.

Sumi-e (monochrome artworks expressed in black ink calligraphy) and the subtle shine of polished Japanese red-and-black lacquer bowls are both art forms that immediately remind their viewers of Japan. If something is japanned, then it has been painted with layer upon layer of black lacquer.

KIIRO – YELLOW

Element: Earth (*Chi*)
Season: Midsummer, a transitional period between two seasons, or late summer.
Direction: Centre
Planet: Saturn
Colour: Yellow
Guardian: Golden Dragon
Virtue: Integrity

In contemporary Japan, shades of yellow are named after Japan's many golden flowers and natural phenomena, such as dandelions, mimosa, yellow kerria, yellow wisteria, gardenia and, especially, sunflowers. Yellow represents the sun's warmth, causing golden wheat and corn to ripen; and it's also the colour of golden steamed chestnuts.

Like purple, the colour *kin iro* or gold has ancient noble and auspicious associations. They were initially mandated for the exclusive use of the Emperor of China, who wore *chaofu*, golden yellow Imperial court robes richly embroidered with sinuous golden dragons. Golden yellow and the five-clawed dragon affiliated with it were his unique signifiers. Japan adopted this tradition connecting dragons with the Imperial household and Buddhism (see page 205). Golden chrysanthemums also became Japan's imperial insignia (see Chapter 10).

MURASAKI – PURPLE

A significant colour in Japanes culture, *murasaki* (the colour purple) is achieved using dye made from the roots of purple gromwell

(*Lithospermum erythrorhizon*), which has been used to dye cloth since ancient times. *Murasaki* covers a spectrum of purple that includes shades of violet, wisteria, iris, bellflower and aster. In the Heian period (794–1185), it was considered the ideal colour due to its connection to royalty and was worn only by the most high-ranking members of society. The colour purple is historically closely associated with Japan's most significant literary treasure, *The Tale of Genji*, because it includes recurring purple floral imagery throughout the book. When Lady Murasaki, the book's heroine, is adopted by the Shining Prince as a child, he calls her Hanachirusato (the Lady of Falling Flowers). Later, eponymously, the author herself was also named Murasaki.

KASANE

The Japanese Art of Colour Layering

The kimono uses the coded language of colour and floral motifs; this layered symbolism reflects seasonality and occasion. Kimono is tied to the natural world and seasonal shifts more so than any other clothing system; as kimono expert Sheila Cliffe writes, kimono is securely "bound into place and seasonal time". This is demonstrated in a practical way by the fact that kimono can be worn to keep cool in the summer and warm in the winter.

Japanese colours are named for the blossoms they emulate or the plant material used to create their dyes (*someiro*). The choice of colours celebrates, echoes or anticipates the upcoming season.

What if you could wear the seasons? For example, robe yourself in the ephemeral shades of a cherry blossom or the delicate blush of a rose? Well, that's precisely what the noble women of the Heian period (794–1185) court did. Women like Sei Shōnagon and Lady Murasaki Shikibu rarely left the cloisters of the Imperial court. Yet, they were surrounded by nature at all times. Through letters, textiles, poetry, seasonal festivals and artworks, they lived lives filled with flowers. The silk of the time was so fine that it was almost translucent, meaning the lining of a garment could be glimpsed from the outside. *Kasane no irome* (layers of colour) was a chart of the various colour-layering combinations worn by the members of the Heian-period court. *Kasane* means "layers", and *irome* means "a colour combination taken from the Japanese word for colour, *iro*". These combinations took their inspiration from the colours of flowering trees and plants of each season, which featured in *waka* poetry. Layers were organized into sets, each with a poetic name for the plant, flower or tree that inspired it, each colour combination alluding to a specific season. In the Heian-period court, having an aesthetic sense of seasonal transitions and choosing suitable kimono to allude to them was considered an important skill.

Then, you could literally wear the seasons by layering unlined kimono in combinations according to the *kasane no irome*. You could suggest a fading chrysanthemum by wearing a pale lavender kimono over a blue-green interior. Using gossamer-thin silk with a white outer layer and darker-coloured inner layers, the kimono takes on certain shades of colour. For example, a kimono worn with a white outer layer and a red inner layer has a pale pink tone, simulating the colour of cherry blossoms.

Celebrated for its classical art, poetry and literature, the Heian-period court was known for the love of poetry. The courtiers also employed colour-layering when writing love letters, exchanging poems between lovers on specially dyed fans or elaborately folded pieces of paper in the shades of the season. They would write a poem containing seasonal sentiments and expressions and then enclose it within several layers of seasonally coloured paper.

Heian-period literature is full of references to the art of colour-layering. One of the most detailed mentions of the art of *kasane* is in *The Pillow Book* (*Makura no Soshi*) by Sei Shōnagon (c.966–1017 or 1025); she was a contemporary of fellow writer and lady-in-waiting Murasaki Shikibu. Her keen observations of Heian-period court life give detailed accounts of the breath-taking seasonal combinations worn by the courtiers; she describes robes of cherry blossom, over spring-shoot green and plum pink, their long sleeves trailing.

Spring combinations suggested the year's first blossoms: plum, cherry, wisteria and yellow kerria. Five layers of kimono are worn to create the *kōbai no nioi* (red plum fragrance) combination, which is built up layer upon layer – a red layer blends into four graduated layers of ever-lightening shades of pink. This colour combination is appropriate for special occasions celebrated in the late winter and early spring. When worn in the late winter, the wearer is anticipating the plums blooming.

What combination of colours would you choose to create inspired by local plants and trees? What colours represent your favourite flower or favourite season?

Spring Colour Combinations

Spring colours are cool fresh greens and delicate pinks, reminiscent of fresh new buds and the anticipation of upcoming blooms. An example is *moegi*, meaning "to sprout", a colour that has been related to spring since the Heian period (794–1185).

Kōbai (Crimson plum): A bright scarlet surface layer with dark crimson, almost purple underneath. There are various opinions about this colour, but it is believed to have been slightly dark pink like the colour of red *ume* (Japanese plum) blossom in the Heian period.

Sakura (Cherry blossom) is created by combining a white surface layer and a pink, almost maroon, interior beneath.

Moegi (Spring-shoot green): A yellowish shade of green, like fresh green shoots, created by overdyeing indigo with yellow. This shade of pale green was lined with a darker shade of green.

Yanagi (Willow) is created by layering white over pale green.

Summer Colour Combinations

Fuji (Wisteria): A pale lavender grey-coloured surface with a spring-shoot green interior.

Hana tachibana (Mandarin orange blossom): A withered leaf (russet-coloured) exterior layer combined with a green interior.

Unohana (Deutzia or Japanese snow flower): A robe of white worn over a layer of spring-shoot green.

Futaai (Lavender): This colour combination could be worn as a double layer of lavender or lavender over white. The shade of purple was achieved by dyeing the cloth with safflower to create scarlet, followed by indigo and could range from one end of the spectrum to the other – from almost all scarlet to all indigo, depending on the season and the age of the intended wearer (generally, the shades people wear get darker and more subtle as they grow older).

Autumn Colour Combinations

Kuchiba (Fallen-leaf ochre): *Kuchiba* is the colour of orange-yellow fallen leaves, and it was a brilliant shade of yellow in the Heian period, created from dyes using gardenia and saffron.

Hagi (Bush clover): A dark red or maroon surface with a spring-shoot green interior.

Utsuroigiku (Fading chrysanthemum): A combination of a light lavender-coloured surface with blue-green underneath.

Momiji (Bright foliage): A warm reddish brown worn with a brown interior layer.

Winter Colour Combinations

Shiragiku (White chrysanthemum): This combination of a white top layer could be worn with either a green or dark red interior.

Kōri (Ice): An elegant light grey surface layer worn with a white interior.

Kareno (Withered field): A yellow surface layer combined with a white or light green interior layer.

KUSAKIZOME

Natural Dyeing With Plants

Since ancient times Japan has been awash in a multitude of colours. Ever since the Heian period (794–1185), artisans have employed the techniques of *kusakizome*, the Japanese term for extracting colour from plants. *Kusaki* means "plants" or "vegetation", and *zome* means "dye". The colours produced through natural dyeing can create a much more delicate, subdued palette than chemical hues; working with these subtle colours is another way of capturing the fleeting beauty of the changing seasons. Natural dyeing has seen a huge resurgence in recent years but in the past all dyes came from natural materials. Still, in Japan, it's a tradition that has been kept alive for over 1,000 years as plants, flowers and even tree bark have been used to dye silk threads for kimono, textiles and *washi* paper since the Heian period.

The *kusakizome* method was used to create the coloured silks used to weave kimono, such as the *jūnihitoe*, the twelve-layered kimono worn by Japanese noblewomen.

Atelier Shimura:
Weaving the Colours of Life

What was it about those roots, which had slept in the earth for hundreds of years, that called out to me so?

FUKUMI SHIMURA

TRANSLATED BY MATT TREYVARD[12]

---

[12] Source: Shimura, F. (2019) *The Music of Color*. Translated by M. Treyvaud. Tōkyō: JPIC.

Atelier Shimura is one of the incredible textile studios keeping the art of *kusakizome* alive. It is the legacy of celebrated textile artist Fukumi Shimura, a *senshokuka* (master of dyeing and weaving, specializing in making kimono and *obi* – the accompanying wide fabric sashes or belts) and a designated Living National Treasure. According to Shimura, nature reveals its secrets to those who pay close enough attention. Her gift is drawing out the colours hidden within the plant. The "colours of life" that Shimura extracts from the roots, bark, leaves and flowers of plants are the "spirits of the flora".

Interestingly, *sakura iro*, the delicate colour of cherry blossoms, is drawn not from its delicate petals but from its gnarled bark. Throughout the year, the atelier works with a unique paintbox of colours only possible to achieve by using Japan's biodiversity, embracing its variety of seasonal plants, trees and grasses. As Shimura explains, "The plum, the peach, the grapevine: without fail, each births its own colour." She describes the dyes made with plants that are just about to bloom, which produce, in her words, "colours of indescribable innocence".

These colours are at their peak due to all the nutrients stored in the plant over the winter. Although the plant gives its life to allow us to dye with it, it lives on through the colour it produces. These colours are the gifts of the trees and grasses. Shimura hears the songs of the wild flora, newly born in the freshly dyed yarns. The voices of these plants are a symphony of the season, singing through the skeins of dyed fibres.

Shimura established Atelier Shimura in Kyōto with her daughter and grandson and showcases hand-dyed fabrics made with seasonal plants to produce kimono, *obi*, scarves and accessories using traditional tools and techniques. The studio is now run by Fukumi's grandson, Shōji Shimura.

JAPANESE MICRO SEASON NO.22
KAIKO OKITE KUWA O HAMU

Silkworms Start Feasting on Mulberry Leaves
21–25 May

The colours of nature are a gift, just as silk is a gift from *kaiko* (silkworms); the English translation of their Japanese name means "heavenly insect". Raw silk (*suzushi*) is also sometimes called the "thread of Heaven". Without silkworms, there would be no kimono. Silkworms are such an important part of life in Japan that they are often spoken about with the honorific prefix O, inserted before native Japanese words (*okaiko sama*), which is a sign of great respect – used when talking about older family members and revered substances like *ocha* (green tea) or *omizu* (water). Given their great gifts and special place in Japanese culture, it's no wonder that silkworms appear as one of the seasonal indicators in Japan's 72 micro seasons.

KIMONO SUSTAINABILITY

I've been collecting vintage kimono since I was a teenager, and one of the things I love about them is their inherent sustainability. Kimono are ingeniously sustainable garments. Made from one bolt of cloth cut into eight pieces, their straight lines make them easy to unpick, clean, dye and resew, which was common practice until the 1960s. Paler-coloured kimono traditionally designed to be worn by younger people could be dyed and redyed ever darker shades as the wearer grew older. This was the work of *shikkai*, Japan's kimono "doctors", who had a network that spread across the country. They were responsible for cleaning, redyeing and maintaining Japan's kimono.

Once older kimono could no longer be worn in their current form, they were transformed into *kanzashi* (hair ornaments) by *shokunin*, Japanese master artisans. Finally, their remaining silk threads were made into *tamari* balls. This ecological reusing and recycling of things is very much in keeping with the slow fashion movement, which, like the kimono, stands in opposition to the irresponsible mass-market fast fashion that is now a global issue.

Why Buy Vintage Kimono?

The kimono industry in Japan is under threat of dying out as many of the artisans who make them are retiring without apprentices, and they're now mostly worn only for special occasions. Daisaku Kadokawa, the Mayor of Kyōto, the hub of Japan's textile industry, is trying to prevent this. He famously wears kimono every day in an attempt to encourage both locals and foreign visitors to wear them. He has also instigated several initiatives in Kyōto, including discounts on visiting famous cultural sites if visitors dress in kimono. Buying vintage is an act of resistance to the fast fashion movement that has swept over our planet. Collecting vintage garments like second-hand kimono is one of the antidotes to fast fashion.

Vintage kimono are readily available; they are affordable, well-made, and have already lasted the test of time. Technically, pieces from the Taisho era (1912–1926), which are 100 years old or more, are classified as antique, whereas anything 50 years old or more is considered vintage.

Reasons to buy vintage kimono include:

- They make wonderful gifts and souvenirs.

- They are an authentic example of Japanese art and craft.

- They are sustainable.

- If you fall in love with a kimono but don't have the confidence to wear it, remember they are also stunning art objects that you can display as well as wear.

- Collecting vintage garments like second-hand kimono is one of the antidotes to fast fashion.

- Kimono are another way to mark the changing seasons. You can embrace the endless seasonal designs of kimono, referencing the flora and fauna of the season with your own combination of colour, symbols and motifs. Remember, a cotton *yūkata* will help keep you comfortably cool in the summer and a lined kimono can be paired with boots and autumnal layers to keep you chic and warm when the seasons shift.

Tips for Buying Vintage Kimono

- If in doubt, a classic minimal black *haori* (kimono jacket) is a great first piece to experiment with wearing and styling. Just like little black dresses, they look chic on everyone.

- Keep an eye out at local flea markets, charity shops and thrift stores – you never know where a kimono in need of a new home might turn up.

- Always check for damage. Are there any marks, holes or stains?

- Next, look for repairs and alterations.

- Make sure you check the length of the sleeves, especially on older pieces, which can be quite short.

- Look at the garment in natural light and be sure to check the lining, which is often in worse condition than the outer shell.

KAMON

Family Crests

Graphic, stylized images of iconic Japanese symbols such as trees, flowers and birds are used not only as kimono designs but also for creating *kamon*. These *kamon* or *mon* are stylized motifs that act as Japanese family crests, much like the European coat of arms. Every family, from nobles to farmers, had their own crest, which was forbidden for others to use. The crests were sewn onto formal black kimono in pure white thread. Depending on the formality of a kimono, it will have one, three or five crests. You'll be able to spot the *kamon* in the middle of the back of the garment. A more formal kimono also bears crests on either side of the chest and the sleeves. *Kamon* hide in plain sight all over modern Japan, incorporated into company logos, used on packaging, fabric and, of course, every Japanese passport, which bears the chrysanthemum seal of the Imperial family.

Create Your Own *Kamon*

Imagine this will be your insignia, your own personal coat of arms. What plant characteristics do you want to embody? Perhaps you're graceful like a weeping willow or strong but flexible like bamboo? You can experiment with creating your crest by drawing or painting your *kamon* design and even turning it into a stencil to print on fabric, sew it on your clothes or use it as a logo for your creative projects.

KIMONO MOTIFS

Kitsuke is the art of dressing in kimono. In the world of *wafuku*, Japanese dress, ideally you wear the motif of a flower just before it blooms, in anticipation of the coming season. Kimono colours and motifs were initially dictated by the seasons. Although seasonal rules are less rigidly adhered to in contemporary Japan, geisha and people practising the traditional arts are still very mindful of them. Ideally, the imagery on your kimono would represent the beauty of the coming season but not compete with it. So, while you might wear plum blossoms as *ume*

Wrapped in peonies
Tightly bound
Kimono's embrace

NATALIE LEON

season approaches, you would not wear them to a plum viewing party because you wouldn't want the flowers on your kimono to compete with the flowers in the garden.

Anthropologist Lisa Dalby summarizes the complexities of meaning in kimono when she explains, "kimono employ a vocabulary of fabric, colour, pattern and form." The kimono is a canvas. Women could express their own aesthetic sensibilities through their kimono. Children's clothes were similar in design, only the decoration changed, reflecting the parent's wishes for their children through auspicious symbols. Kimono coordinations can be whimsical, elegant, playful or edgy because they reflect their wearers' personal tastes and unique styles.

There are textbook meanings for certain flowers, but then there are also our own personal meanings, which add another layer of significance to our favourite botanical imagery. For vintage kimono dealer Sonoe Sugawara that's *shōbu* (irises) or *shōbu iro* (iris-coloured) kimono. While Japanese irises are traditionally an auspicious motif associated with winning a game or defeating an opponent, growing up in Japan with two brothers, Sonoe san has a particular fondness for them because of her vivid childhood memories of iris baths, visiting gardens and eating *kashiwa mochi* during iris season. She wears an iris-patterned or -coloured kimono all year round, especially for important meetings when she needs a little extra luck! (You can read more about iris symbolism in Chapter 5.)

ITCHIKU KUBOTA

On the shores of Lake Kawaguchi in the shadow of Mt Fuji, is a beautiful and unique kimono museum dedicated to preserving and sharing the work of textile artist Itchiku Kubota (1917–2003). Kubota used the kimono not just as his canvas of choice but conceptualized the kimono as panels of a folding screen or a Renaissance triptych. He designed them to fit together so that they become one canvas on which the beauty of Japan's four seasons played out in one continuous landscape, unbroken from one garment to the next. He called this masterpiece "The Symphony of Light". Kubata's lifelong love of nature and adoration of Mt Fuji feature prominently in his panoramic masterpieces, which depict the many colours and faces of the sacred mountain as it changes throughout the year. Sadly, Kubota passed away before he could complete the 80 works he envisaged as part of "The Symphony of Light". However, the museum gives visitors the opportunity to still see his exceptional nature-inspired work.

KITSUKE

A Kimono for Every Season

Spring
Spring kimono feature the imagery and colour palette of spring flowering trees, such as plum, peach, cherry, wisteria and magnolia. At this time of the year, people are still wearing *awase* (lined) kimono,

which are worn from the autumn onward throughout the winter until spring arrives, or October to May.

Summer

Summer is the time of *hitoe* (unlined summer kimono), which are generally worn from June to September and made from lightweight and sheer fabrics such as *asa* (hemp), *ro* (a fine translucent silk, loosely woven with skipped rows which create natural gaps in the weave) and *sha* (a stiffer transparent silk gauze, similar to *ro*, woven with equidistant spaces between the threads, which allows the fabric to breathe and is ideal for the hottest months of the year).

Another quintessential Japanese summer image is the *yūkata*, worn throughout the summer festival season. *Yūkata* are lightweight, more informal cotton garments. They are traditionally worn in shades of blue and white, and depict ocean waves, flowing streams and various types of water imagery to give the impression of coolness and freshness to counter the heat of the humid Japanese summer.

Autumn

As autumn begins, September signals the transition from unlined single-layer summer kimono, *hitoe, back* to lined kimono or *awase*. Then on 1 October, people take part in *koromogae*, the seasonal changeover of clothing, putting away their *yūkata* and *hitoe* kimono to replace them with thicker, lined kimono in warmer, rich autumnal colours. Autumnal kimono imagery includes changing leaves, the moon, rabbits, autumn grasses and chrysanthemums.

Winter

To help keep warm in the winter months, people sometimes add thermal elements underneath their lined or woollen kimono and layer western elements that coordinate with their outfits, such as scarves, a fake fur stole, a shawl or winter boots. Winter kimono often feature the Three Friends of Winter (plum, pine and bamboo, see page 312), camellias, snowflakes and snow-covered landscapes.

DESIGN YOUR OWN KIMONO

In the Edo period (1603–1868), artists created woodblock-printed kimono pattern books called *kosode hinagatabon* or *hinagatabon*, which were full of page after page of detailed illustrations of the design of a sleeve or an entire kimono, both in colour and monochrome. These kimono design books were like early fashion magazines, which became indispensable guides. They were used as inspiration by both consumers and manufacturers of kimono. Meanwhile, *shikkai* (specialist kimono coordinators) would visit samurai families in their homes and create individual hand-drawn ink sketches of proposed kimono designs based on their customers' requests, often inspired by *hinagatabon*.

Fast forward to the 2020 Tōkyō Olympics when Japan unveiled one custom-made kimono for each of the 213 nations competing. Each garment wove together key colours, symbols, flora and fauna from that country's unique history. India's, for example, featured peacocks, elephants and lotus blossoms. This herculean undertaking, years in the making, was the work of the One World Kimono Project led by Yoshimasa Takakura, which began in 2014 and was completed in 2021. Now it's time to design your own kimono.

STEP 1. Find your inspiration – you could take it from the imagery covered in this book and the outline at the beginning of this chapter. You could even create one for each of the four seasons.

STEP 2. Next, consider your colour palette. Will it be a classic blue and white summer *yūkata* or a silk robe of fiery autumnal tints? What colours represent you and your favourite season?

STEP 3. And finally, add birds, plants and auspicious motifs. Take inspiration from indigenous plants and wildlife that are meaningful symbols for you.

Birds and Insects on Kimono

Highly elaborate and stylized natural motifs decorate the silk canvas of the kimono, turning this traditional form of dress into a wearable art form. Many of the motifs are seasonally specific and would not typically be worn out of season. These are some of the myriad of kimono design elements you may come across.

Chōchō (Butterfly)

Butterflies are a spring motif that represents joy and longevity; a pair of butterflies, like mandarin ducks (see below), often appear in wedding imagery. They are also said to be the souls of those who have passed on.

Yatagarasu (Crow)

The mythical three-legged crow is linked to both Japan's first legendary Emperor, Jimmu, and several Shintō shrines. It was a fashionable motif in the Taisho period during the 1920s and can be worn all year round.

Oshidori (Mandarin ducks)

A pair of mandarin ducks on a kimono or an *obi* belt represent joy, a married couple or marital bliss.

Kumonosu (Spider's web)

This trans-seasonal motif can be worn all year. It's good for business because it symbolizes catching or attracting luck, money or customers. It was especially popular with *moga* (modern girls), the Japanese equivalents of the western flapper girls, who flocked to the cities to work as café waitresses in the 1920s.

Tsubame (Swallow)

These early migratory birds appear in the spring, making them one of the representatives of that season. The swallow is also an auspicious symbol representing good fortune and good luck for travel.

SHIKUNSHI

The Four Philosophers

The Four Philosophers is an artistic grouping of plants that originated in China, like the Three Friends of Winter (see Chapter 11). When combined, the wild orchid (*ran*), plum (*ume*), chrysanthemum (*kiku*) and bamboo (*take*) are known in both China and Japan as the Four Philosophers or the Four Gentlemen. They are a recurring theme in East Asian art. Each flower symbolizes a virtue, such as uprightness, purity, humility and perseverance in harsh conditions. Each also represents a different season (the wild orchid, spring; the bamboo, summer; the chrysanthemum, autumn; and the plum, winter). Together, the four are used to depict the unfolding of the seasons throughout the year and this auspicious trans-seasonal motif can be worn at any time of the year.

SEIJIN NO HI

Coming of Age Day
14 January

Seijin no Hi, or Coming of Age Day, is perhaps the single most important day in a Japanese woman's life, other than her wedding day. It takes place on the second Monday of January each year when Japan's 20-year-olds celebrate officially entering adulthood. Young women all over the nation dress in *furisode*, the most formal kimono, with long flowing sleeves, and men wear *hakama*, wide-legged pleated trousers, fastened by straps tied at the waist, to mark the occasion. *Seijin no Hi* is one of the few annual occasions where you will see hundreds of people dressed in kimono of all imaginable colours and designs in both modern and traditional styles. During the early Edo period (1603–1868), the *furisode* became standard formal wear for young unmarried women to wear to weddings and other key events. These special kimono, often covered in auspicious designs, are said to protect against disaster by shaking off any misfortune with their flowing sleeves.

KARYŪKAI

The Flower and Willow World

In contemporary Japan, very few people wear kimono every day. Only those that practise the traditional arts, such as *Chadō* (the Way of Tea) and geisha, wear kimono daily and not just once or twice a year for special events. As anthropologist Liza Dalby wrote, contemporary geisha are now "curators of tradition", actively preserving traditional Japanese culture. Kimono terminology is often used as a metaphor for the life of geisha. To pick up one's hem (*tsuma o toru*) means to join the geisha profession. However, there are less than 1,000 geisha left in contemporary Japan.

Geisha and maiko – those in training to become geisha – are the true flowers of the *hanamachi* (flower district) or *kagai* (flower town), the districts where all Kyōto's geisha live. There are five of these districts in modern-day Kyōto. The yearly calendar of the flower town is dictated by the seasons, annual festivals and local events; they are often closely linked to local shrines. Geisha and maiko exist in a world beyond our own called the *karyūkai*, the flower and willow world.

KIMONO ACCESSORIES

As already noted, a kimono is a form of wearable art closer to a painter's canvas than a fashion garment. Every element of a maiko or geisha's *kitsuke* (kimono coordination) references the upcoming season. Her kimono is just the first layer, accented with an embroidered or coloured *haneri* (half collar) and a wide fabric *obi* sash or belt. Finishing touches include her *obidome*, a jewelled pin or brooch threaded onto an *obijime*, a decorative woven cord that ornaments the *obi* and keeps it in place. These accessories all relay subtle messages using the layered imagery of flora and fauna.

However, perhaps the most striking adornments are the *hana kanzashi*, ornate seasonal hair ornaments constructed from folded pieces of kimono silk that have been painstakingly dyed, piece by piece. The most elaborate *kanzashi* are worn by maiko (apprentice geisha).

They depict Japan's many seasonal flowers and change according to the months of the year.

THE *MIYAKO ODORI*

If you're in Kyōto at the right time, a wonderful seasonal activity is to see the maiko perform eight seasonally themed dances, which progress from spring through the four seasons. This performance is called the *Miyako Odori*. *Miyako* means "a capital city" and *odori* means "dance", so *miyako odori* literally translates as "capital city dances." The event takes place each spring throughout April in the Gion district of Kyōto. It gives both tourists and locals a rare opportunity to enjoy a stunning theatrical performance by a group of maiko, all dressed in exquisite, seasonally themed kimono, *obi* and *kanzashi*.

KOROMOGAE

The Seasonal Change of Clothing

1 June

1 October

Koromogae occurs twice a year: on 1 June and then again on 1 October, and this practice acknowledges the change in seasons. Traditionally, everything in the Japanese home was changed on 1 June to prepare for the extreme summer heat and the custom continues today with clothes and also fabrics, bedding and tableware, which are all replaced with lighter summer alternatives. At this time of the year, civil servants and schoolchildren change into their summer uniforms. People pack away their heavy winter jumpers and coats and replace them with light, bright, airy clothes in anticipation of the summer, only to reverse the whole process on 1 October in anticipation of the seasonal shift back to the colder months.

KIMONO NO HI

Kimono Day
15 November

Kimono no Hi or Kimono Day, is held annually in Japan on 15 November. It was created in 2015 by the Japan Kimono Revitalization Committee, in an effort to help support the kimono industry and encourage more people to wear kimono as casual everyday wear. Meanwhile, throughout November, kimono lovers around the world come together online and express their love for kimono. They share their unique kimono style by dressing in kimono every day or as many times as they like throughout November.

KADŌ

The Way of Flowers

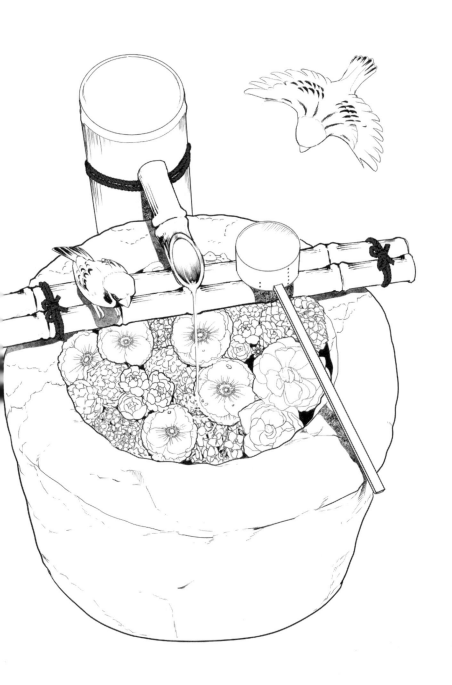

Living with Flowers

A love of flowers is something that transcends all boundaries, national and cultural. As Tenshin Okakura, the author of *The Way of Tea*, wrote, "In joy and sadness, flowers are our constant friends." Flowers are our companions through good days and bad, present at our births, deaths and marriages. Flowers are always with us. Their presence in our lives cannot be overstated. We name ourselves after them and use them in cooking, baking and medicine. We dye our clothes with them and adorn our homes in floral prints and garland our heads with flower crowns.

Japan celebrates flowers in all their forms whether edible, artfully placed in a vessel, growing wild or found in carefully manicured gardens, both indigenous and imported varieties. Japan cherishes them all, immortalizing them in food and myriad art forms including ikebana, ceramics, ink painting, woodblock prints, painted screens and sliding doors, textiles, stationary, tea, and sweets – the list is never-ending. In Japan, examples of primary nature such as gardens, bonsai and flower arrangements are enjoyed alongside secondary nature such as painted screens, woodblock prints, ceramics and textiles. The two mingle together, enjoyed simultaneously in every home and temple.

I am rarely without the presence of flowers, and that's just how I like it, whether it's in the form of a vintage ring, something plucked from the garden or the side of a country lane or a bunch of flowers from the local supermarket. I have always been a flower child, happiest in the garden making perfume from my mother's beloved roses or pressing petals between the pages of books. Later my mum would teach me the names of the flowers in her garden, and how to cut and arrange them properly so that they would last a little longer. She taught me the basics of western-style flower arranging, how to create an arrangement that your gaze would alight on and move around the different elements like a bee or a butterfly searching for nectar. Now, I delight in growing flowers in pots on my patio and drying the precious bouquets I receive from loved ones. So, it only seems natural that chasing the spring blooms across Japan has become one of my favourite pastimes.

Bringing flowers into our homes means living with nature. Flowers bring glorious colour, vitality, scent and a myriad of elegant forms into our lives. They also remind us of the passage of time and the evanescence of life. Florist Amy Merrick put it beautifully when she wrote, "To love flowers is to revere nature and to revere nature is to honour the seasons."

Friendship through Flowers

Appreciation of flowers and, in the broader sense, natural beauty is a global pastime that transcends language barriers. I grew up in Britain, a nation of nature lovers, the birthplace of floriography – a country renowned for its parks, cottage gardens and areas of outstanding natural beauty. Nowhere else in the world have I felt such an affinity for flowers except in Japan where people dedicate their lives to the practice of bonsai, the art of flower arranging, and the creation of exceptional gardens. They make pilgrimages to see flowers, not just once in a lifetime but annually. Kyōto, the ancient capital of Japan, is sometimes called *hana no miyako* (the capital of flowers). This is perhaps because in Kyōto there are temples dedicated to the enjoyment of cherry blossoms, irises, wisteria, camellias, mosses and fresh green leaves. It's no wonder that Kyōto is also the birthplace of ikebana, the Japanese art of flower arranging.

IKEBANA

Giving Life to Flowers

Flower arrangement has been practised in Japan for over 1,000 years. Ikebana, which means "arranging flowers" or "giving life to flowers", dates back to the Heian period (794–1185). Ikebana is the marriage of the ritual use of branches of sacred evergreens in Shintō and the tradition of colourful floral offerings placed on Buddhist altars throughout East Asia. This sacred art was initially practised by monks who gathered fallen branches from their temple surroundings to create offerings without harming any living things. Ikebana can be a form of art, mindfulness, a floral meditation and a sacred offering. As Buddhist author and ikebana teacher Joan Stamm explains, to practise ikebana is to "become absorbed into the deep essence of the flower" and, in doing so, to forget yourself.

There are now over 3,000 ikebana schools in Japan. The three most well-known *ryū* (schools) are Ikenobō, Ohara and Sōgetsu. The Ikenobō School is the oldest and the most traditional of the three. Senno, the Buddhist monk who founded the Ikenobō School in the 15th century once said, "With a spray of flowers, a bit of water, one evokes the vastness of rivers and mountains." The Ohara School celebrates colourful western flowers and natural scenery, while the Sōgetsu School is the home of *zen'ei* (avant-garde) flower arranging, which focuses on freedom of expression and incorporates artificial materials. The idea is that Sōgetsu-style ikebana can be practised by anyone, anytime, anywhere.

Heaven and
Earth are flowers.
God, as well as
Buddha, are flowers.
The heart of man is also
the soul of flowers.

TRANSLATED BY MARY AVERILL

The Principle of Three

Most ikebana arrangements are built around a three-branch structure, which is based on the teachings of the Chinese philosopher Confucius, whose ethical ideals form part of the foundation of East Asian society, especially in China, Korea, Japan and Tibet. The core virtues of Confucianism included a focus on empathy, family loyalty, ancestral worship, reciprocity, the cultivation of knowledge and respect for one's elders. According to Confucianism, there are three realms: Heaven, Earth and humanity. Each one is represented by a different element within the floral arrangement. Heaven is represented by the *shin* (the tallest branch), *soe* (the medium stem) signifies humanity and *hikae* (the shortest flower) symbolizes Earth. In the sacred art of *kadō*, humanity is caught between the flowers of Heaven and Earth. In ikebana, white chrysanthemums represent Heaven, purple symbolize humanity and yellow signify Earth.

Japanese flower arrangements are often based on lines. They focus on the beauty of a single branch or stem. These restrained, often minimal designs use the space around the arrangements and within it as part of the composition. They seek to create harmony and balance through the union of opposites and clean-flowing lines. Like many other Japanese art forms, ikebana favours asymmetry, which helps create more dynamic and natural arrangements. Incompleteness, unevenness and odd numbers are all essential elements of the Japanese aesthetics of beauty.

RINPA

Nature in Japanese Art

According to curator John Carpenter, *rikka*, the standing-flower style of ikebana created by the Ikenobu School, inspired one of my favourite Japanese art styles – Rinpa. Unlike the Tosa or Kano Schools, the Rinpa or Rimpa School (sometimes called the School of Korin) was unusual because it was not based on student-teacher lineages. There was no hierarchical structure or formal school to speak of. Anyone could become a Rinpa artist simply by working in the Rinpa style. Rinpa's works alluded to the four seasons, incorporating popular natural and botanical motifs such as combinations of trees, birds, waves and flowers, particularly irises. These were all produced in various media, including screens, ceramics and lacquerware, through the patronage of the wealthy merchant class and courtiers, much like Italian Renaissance artists. Rinpa pieces were also heavily inspired by classical *waka*, elegant court poetry composed of 31 syllables. *Waka* focuses on themes such as the flowers of the four seasons, love, parting and works of the Heian-period *monogatari* (court tales).

The highly stylized graphic images of nature and the refined use of gold, silver and vivid mineral pigments such as powdered azurite, coral and malachite is what first attracted me to Rinpa. Both their subjects and their pigments came from nature. Rinpa artists were creating nature-inspired graphic art 450 years ago, long before graphic art as we now know it existed. Japan's most renowned Rinpa artist, Ogata Kōrin (1658–1716), created one of Japan's national treasures and most iconic artworks, *Red and White Plum Blossoms*, an eternal image of early spring, painted across a pair of folding screens (*byōbu*) decorated with silver and gold leaf. It elegantly depicts a blossoming white plum tree on the left screen and its twin in red on the right, separated by a winding river painted in silver and midnight blue. It's no surprise that Rinpa's flowing lines and bold decorative style significantly influenced one of my favourite European art movements, Art Nouveau.

AN ARRANGEMENT FOR EVERY SEASON

Study how plants and flowers grow in different environments such as in your garden, in the forest and in fields and hedgerows. As Tatsuo Ishimoto wrote, "Here nature is making her own arrangements", and you can use these natural configurations as inspiration for your own arrangements. Flower arrangements are ephemeral sculptures or living artworks.

Practising ikebana or any form of flower arranging is also an excellent lesson in non-attachment. The bouquet you have lovingly selected and painstakingly arranged will wither and fade within a matter of days, but this doesn't make them any less beautiful or mean that your time was wasted. In fact, it's just the opposite. Spending that time acutely aware of the flowers, from handpicking them in the field or florist to quietly trimming and arranging them at home, from noting which way they wish to bend to enjoying their perfume and blooms as they slowly unfold over the coming days – none of this time is squandered. You have created a seasonal artwork that expresses the passage of time through flowers. In the process, you have become intimately familiar with those flowers, and they have become a vehicle for your expression.

As Mary Averill explains in her book *Japanese Flower Arrangement for Western Needs*, in Japan, as a plant grows and develops, its soul moves from "flower to leaf and from leaf to fruit, according to the four seasons of the year". So, in the spring, the soul resides in the flowers; in the summer, it dwells in the leaves; in autumn, it lives in the fruit; and finally, in winter, it moves into the branches.

The word *hana* or flower is used liberally in Japanese flower arranging; it can also refer to leaves, flowering fruit trees, branches of evergreens, shrubs and grasses such as bamboo, which can all be used for ikebana. Japan celebrates the elegance of swaying autumn grasses, the delicacy of cherry blossoms and the vibrant blooms of the chrysanthemum. They all have their place in the floral calendar of the year and in our hearts. So even if you don't have access to a garden to pick from or the funds to buy from a local florist, you can still create imaginative arrangements using a few carefully chosen fallen branches or foraged wild grasses.

Haru (Spring)

Spring arrangements often feature unfurling buds, representing the promise of spring blossoms to come, such as cherry or peach. Their branches are symbolic of the *ki* or life force of spring.

Natsu (Summer)

Cooling, refreshing summer arrangements are designed in shallow vessels so that their water source is clearly visible. They include lots of fresh green foliage, and blooms such as cosmos or Japanese anemones.

Aki (Autumn)

Autumn brings with it the suggestion of harvest time. Seasonal favourites include rustic baskets of grasses and branches of iconic red maple leaves and golden yellow ginkgo.

Fuyu (Winter)

Winter arrangements may feature bare branches accented by a single camellia bud. Popular combinations include evergreens such as bamboo, pine and nandina with chrysanthemums and roses.

Flower Arranging Tips

- Try to pick your flowers first thing in the morning or after sundown.

- Make clean, sharp slanted cuts in the stems to allow for better water absorption. Ideally, cut them underwater.

- Allow your stems to soak. Give them a good drink for at least an hour, if possible, before arranging them.

- Keep them cool, with access to fresh air. Your arrangements will last longer if you keep them away from direct sunlight and heat sources such as radiators.

- Remove everything below the water line; removing these leaves helps keep the water clean.

- Change the water regularly, if not daily.

Essential Flower Arranging Tools

You don't need much equipment to begin practising flower arranging at home, but these essentials will help get you started.

- A pair of Japanese steel floral scissors, traditionally used for ikebana and bonsai.

- A *kenzan* (sword mountain), which is often called a flower frog. These circular or square Japanese flower-pin holders have sharp metal teeth that help to hold the flowers upright. They come in various sizes to fit different vessels.

- A pair of floral or garden shears for cutting softer stems.

- Baskets of different woven materials and proportions.

- Pruning shears or secateurs that can handle tougher jobs like cutting roses, small trees and other thick, woody stems.

- Ceramic and glass vessels of different shapes and sizes. You can find wonderful things for little expense in charity shops and thrift stores. For ikebana, look specifically for shallow, open-shaped dishes.

TSUTSUJI

Azaleas

Azaleas or *azalea japonica* are indigenous to Japan and have been cultivated since the 1600s. The ancient Japanese name for May is *Satsuki*, meaning "the month of azaleas", when Japan's *satsuki* azaleas flourish. More flowers blossom in Japan in May than in any other month. *Tsutsuji* (azaleas), *fuji* (wisteria), *botan* (peonies) and *shōbu* (irises) are just some of the flowers you will encounter in Japan in the late spring/ early summer.

Mifuneyama Rakuen
3 April–7 May

How do you talk about a place that's so beautiful it feels unreal? That's the overwhelming experience I had when I first visited Mifuneyama Rakuen in Saga, where 200,000 Kurume azaleas bloom on the hillside annually. After the delicate hues of the cherry blossoms, the rainbow hues of azaleas seem almost blinding in their brilliance. They dye the garden's 120 acres kaleidoscopic shades of hot pink, purple and orange red. The result is a landscape of dreams. Azaleas are possibly the most overlooked flower of late spring. However, here they put on a spectacular show, creating a carpet of flowers that draws crowds from all over Japan.

I suggest visiting early in the morning and then enjoying some freshly made *dango* (rice dumplings) at Hagino Ochaya tea house. At the same time, you can enjoy a view of their 170-year-old wisteria. If Kyushu is beyond your reach, then the Isabella Plantation in Richmond Park, London, is the best place to see azaleas in the UK, as it is home to 50 Kurume azaleas, which were initially introduced to the West from Japan in the 1920s by the plant collector Ernest Wilson. Here the azaleas surround a shining pond creating a fairy glade with magical mirror-like reflections. If you're in the USA, you can visit the National Arboretum in Washington, DC and take their stunning azalea trail up Mt Hamilton.

KADŌ MATSURI

Flower Arranging Festival
⁂〜 *Mid-April* 〜⁂

This festival dedicated to flower arranging takes place every April at Daikakuji in a quiet corner of Arashiyama – the headquarters of the Saga Goryū School of Flower Arrangement. The festival celebrates the temple's long association with *Kadō* (the Way of Flowers). Monumental ikebana installations are showcased throughout the temple grounds against the backdrop of their exquisitely painted screens. This is also one of only two opportunities a year when you can ride the dragon-headed boats out onto Osawa Pond, just as the Heian-period court ladies did in the "Butterflies" chapter of *The Tale of Genji*.

JAPANESE MICRO SEASON NO.32

HASU HAJIMETE HIRAKU

The First Lotus Blossoms
⁂〜 *12–16 July* 〜⁂

We are now entering no.32 of Japan's 72 micro seasons when the first lotuses bloom. There are over 800 varieties of *hasu* or *ren* (lotus), and *kanrensetsu* (lotus flower viewing) is an annual summertime activity in Japan. There, and throughout East Asia, lotus flowers are revered because of their connection to Buddhism and their ability to rise from the depths of dark, murky waters to bloom. This process is said to symbolize the Buddhist journey to attaining enlightenment. The idea is that humanity can rise above suffering in the same way as the lotus, moving from the lowest to the highest state of consciousness. When many flowers achieve enlightenment simultaneously, it's said you can hear the blooms as they "crack" open.

Iconic throughout Asia, the sacred lotus (*Nelumbo nucifera*) is the representative flower of Buddhism, the floral throne on which the Buddha sits. The *Lotus Sutra* is one of the most venerated Mahayana Buddhist texts, which has influenced art, literature and philosophy throughout East Asia for more than 1,400 years. It states that anyone has the potential to reach enlightenment. The heart of each sentient creature is represented by an unopened lotus, which contains within it everything they need to bloom. Once they achieve enlightenment, the lotus blossoms. In Buddhist imagery, the lotus represents transcendence, creation, compassion, purity, longevity, regeneration and enlightenment.

JŌDO

Pure Land Buddhism

Mahayana or Pure Land Buddhism, which became popular in the Heian period (794–1185), is one of the most widely practised schools of the Buddhist tradition in East Asia. Forms of Pure Land Buddhism are practised in China, Korea, Japan, Vietnam and Tibet. Japanese Pure Land Buddhism (*Jōdo*) is devoted to the worship of the Amitabha or Amida Buddha (the Buddha of Infinite Light). Pure Land teachings are full of floral imagery and state that anyone can be reborn in the Amitabha Buddha's Western Paradise, known as the Pure Land or Land of Bliss, where they can work toward reaching enlightenment. When the Buddha was born, according to legend, he was enveloped in flowers of the field. Pure Land Buddhism portrays paradise *(Gokuraku Jōdo)* as a place of wish-granting trees where the air is full of birdsong and heavenly music and, according to anthropologist Emiko Ohnuki-Tierney, is "overflowing with flowers blooming throughout the four seasons".

SŌMOKU JŌBUTSU

The Buddhahood of Plants

The indigenous Shintō belief that plants, trees and animals contained spirits predates the introduction of Buddhist literature to Japan. Examples of talking plants can be found in the *Manyōshū (Collection of Ten Thousand Leaves)*, the oldest existing anthology of Japanese poetry, compiled during the Nara period (710–794). As Professor Mark

Cody Poulton writes, "both Shintō and Buddhism acknowledge that sentience can exist across a broad spectrum of life." Shintō and Pure Land Buddhism both hold that all living things have spirits. If they have a spirit, then they are capable of reaching enlightenment, just like humanity.

The *Manyōshū* is a collection of 20 volumes, which contains over 1,000 *waka* poems dedicated to more than 150 species of flowers, trees and grasses. There are several Manyo botanical gardens in Japan, which aim to include every single variety of plant mentioned in the *Manyōshū*; these gardens are called *Manyōshū shokubutsu-en*. One of the things that makes the *Manyōshū* so unusual is that it contains poetry written by people from all walks of life: men and women, young and old, from emperors and princes to humble townsfolk. According to Professor Hideo Shintani, the curator of the Takaoka Manyo Historical Museum in Toyama, we are no different from the poets of the *Manyōshū*, which was written over 1,200 years ago. Instead of composing poems to celebrate the infinite beauty of nature and sending them to our friends, we compose photographs and social media posts to share them with our loved ones. We are just as in awe of the natural world as those who lived over 1,000 years ago – proving that our appreciation for nature and desire to connect with the natural world transcends time.

NOH THEATRE

The Flowering Spirit

Noh is the classical theatre of Japan. A form of Japanese musical drama known for its highly stylized dances and iconic masks, it is one of the world's oldest performing arts. The language of Noh is rich in imagery of Japanese flora and *kigo* (seasonal words). Many Noh plays contain a fusion of Shintō and Buddhist attitudes toward nature, referencing the colours, fragrances, and forms of various flowers and plants that are immediately recognizable to those versed in poetry and Buddhist philosophy.

The origins of Noh theatre lie in ancient shamanistic ritual practices, the nature-focused belief structure of Shintō and the floral language of *waka* poetry. These are combined with the Mahayana Buddhist concept of *sōmoku jōbutsu*, the Buddhahood of plants, an idea that originates from the *Lotus Sutra*, stating that all natural things, both sentient and non-sentient, can achieve Buddhahood. This is the theme of more than 40 Noh plays. Noh gives these spirits a voice. In the dramas the spirits of flowers often appear as beautiful young women and recite poetry to weary travellers.

Zeami Motokiyo (1363–1443), the father of Noh, described this form of theatre in abstract floral terms, writing that "leaves of words are drops of dew that turn into seeds that illuminate the heart." He spoke of the illusive *hana* (flower), which signified beauty or perfection inspired by the *Lotus Sutra*, in which the lotus flower represents supreme truth and enlightenment. The *jibun no hana* (temporary flower) is the natural beauty of youth, whose petals will eventually fade and scatter. Zeami's ultimate goal was to achieve what he called the *makoto no hana* or the true flower, the blooming of the perfect moment on stage – something that takes years to master and requires perfect timing to unite both actor and audience.

Fuji Musume
The Wisteria Maiden

Symbolic natural imagery is at the heart of many Japanese traditional art forms, and Noh theatre is no exception. Noh plays are often set in a specific season, each with its own seasonal imagery. The spirit of trees and flowers that feature in classical Japanese poetry appear in human form in several Noh plays as the *shite* or masked protagonist. In ancient Japan, pine trees symbolized men, and wisteria represented women. The *shite* is the leading actor in any Noh performance; they wear the most elaborate costumes, deliver the most poetic lines and express their emotions through dance. These types of plays are called *mugen no* (dream Noh), and they take place in a world of illusion where the lines between dreams and reality are permeable, allowing ghosts and spirits to interact with mortals.

One example is *Fuji* (*Wisteria*), in which a beautiful woman appears to a travelling priest who stops to admire the Tagonoura wisteria in flower and recites a poem but does not praise the beauty of the flowers.

A local woman suddenly appears and scolds him for not mentioning the famous local wisteria after revealing that she is, in fact, the spirit of the ethereal flowers; she then promptly disappears. She returns to find the sleeping monk in the middle of the night, performs a dance and tells him that she has reached enlightenment and become the Boddhisatva of flowers. As daybreak begins, she vanishes with the sun's first rays.

Fuji
Wisteria

As spring gives way to summer, the pink clouds of blossoms fade and are replaced with lush green foliage and a haze of purple tendrils. The first and most beloved of the *murasaki* (purple) flowers to bloom is wisteria, followed by water-loving irises and later hydrangeas, the iconic flower of Japan's rainy season. In the countryside, wild wisteria climbs through the trees and sprinkles the mountains with a dusting of purple flowers, perfuming the air. As Heian-period noblewoman Sei Shōnagon wrote in *The Pillow Book*, the sight of "long, richly coloured clusters of wisteria blossoms" is a truly splendid thing.

In Japan, when flowering trees bloom, people don't just sit beneath them; they make sweets to represent them, photograph them, compose poems about them and cherish a single flower or branch that graces a vase. Wisteria flowers are the floral emblem of Nara's Kasuga Shrine. At the Manyo Botanical Gardens in Nara, a maze of interconnected trellises leads visitors on a journey through the gardens, home to twelve kinds of wisteria, from pure white to the deepest purple, where each May metallic orange koi swim lazily beneath the heady sweet scent of the flowers.

JAPANESE MICRO SEASON NO.18
BOTAN HANA SAKU
Peonies Bloom
≫— 30 April–4 May —≪

Treasured throughout East Asia, *botan* (peonies) were introduced to Japan from China over 1,000 years ago. In Japan they are known as the "King of Flowers" or the "Goddess of Flowers". Initially prized for their medicinal properties and later for their extravagant beauty, peonies appear in all forms of Japanese art. Popular with both the Chinese nobility and the Japanese Imperial court, peonies retained this majestic association through symbolism; they represent honour and nobility.

Japan is home to two different kinds of peonies, those that bloom in April/May following after the *sakura* and wisteria and those that bloom in the winter. Japanese tree peonies known as *kan botan* (cold peonies) and *fuyu botan* (winter peonies) need to be protected from heavy snowfall. Japanese gardeners do this by lovingly creating small huts made of woven straw. The sight of the vibrant peonies under their conical winter hats covered with a dusting of snow is an iconic winter image.

Japan's Peony Island

Last year I celebrated this late spring micro season in the perfect place: Japan's peony island. Yuushien is a stunning traditional garden entirely devoted to peonies that dominates Daikon Island, about an hour outside Matsue City. Each Golden Week, the garden celebrates by holding its annual *Botan Enyukai* (peony garden party). The highlight of the event is a river of peonies.

Like cherry blossoms and roses, peony petals are edible; the chefs at Yuushien use them to make *botan soba*, petal pink soba noodles coloured by the flower petals kneaded into the dough. This spring dish is served chilled on a bed of ice in a heavy glass dish so you can enjoy the delicate colour and flavour of this seasonal delight.

The Japanese Floral Calendar:
A Year in Flowers

Flowers are a living, breathing calendar. Although we can now quickly and easily source flowers from all over the world and enjoy them all year round, flowers are still nature's calendar for those who want to attune themselves to the seasons. Throughout the year in Japan, one flower passes the baton to another. Japan's many floral festivals and gardens mean that there is always something in bloom to enjoy and look forward to every month of the year.

Here is a list of the key blooms to look out for if you're planning a trip to Japan. These are the plants and trees traditionally associated with each month of the year, which will appear on kimono, in the form of sweets or stationary and give you a gentle floral reminder of each season. The cycle repeats anew year after year. Changing temperatures will, of course, have a significant effect on this and dates can fluctuate annually. So, it's always best to check the annual *sakura zensen* (cherry blossom forecast) if you plan to go cherry blossom hunting in Japan.

How does this compare with the flowers that bloom in your neighbourhood?

• January – *Matsu* (Pine)

• February – *Ume* (Plum)

• March – *Momo* (Peach)

- April – *Sakura* (Cherry)

- May – *Tsutsuji* (Azalea), *Fuji* (Wisteria) and *Botan* (Peony)

- June – *Shōbu* (Iris)

- July – *Asagao* (Morning Glory)

- August – *Ren* or *Hasu* (Lotus)

- September – *Aki no Hanakusa* (Seven Autumn Grasses)

- October – *Kiku* (Chrysanthemum)

- November – *Momiji* (Maple leaves)

- December – *Tsubaki* (Camellia)

TSUBAKI

Camellia

The *tsubaki* or camellia is one of Japan's most iconic flowers. Native to both China and Japan, it has been grown in East Asia for over 1,000 years and was considered sacred in Japan during the 4th and 5th centuries. *Tsubaki* are also sometimes called "Japanese roses", named by the German botanist Engelbert Kaempfer in c.1712. Later during the early Edo period (1603–1868), interest in *honzōgaku* (medical botany – the growing of plants for medicinal purposes) had a significant impact on the development of Japanese horticulture and resulted in the cultivation of many exquisite privately owned gardens. These were created by the Japanese nobility, who especially loved camellias and documented over 200 varieties.

All camellia varieties originate from the genus of flowering plants in the *Theaceae* family – the same family as the tea plant *Camellia sinensis*. Therefore, camellias are closely linked to *Chadō* (the Way of Tea). The single-flowered, paler varieties called *waki-suki* are often used in tea gardens. There are two varieties of Japanese camellia or *tsubaki*: *Camellia japonica* and *Camellia sasanqua*. *Camellia japonica* blooms from late October through to April, while in Japan's temperate winter, *Camellia sasanqua* begins to bloom in the autumn and represents November and December in Japan's traditional floral calendar. This means they can be both a precursor to spring and a symbol of winter. On Cape Ashizuri, in Shikoku, 150,000 camellias bloom every year.

Beauty and the Camellia

Since the 7th century the camellia has symbolized strength and longevity in Japan. Camellia leaves, stems and seeds are used to make dyes, essences and oils. The essence extracted from the seeds is used to make hair oil, which has been a part of the Japanese beauty regime for over 1,000 years. In the Heian Era (794 –1185) *osuberakashi* (long, free-flowing lustrous black hair) was considered the epitome of Japanese beauty. Noblewomen used rice water (water left over from washing rice before cooking) and camellia oil to maintain their hair and the oil remains one of Japan's most popular beauty products to this day.

AISATSU

Seasonal Greetings

Japanese letters always begin with a reference to the current season. This seasonal greeting is called *jikou no aisatsu*. Letter writing, poetry composition and calligraphy were some of the most highly regarded skills of the Heian Imperial court and an integral part of courtship rituals. Long before envelopes existed, members of the Japanese aristocracy would write their *koibumi* (love letters), then fold them and tie them to the branches of flowering trees to be hand delivered by elegantly attired attendants. Each piece of paper was dyed with natural plant materials to represent the specific season. Both the content of the letter and the colour of the paper itself referred to the season. This elegant traditional method of communication also involved letters sent to friends, who often included pressed seasonal flowers or plants. Can you imagine receiving one of these letters? How romantic!

This custom of sending fragrant missives written on coloured sheets of paper is introduced by Sei Shōnagon, a lady-in-waiting to the Japanese Empress, in her novel *The Pillow Book*. She lists things of elegant beauty, including "a letter of fine green paper, tied to a sprig of willow covered in little leaf buds". The Shining Prince (Genji) does the same thing in Murasaki Shikibu's *The Tale of Genji*. After composing his last message to the crown prince, he ties it to a cherry tree branch and sends it via a go-between. This elegant practice of *musubi fumi*, or knotted letters tied to branches of seasonal plants, persists in the custom of *omikuji* (paper fortunes), which you receive when you visit a shrine. Visitors often tie their fortune slips onto a tree branch in the shrine's grounds, especially if their prediction wasn't as fortuitous as they had hoped.

Send a Seasonal Greeting

This is a beautiful tradition we can incorporate into our modern lives. As anyone who has wandered into a Japanese stationery shop knows, the art of letter writing is alive and well in Japan. Snail mail is still one of my favourite ways to communicate, and there's nothing better than receiving a real handwritten letter.

Here are some ideas for seasonal greetings.

- Select some beautiful stationery, and look for pastel spring flowers, cooling summer imagery or warming autumnal hues.

- Paint a postcard depicting a seasonal image.

- Add a salute to the season in the form of a poem.

- Decorate some plain stationery and write to a friend.

- Include a pressed flower inside.

- Get creative and dye some sheets of white paper with your favourite colours of the season.

- Use handmade paper or make your own.

HANACHŌZU

Flower Water Basin

Traditionally when you visit a Shintō shrine in Japan, one of the first things you do is called *temizuya*, a water-based purification ritual, to cleanse yourself before entering the shrine's innermost and most sacred spaces. This involves washing and rinsing your hands and mouth with one *hishaku* (bamboo scoop) of water. You do this at the *chōzuya*, the stone fountains or water basins typically found near the entrance of a Shintō shrine. Since this practice was not possible during the Covid pandemic, more and more shrines have taken up the practice of *hanachōzu*, which means "flower basin". This beautiful practice involves decorating the water's surface with seasonal cut flowers, which are changed regularly. I like to visit my favourite temples, such as Yanagidani Kannon in northern Kyōto, to see their exceptional seasonal displays.

❀ MAKE YOUR OWN ❀
HANACHŌZU

You don't need to be in Japan to experience the simple beauty of seasonal flower displays. Try making one in your own home or garden. You can use this as a new way to enjoy flowers from the garden or support a local florist. Making a new *hanachōzu* to celebrate your favourite flowers of the season could be your new seasonal ritual.

STEP 1. Select your vessel. A stone water feature or an empty flower planter will do nicely if you're making one in the garden. If you're making a smaller *hanachōzu* to enjoy inside your home, look for a plain white bowl or a simple dish that won't detract from the beauty of the flowers. See if you can find a vintage cut glass bowl in a charity shop or thrift store.

STEP 2. Choose your flowers. The options are endless, but I like to use seasonal flowers wherever possible. Choosing a single flower or a limited colour palette works especially well. For a clean, fresh look, use only white flowers with a touch of green. Try a combination of seasonal pastels in shades of pink, green, purple and yellow for a delicate spring feeling. If it's autumn, why not celebrate the Chrysanthemum Festival with a bowl of jewel-like *kiku* (chrysanthemum) flowers in shades of white, gold and purple?

STEP 3. Fill the vessel to just below the lip of the bowl with clean, fresh water.

STEP 4. Using a pair of sharp scissors or gardening shears, cut the stems off your flowers, leaving only the flower heads and place them one by one into the bowl.

STEP 5. Use smaller blooms to fill in any gaps where water is still visible. Play with your composition, experimenting till you're happy with the balance of the overall design you've created.

STEP 6. To keep enjoying your flowers for as long as possible, change the water regularly and keep them away from direct heat sources.

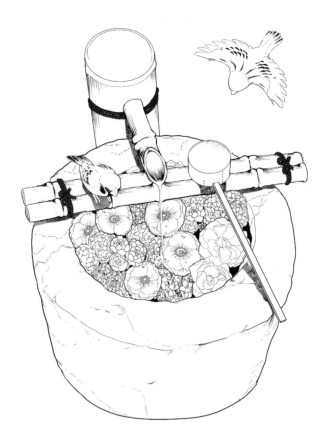

HANAKOTOBA

The Japanese Language of Flowers

Often called the Japanese language of flowers, *hanakotoba* literally means "flower words". It was created in the Meji period (1868–1912), only decades before its western equivalent, floriography, which became incredibly popular in Britain during the reign of Queen Victoria. Each flower symbolizes specific character traits or seasons, and by using the imagery of certain plants, you can communicate your sentiments through the language of flowers.

Six Japanese Flowers and their Meanings

Botan (Peony)
The King of Flowers – the opulent peony – is symbolic of spring. It also represents honour, wealth and prosperity.

Yanagi (Willow)
The weeping willow is a popular motif in Japanese art, representing femininity and spring.

Himawari (Sunflowers)
Vast fields of these large, sun-loving blooms represent summertime in Japan. Their golden colour symbolizes sunshine, warmth, wealth and progress, so they're often given in bouquets to represent good luck and prosperity.

Asagao (Morning Glory)
Asagao means "face in the morning", referring to the fact that the flowers bloom first thing in the morning and close in the evening. Grown by school children throughout Japan, the flowering vines of vivid blue and purple morning glory are an iconic image of the late summer/early autumn. This short-lived flower also symbolizes innocence and ephemeral love.

Kiku (Chrysanthemum)

The chrysanthemum – Japan's national flower – symbolizes the sun, longevity, autumn and Japan as a nation. Along with the paulownia, the Japanese Imperial family uses the *kiku* as their crest.

Tsubaki (Camellia)

Camellias are in bloom from late winter till the early spring in Japan, so they can be used to refer to either season. They traditionally represented virtue and a noble death to members of the samurai class. However, like many red flowers, red camellias also represent love.

HANA KIGO

Beautiful Japanese Words for Flowers

Hanadoki – Meaning "the flowering season", when everything is in bloom, this refers specifically to spring when the cherry blossoms are in bloom.

Shiki-e – Japanese paintings depicting the flowers of the four seasons.

Mansaku –The first flowers to bloom.

Kafu no Michi – "The scented wind road" – this phrase refers to the profusion of spring flowers that perfume the air.

Haru no no – Spring fields full of new green shoots, violets and dandelions.

Hanakotoba – The Japanese language of flowers.

Fujinami – Waves of wisteria – the long clusters of the purple wisteria caught swaying in the breeze resemble waves.

SPEND TIME WITH FLOWERS

A life filled with flowers is a life full of poetry. Here are some suggestions for how to spend more time with flowers.

- Walk through a field of wild flowers.

- Grow flowers from seeds.

- Visit a botanic garden.

- Draw the flowers that inspire you.

- Learn about the life cycle of your favourite flower through botanical art.

- Find your nearest flower market.

- Select flowers from a florist and create your own seasonal bouquet.

- Photograph flowers that catch your eye on your walk to work or school.

- Study how flowers grow in a garden, a field or the forest.

- Use a cyanotype kit to capture the silhouettes of your favourite flowers and leaves. Sunlight will develop the image, creating a rich, indigo blue print.

OTSUKIMI

The Ritual of Moon Viewing

Japan's early autumnal rituals centre around three key elements, *tsuki* (the celestial moon), *kiku* (chrysanthemums, the iconic flowers of autumn in Japan) and *aki no nanakusa* (the seven autumn grasses).

September is Japan's designated moon viewing season. The whole month becomes a celebration dedicated to appreciating the moon's beauty. An endless source of poetic inspiration in Japanese art and literature, imagery of the moon can mean many things: a symbolic representation of autumn, a metaphor for truth, enlightenment or even love.

Tsuki is the Japanese word for moon, and the character is a pictograph of a crescent moon hidden behind clouds. *Tsukimi* means "to look at or admire the moon". The autumnal rite of moon viewing has been practised in Japan for over 1,000 years. *Otsukimi* or *tsukimi* is the Japanese equivalent of China's Mid-Autumn Festival.

The custom was initially introduced to Japan from China and dates back to the Nara period (710–794). In Japan, every

Otsukimi people celebrate by making offerings of seasonal fruits and vegetables, attending moon viewing parties and eating rabbit-shaped delicacies while looking up at the harvest moon. The imagery of rabbits gazing up at the moon among autumn grasses combines the three key seasonal images that represent autumn in Japan. You'll see these three elements separately and combined on stationary, *tenugui* (decorative cotton towels) and sweets throughout the country each September.

There are endless beautiful names for the moon in Japanese. As the moon dances across the sky throughout the year, each season and phase has its own *tsuki* or moon.

Haru no tsuki – The spring moon

Natsu no tsuki – The summer moon

Aki no tsuki – The autumn moon

Fuyu no tsuki – The winter moon

HAZUKI JŪGOYA

The Clearest Night

Otsukimi is sometimes also called *jūgoya*, meaning the fifteenth night. According to the ancient Japanese lunar-solar calendar, the full moon appeared on the fifteenth night of each month. This was considered the best night of the year for observing the moon at its fullest and brightest. The fifteenth night of the eighth month of the old lunar calendar is known as *jūgoya no tsukimi*.

Tsukimi Kigo
Seasonal Words for Moon Viewing Season

Meigetsu – Meaning "renowned moon" or "bright moon", this phrase refers specifically to the majesty of the harvest moon of mid-autumn.

Tsuki yo – A moonlit night or moonlight.

Shinmai – The name given to the rice from the year's first harvest, meaning "new rice".

Kikuzuki – The month of chrysanthemums.

Shusei – The songs of autumn, such as a choir of insects singing, the sound of rustling leaves.

Shūshoku – Meaning "autumn colour" – the atmosphere created by the many glorious hues of autumnal foliage.

TSUKI NO USAGI
The Moon Rabbit

Myths about the moon have existed worldwide for thousands of years. The moon rabbit is a popular legend that exists throughout East Asia and among many of the First Nations in America, Canada and Mexico. Japan's lunar legend is inspired by the craters of the moon that are said to look like a rabbit pounding glutinous rice to make *mochi* (sweets). According to the Chinese zodiac, rabbits are peaceful, cooperative creatures. Rabbits embody yin, which manifests in their elegance, quiet contemplation and kind ways. They are known as the gentlest and the luckiest of all the animals in the Chinese zodiac. In Japanese, the word *eto* refers to all twelve animals of the Chinese zodiac, which are an inherent part of daily life in Japan.

Each September, to celebrate *Otsukimi* in my own small way, I like to buy a rabbit-themed sweet to enjoy while I try to catch sight of the harvest moon. You'll see lots of rabbit-themed *wagashi* in Japanese sweet shops at this time of the year because they represent *tsuki no usagi*, the moon rabbit or moon hare. He is a popular folklore figure in China too, where he's called the Jade Rabbit.

The moon rabbit's story tells that one day, the man who lived on the moon grew lonely. He looked down at the Earth, and in a forest he saw a rabbit, a fox and a monkey. He decided that the kindest animal could come and live with him on the moon. Disguising himself as a starving beggar, he came down to Earth and approached the animals in the forest and asked if they could help feed him. When the rabbit lit a fire and offered his own life to provide for the elderly man, he was rewarded with a place by his side for eternity.

Tsukimi Dango
Sweets for Moon Viewing

Certain traditional dishes are made as offerings to celebrate the moon viewing festival, including moon-shaped *wagashi* called *tsukimi dango*, which are displayed in a pyramid alongside sprays of golden *susuki* (pampas grass), another of the archetypal symbols of autumn in Japan. Round moon-shaped sweets and fruits are presented as a harvest offering. Fifteen dumplings are arranged in a pyramid shape on top of a small stand called a *sambō*.

In Kansai, *tsukimi dango* are plain white and shaped like the moon, whereas in the Kanto region, they are filled with red bean paste and made in an oval shape to resemble *satoimo* (taro, a root vegetable) because it's time to give thanks for the autumn harvest, and the potatoes are the *shun* (seasonal food at its best) of the season. The *anko* (red bean paste) represents the clouds, so the *mochi* is the moon hidden behind the clouds.

MEIGETSU

The Harvest Moon

The autumn moon is one of Japan's representative seasonal images. Lunar legends and moon myths exist the world over – for example, Indigenous North Americans have poetic names for every moon of the year. Members of the Ojibwe, one of the biggest remaining Algonquin tribes based in the Great Lakes area of the United States, call the moon closest to the autumnal equinox the corn moon or the harvest of fruit moon. The equinoxal moon marks the mid-point of autumn when yin and yang equalize, as do the hours of light and dark. Of all the full moons that wax and wane throughout the year, it is autumn's full moon or harvest moon that is considered to be the most sublime. The term *meigestu*, meaning "splendid moon" or "harvest moon", refers to the nearest full moon to *shūbun* (the autumn equinox), which appears on the fifteenth night of the eighth month, according to the old lunar-solar calendar. Transposed onto the Gregorian calendar, this is now September, the ninth month of the year.

Chūshū no Meigetsu
The Harvest Moon Festival

Chūshū no Meigetsu, Japan's harvest moon festival, is descended from China's Mid-Autumn Festival. Since ancient times, people have enjoyed one of autumn's most beloved traditions, gazing up at the full moon in Kyōto. At this time of the year, *kangetsu no yūbe* (moon viewing parties) are held to celebrate the beauty of the harvest moon. This has been an annual tradition at Daikakuji since Emperor Saga (786–842) first set sail on a dragon boat across the temple's Osawa Pond during a lavish party on the night of the harvest moon, which enabled his guests to enjoy two moons, the moon in the sky above and the reflection of the moon in the waters below.

The celebration involved the creation of dedicated moon viewing platforms through the temple gardens, an extravagant banquet and a lunar-themed poetry competition.

How to Enjoy Moon Viewing Season at Home

- Compose a poem inspired by the beauty of the moon.

- Make a moon-themed seasonal display.

- Learn about global lunar legends and rites. Why not read about a new one each year during September?

- Take a moment to reflect on all the joys of summer and think about what you're most looking forward to about autumn.

- Invite some friends for a harvest feast of seasonal delights under the light of the autumn moon; if the weather allows, you could even eat outside.

- Enjoy some *mochi* and make an offering to the moon.

Apples, persimmons and other round, harvest-season fruits and vegetables are perfect if you can't easily access *mochi*.

- Fill a vase with autumnal grasses gathered from nearby fields and riverbeds or source some dried pampas grass. Position it by the window so you can look past the grasses to see the moon.

- Find out if there are any moon-themed events taking place near you. One of my favourites is Luke Jerram's travelling artwork, the *Museum of the Moon*, which continually tours the world. You can check the tour dates on their website.

YEARNING FOR THE MOON

Since the 8th century, Japan has been a nation of selenophiles – those who adore the moon. The Japanese phrase *kyōka suigetsu* means "flower in the mirror, moon on water". Neither the flower in the mirror nor the moon's reflection in the water can be touched. This expression refers to something that's visible but is just beyond our reach. It is something you can feel (a sense of beauty or an emotion) but can't easily put into words; this is one of the definitions of the Japanese term *yūgen* or "mysterious depth".

As writer Matsuoka Seigō explains, "We all possess a yearning for the unknown", and that desire for an "indescribable somewhere" often manifests in our love for the moon. Seigō wrote eloquently on the subject of the moon in Japanese art and culture, explaining that we walk through life with a sense of incompleteness within ourselves, missing some vital "other half" that prevents us from being whole. This is not another person but a yearning for something that we cannot name or give voice to. The moon is one manifestation of that *hoka* (other).

In Japan, when people talk about the moon, they're often saying something else, like "I love you". Yasunari Kawabata, who won

Japan's first Nobel prize in literature, explains that "seeing the moon, he becomes the moon, becoming one with nature". Looking at the moon can make us feel whole; in that brief shining moment, we tap into something greater than ourselves, connecting momentarily with the moon, nature and perhaps even the universe itself. Even long after the moon disappears from our sight, the impact of it echoes within us. That sense of awe is akin to the feeling of walking in an ancient forest or looking out over an exceptional landscape. When we are one with nature, we are home. It is in these moments that we feel both part of a wider community and experience communion with the natural world.

THE BEAUTY OF THINGS OBSCURED

Buddhist monk Urabe Kenkō (1283–1350) believed that beauty is to be celebrated, even though it will ultimately fade as all things do. He asked, "Are we to look at cherry blossoms only in full bloom, the moon only when it is cloudless?" believing instead that "Branches about to bloom or gardens strewn with faded flowers are worthier of our attention." Kenkō's words eloquently explain that Japanese aesthetics prizes both anticipation and mystery of things that are slightly obscured or incomplete, things left unspoken, things unsaid or undone – such as the beauty of the moon peeking out from behind the clouds. The view is slightly obscured but full of anticipation and suggestion; waiting for the luminous moment, the moon emerges and breaks free of the clouds. There is beauty at every stage of its waxing and waning. *Yoin* is the Japanese word for a feeling that lingers after something ends, like an echo. Zeami, Japan's most famous playwright, echoes this, saying that the "enjoyment lies in the undone" the moment before a kiss or once our love disappears from view. Ask yourself honestly, do you ever notice the waxing and waning of the moon? Taking a moment to observe the stages of the moon grounds you firmly in the present moment.

JAPANESE MICRO SEASON NO.50
KIKU NO HANA HIRAKU

Chrysanthemums Bloom
✽⁓ *13–17 October* ⁓✽

East Asia is the chrysanthemum heartland. *Kiku* or chrysanthemums came to Japan from China and were originally cultivated for their medicinal properties. They have been cherished in Japan for over 1,000 years. Since the Heian period (794–1185), the *kiku* has represented autumn, longevity and Japan as a nation, appearing throughout Japanese art as a symbol of autumn and as one of the Four Gentlemen alongside the orchid, plum and bamboo (see page 188). In Japan, you'll encounter chrysanthemums everywhere: as sweets; on textiles, family crests and coins; and painted on ceramics, as well as lobed dishes called *kikuwari*, shaped like overlapping petals, which emulate the form of the chrysanthemum seal.

KIKUMON

The Chrysanthemum Seal

The Mikado or Emperor of Japan sits upon the chrysanthemum throne. This autumnal flower is the Imperial standard in Japan, equivalent to the English Rose. While the *kiri* or paulownia flower is the emperor's personal crest, the *kikumon* (chrysanthemum seal), a stylized sixteen-petalled chrysanthemum, is the official emblem of Japan's royal family. The golden chrysanthemum insignia is also used as Japan's national crest, which appears on Japanese passports. The Supreme Order of the Chrysanthemum is Japan's highest honour, established in 1876 and was bestowed upon the late British monarch, Queen Elizabeth II, in 1962.

The Story of Lady White and Lady Yellow

According to *Myths and Legends of Japan* by F Hadland Davis, this is one story of how the *kikumon,* or the sixteen-petalled chrysanthemum crest, came to be.

Long ago, two chrysanthemums stood in a meadow side by side. One was white and the other yellow. One day, a farmer walking by became enamoured by Lady Yellow; he told her that if she came home with him, she would enjoy fine foods and he would give her beautiful clothes to wear. Charmed by his words, she left the meadow to grace his garden, leaving poor Lady White all alone in the field, weeping for her lost sister.

Lady Yellow's long curled petals grew more and more beautiful each day in the farmer's garden. One day, the village chief came to visit the farmer on a quest to find the perfect chrysanthemum specimen to be used as inspiration for his lord's crest design. The farmer took him to see Lady Yellow in the garden, but what he wanted was a simple, pure white chrysanthemum with sixteen petals.

On his way home, the village chief cut across a field and came across Lady White crying. She told him her sad story, and when she finished, he exclaimed that he did not find her sister half as beautiful, and he wanted her to be on the crest of his lord, the Daimyo. Lady White dried her eyes; she was delighted. Soon afterwards, she was carried away to the Daimyo's palace on a palanquin, and there she was visited by artists from far and wide, who came to draw her and praise her beautiful form. Everywhere she looked, she saw herself reflected in the Daimyo's belongings: on his robes and his armour, on lacquered boxes and great carved panels on the ceiling. This is how Lady White's quiet beauty and her pretty white face were immortalized forever as the chrysanthemum seal.

Sadly, Lady Yellow met with a different fate. She bloomed alone in the farmer's garden. Although she was much admired and drank in her visitors' praise like dew, she eventually began to feel weary. Finally, one day, when her proud head fell forward, the farmer carried her off to the compost heap.

Amaterasu Ōmikami
The Sun Goddess

With its golden petals outstretched, the chrysanthemum mimics the rays of the rising sun. This is a key motif in Japan's mythology, which harks back to its legendary matriarch, Amaterasu Ōmikami, the celestial Sun Goddess, daughter of Japan's mythical creators Izanagi and Izanami. Her fabled descendants include Emperor Jimmu, the first Mikado of Japan. Her name comes from the Japanese word *amateru*, meaning "to illuminate the sky", a combination of the words *ama,* or Heaven, and *teru,* to shine.

In the most well-known myth about the Sun Goddess, Amaterasu's brother Susanowo, the god of storms and oceans, was sent to rule the land of Yomi. On his way to the underworld, he made a detour under the pretence of innocently visiting his sister in Heaven. Instead, soon after his arrival, he destroyed her sacred rice fields and wreaked havoc in her heavenly domain. Appalled by his behaviour, Amaterasu locked herself

Dew-dappled
Let us pluck and wear
Chrysanthemum blooms
That an Autumn of eternal youth
Should last forever!

KI NO TOMONORI
TRANSLATED BY DR THOMAS MCAULEY
EXCERPT FROM *AUTUMN,*
BOOK FIVE OF THE *KOKIN WAKASHŪ*

away in a cave to escape her younger brother, but of course, once the Sun Goddess hid herself away, the world was plunged into darkness; there was no day, only endless night.

Japan's myriad gods gathered on the banks of the River of Heaven to discuss how they might appease Amaterasu and convince her to return and bring light back to the world. They prepared to enact a plan, making offerings of jewels and a mirror in a sacred tree. In the end, the Great Persuader, Ama no Uzume, the goddess of dawn, mirth and patron of the arts, performed a provocative dance outside Amaterasu's cave, making all eight million gods roar with laughter, and enticing the goddess to venture outside to discover what all the noise was about. As soon as she peeped out from the rocks, the other gods tied a sacred rope across the cave's entrance so she could not retreat, and the world was once again filled with her golden light.

KIKU NO SEKKU

The Chrysanthemum Festival
9 September and 14 October

Japan's many gorgeous flower festivals punctuate the calendar, signalling the changing seasons throughout the year. They begin with rejoicing over the arrival of the first blooms – the plum blossoms that appear in February – then they move on to *sakura* season in late March or early April, followed by celebrations of wisteria, azaleas, peonies and irises. The rainy season brings hydrangeas, and summer is the season of lotuses and sunflowers. Then autumn begins with delicate grasses and pink cosmos, but it is the regal chrysanthemums that steal the show.

Kiku no Sekku is one of the five ancient sacred festivals, or *Gosekku*. On 9 September, Japan celebrates the Chrysanthemum Festival, known as *Kiku no Sekku* or *Chōyō no Sekku*. The ninth day of the ninth month is dedicated to praying for longevity and good health. People across the nation celebrate by enjoying chrysanthemums in all their forms, visiting stunning chrysanthemum displays, drinking chrysanthemum petal tea and sake with petals floating on its surface. Restaurants serve dishes like *shungiku*, chrysanthemum greens. Or they use the petals, both of which are edible, to make a dish called *kikka no ohitashi* made with blanched, vinegared chrysanthemum flowers. At this time of the year, you might come across boxes of small flaxen-yellow chrysanthemums in local supermarkets in Japan. The whole flowers are used to garnish *sashimi*, and the petals are sprinkled on salads. One autumn several years ago, I was served a bite-sized piece of salmon delicately wrapped in a layer of bright yellow chrysanthemum petals. Did you know that you can eat chrysanthemums?

According to the philosophy of yin and yang, odd numbers are considered lucky. Hence, the ninth day of the ninth month is doubly auspicious. The Double Ninth is a festival celebrated throughout East Asia, including in Hong Kong where it's called the Chung Yeung Festival and in Vietnam, where it's named Tet Trung Cu'u.

Celebrate the Chrysanthemum Festival at Home

To celebrate the chrysanthemum festival, people consume chrysanthe-mums in their many forms, both savoury and sweet, and adorn their houses with these regal flowers. Why not fill a vase with *kiku* or their cousins, dahlias, in September and enjoy this autumnal ritual at home? You can also:

- Drink chrysanthemum tea.

- Create a seasonal floral display featuring chrysanthemums.

- Taste chrysanthemum greens.

- Grow some chrysanthemums.

- Decorate your living space with chrysanthemum-themed imagery and homewares.

- Make a *hanachōzu* (flower water basin) with chrysanthemum flowers (see Chapter 7).

- Visit a chrysanthemum show or a dahlia garden.

Kiku no Kisewata
Chrysanthemum Silk Floss

During the Heian period (794–1185), it was customary on 8 September, the eve of the Chrysanthemum Festival, to cover chrysanthemum flowers with a delicate cotton silk floss designed to catch the precious morning dew that would form on the petals overnight. On the next day, the ninth day of the ninth month, the women of the Imperial court would wipe the chrysanthemum-infused dew across their faces and bodies, wishing for beauty and everlasting life.

Kikuju
Chrysanthemum Longevity

According to Haruo Shirane, Shincho Professor of Japanese Literature at Columbia University, the chrysanthemum "was often believed to hold the power to transcend time". Throughout East Asian lore these flowers have always been closely linked to myths and legends about the quest for immortality. Their many petals or florets symbolize a long life. One of these is the story of *Kikujido*, the chrysanthemum boy or child. The fable states that he was exiled from the court of Emperor Mu and became immortal by drinking from the crystal waters of the heavenly Chrysanthemum River. These fabled river waters were especially sweet because they were imbued with the essence of the chrysanthemums that grew on its banks, shedding their precious petals into the waters below.

According to other Daoist and Japanese legends, if you drank dew from the petals of these immortal flowers, which grow high up in the mountains, you could achieve everlasting life. The next best thing was to drink *kikuzake* (chrysanthemum petal sake), served with floating fresh chrysanthemum petals. This tradition stems from the belief that *kikuzake* was the libation of the Daoist immortals and gave the drinker a long life.

Kikuzake
Chrysanthemum Petal Sake

Kikuzake is the subject of numerous legends; in some, it's a kind of fairy wine that causes forgetfulness; in others, it's the secret to everlasting life. *Kikuzake* is a drink traditionally served during the Chrysanthemum

Festival (*Kiku no Sekku* or *Chōyō no Sekku*). Its name is a compound word comprising *kiku* (chrysanthemum) and sake – the Japanese term for sake served with a garnish of fresh chrysanthemum petals. *Kikuzake* was believed to protect the drinker from sickness and bestow long life. Numerous cups of chrysanthemum petal sake are exchanged during the Chrysanthemum Festival celebrations.

Another example is *Kaga no kikuzake,* a type of sake which is made from water the chrysanthemum blooms have been steeped in. *Kaga no kikuzake* sake is named after the Kaga Province, where it is produced using this method. In some recipes, chrysanthemum-scented rice is used to make sake. Another technique, similar to the recipe for making *umeshu* or plum wine, involves soaking dried chrysanthemum petals in *shōchū* (a popular distilled drink usually made from rice, barley, sweet potatoes or buckwheat), and rock sugar.

Kikuzake has been a part of the Chrysanthemum Festival since the Heian period (794–1185) and the tradition continues today. In contemporary Japan, restaurants still serve sake with floating edible chrysanthemum petals during the Chrysanthemum Festival. So, if you're in Japan during September, you might be able to sample this festive drink for yourself!

Kiku Wagashi
Chrysanthemum Sweets

Kiku Monaka (Chrysanthemum Wafer)
A crisp, round chrysanthemum-shaped wafer or a wafer stamped with the chrysanthemum seal, this sweet is filled with red bean paste and traditionally enjoyed as part of the Chrysanthemum Festival.

Kiku no Tsuyu (Chrysanthemum Dew)
A moist sweet handmade from white bean paste and artfully shaped into a dew-dappled flower. It emulates the delicate dew drops that form on the flowers overnight which, according to legend, are believed to have magical healing properties.

Nihonmatsu Chrysanthemum Festival
❀〜 *Mid-October–late November* 〜❀

Chrysanthemums arrived in Japan from their native China and, in c.910, the Imperial household held Japan's first chrysanthemum viewing event in the grounds of the Imperial Palace. Since then, the *kiku* has been the representative flower of autumn in Japan. During the Edo period (1603–1868) cultivating chrysanthemums became a popular pastime that persists today. At this time of the year, chrysanthemum exhibitions take place all over Japan, showcasing a kaleidoscope of colours and varieties and seemingly impossible flowering bonsai. These seasonal displays are similar to competitive western flower shows.

One of Japan's largest chrysanthemum festivals takes place in the town of Nihonmatsu, in Fukushima Prefecture, home to *kiku* lovers since the feudal era. They take the annual chrysanthemum *matsuri* to new heights by decorating the entire town in a month-long celebration of these autumnal flowers, creating *kiku ningyō* (chrysanthemum dolls) in life-size displays of figures from Japanese history and legend called *gaku* (scenes or tableaux), made entirely from flowers.

NIINAME NO MATSURI

The Imperial Harvest Ritual
❀〜 **23 November** 〜❀

Most Japanese *matsuri* (festivals) can be divided into two groups. While the spring festivals focus on praying for successful crops, the autumn festivals are about giving thanks for a bountiful harvest with new-season rice and freshly brewed sake. The purpose of the summer festivals in between is to pray for rain and protection from natural disasters. Kyōto's most famous festival, Gion *Matsuri*, began as a rain festival.

According to legend set down in *The Nihon Shoki* (*The Chronicles of Japan*), the Sun Goddess Amaterasu presented her grandson Ninigi no Mikoto with ears of rice from one of her sacred heavenly fields. In gratitude for the annual rice harvest, *yudane* (sacred rice) is grown as an Imperial offering to be presented to the gods each November in a Shintō ritual called *niinamesai*. *Niiname no Matsuri* is possibly the most important agricultural ritual of the year, when the Emperor of Japan personally gives thanks to the deities for the previous harvest and prays for a good harvest for the following year. The ritual takes place at the Imperial Palace, Ise Jinja and Izumo Taisha, Japan's oldest Shintō shrine.

KURI NO SEKKU

Day of Sweet Chestnuts

Minori no Aki (harvest season) in Japan brings with it a cornucopia of culinary delights in the form of *kaki* (persimmons), *yaki imo* (sweet potatoes), *nashi* (pears), *kabocha* (pumpkins), *ringo* (apples) and of course, *kuri* (sweet chestnuts). *Kuri* are one of Japan's most popular autumnal delicacies, coming into season from September till October. Another name for the ninth of the ninth, celebrated in mountain hamlets and farming communities, is *Kuri no Sekku*, the Festival of Sweet Chestnuts. The season's savoury rice dish *kuri gohan* (chestnut rice), to which *mottenohoka* (edible chrysanthemum petals) are sometimes added, combines chestnuts and seasonal flowers for an extra festive touch.

You'll find chestnuts used in both traditional *wagashi* (sweets), such as *kuri yokan*, and contemporary Japanese fusion patisserie, such as the French-inspired Mont Blanc. The classic autumnal *kuri* sweet is *kuri kinton*, which is a traditional type of Japanese confectionery made by steaming whole chestnuts and cooking them down with sugar till they become candied and then wrapping them in pureed sweet potato, which is then shaped with a cloth. This dish also features in Japanese New Year celebrations (see Chapter 11). Another lovely sweet you might come across is *kuri konashi,* which is shaped like a chestnut. Its poetic name is *yamazato*, which means "mountain hamlet".

KAKI

Persimmons

In the autumn, persimmon trees put on their annual display – their leaves turn a vibrant red and then, as their fruit ripens, they become a burnished orange. Japan made me appreciate the beauty and culinary delights of persimmon in ways I never could growing up in England, where we don't have access to the astringent type of *kaki*, which, as they slowly ripen, become sweeter and sweeter; eventually, you can simply the cut off the top and eat their jammy flesh with a spoon.

Although there are many kinds of *kaki*, they can generally be divided into two main types. *Fuyu* persimmons look like an orange tomato. These fruits can be eaten as they are, sliced like a crisp apple. Then there are *hachiya* persimmons, the so-called astringent variety, shaped like a giant fiery acorn. These are my favourites. If you can, leave them alone till their skin becomes translucent. Then, when they're almost overripe and ready to fall apart, you will be rewarded with an exquisite *kaki* experience. This process is called bletting, which involves letting fruit soften and ripen off the tree; it's also done with medlars and quinces.

Hoshigaki are an autumnal delicacy people all over Japan eagerly await each year. In countryside villages, you can see row upon row of peeled amber fruits strung from the eaves of people's homes like orange curtains, air drying in the autumnal sunshine while slowly growing sweeter and sweeter as their sugar blooms. It can take three to five weeks of care, patience and daily massaging of the fruit to make this sought-after gourmet speciality. Japanese persimmons make lovely jams and are delicious in autumnal salads. In their dried form, as *hoshigaki*, they are an excellent addition to a seasonal cheese board.

THE SMALL
SEASONS
OF AUTUMN

Risshu – Sekki No.13
The Beginning of Autumn
8 August

In Japan, autumn officially begins on the seventh or eighth of August. *Risshu* means the first day of autumn or the establishment of autumn. However, in reality this micro season brings with it some of the hottest days of the year. These are called "leftover heat".

Shōsho – Sekki No.14
Manageable Heat
23 August

Shōsho, meaning "subduing heat", signals the end of summer and marks the beginning of the rice harvest in certain parts of Japan. The first day of September is considered unlucky because of its relationship to the typhoon season, which begins in late August and continues throughout September. This dramatic season brings rain, storms and strong winds, and *kazamatsuri* (wind festivals) are still held throughout the country to appease the storms.

Hakuro – Sekki No.15
White Dew
8 September

Hakuro means white dew. As autumn deepens, temperatures begin to cool, and dew forms overnight on blades of grass, like jewels in the fields. In Japan, dew drops are more than a seasonal marker, they are an ancient metaphor for teardrops and our brief, fragile existence. After the tragic death of his young daughter, poet Kobayashi Issa (1763–1828) famously wrote a haiku about *tsuyu no yo,* our fleeting dewdrop world. According to anthropologist Liza Dalby, autumnal dew drops called *shiratsuyu* (white dew) have been referred to in Japanese poetry since the first anthologies were compiled; this is because the dew appears white when it reflects sunlight. The Japanese phrase *tsuyu no inochi* means life is as evanescent as the dew.

Shūbun – Sekki No.16
The Autumn Equinox
❀〜 *23 September* 〜❀

The Autumn Equinox is celebrated around the world as the Celtic Festival of Mabon, the Snake of Sunlight in Mexico, *Chuseok* in Korea and the Mid-Autumn Festival in China and Vietnam. *Shūbun* is the Japanese term for the Autumn Equinox, which falls on either 23 or 24 September. As the days begin to shorten, the nation celebrates one of the year's most important seasonal markers.

Kanro – Sekki No.17
Cold Dew
❀〜 *8 October* 〜❀

Kanro means "cold drops of dew" or "heavy dew". Now, there is a definite chill in the morning and evening air. Can you feel it? Once the air begins to cool, the conditions are ideal for what astronomers call observing season because it's one of the best times of the year for stargazing.

Sōkō – Sekki No.18
Frost Falls
❀〜 *23 October* 〜❀

We wake up to a shimmering crystalline world. The first frost of the year is a beautiful seasonal signifier the world over, indicating that winter is coming. Around this time of the year in Japan, the first leaves have also begun to change into their deep autumnal colour palette and *mikan*, small tangerine-like oranges, are available in supermarkets.

KANNAZUKI
The Month without Gods

An ancient Japanese name for October is *Kannazuki*, meaning "the month of no gods" or "the month when the gods are absent". This is because each year, during the tenth lunar month of the ancient Japanese lunar-solar calendar (which now falls in October), after the harvest is finished Japan's eight million Shintō gods have completed their duties for the agricultural year, and so they leave their local shrines, disappearing for a short time to travel cross-country and attend an audience at Izumo Taisha, Japan's most important Shintō shrine. According to myth, they discuss the previous year's events and the destiny of all living things, briefly leaving Japan without its gods. This idea is most famously and brilliantly depicted in Hayao Miyazaki's animated film *Spirited Away* (2001), set in a bathhouse that serves the gods.

JAPANESE MICRO SEASON NO.41
TENCHI HAJIMETE SAMUSHI
Heat Starts to Die Down
28 August – 1 September

The mornings and evenings are getting cooler, have you noticed? It feels like autumn is just around the corner, waiting to greet us like an old friend with a warm embrace and a steaming cup of tea. We are now entering no.41 of Japan's 72 micro seasons, Heat Starts to Die Down.

In my garden, the Japanese anemones are in bloom, and when I see their tightly closed buds begin to unfurl, I know summer is almost over. They mark a shift in the seasons as summer ends and autumn begins. These flowers naturally close at night and open again each morning, which has led to them symbolizing anticipation for something soon to arrive. This species was first named and described by Carl Thunberg in *Flora Japonica* (1784). Anemones are sometimes also called windflowers because their name "anemone", which originates in the Greek word of the same spelling, means "the wind's daughter".

HANA NO

Autumn Fields of Flowers

Japanese springtime imagery and symbolism is devoted to showcasing the beauty of flowering trees, whereas *aki* (autumn) illustrates the understated elegance of autumn grasses, the *aki no nanakusa*. Autumn's fields are ablaze with wild flowers and under a watchful silver September moon, waves of pampas grass sway like a shimmering sea. Grasses are the most abundant flora on Earth and have been around for 55 million years. In contrast, humanity has only been around 0.5 per cent of that time. Japan's seven autumn grasses are twinned with the seven spring herbs gathered at the start of the New Year (see page 88). The seven flowers of autumn originate from a poem by Yamanoue no Okura (660–733), which appeared in the 8th-century poetry collection, the *Manyōshū*. *Kaya* is the collective Japanese term for long grasses, sedges and pampas grass. Chances are you have some beautiful native grasses growing on your doorstep. What are their names? I especially love the deep, rich purple wheat-like grass that lines riverbeds throughout the Kentish countryside in the autumn.

The Seven Autumn Grasses

Spring and autumn are historically by far the most popular seasons in Japan, especially for artists and poets. Japan's seven autumn grasses are twinned with the seven spring herbs or *nanakusa* (see Chapter 11).

Hagi – Bush clover (*Lespedeza thunbergii*).

Kudzu – The flowering arrowroot vine (*Pueraria lobata*).

Nadeshiko – Dianthus, fringed pink or wild carnation (*Dianthus superbus*).

Ominaeshi – Golden valerian or maiden flower (*Patrinia scabiosifolia*).

Fujibakama – Thoroughwort or boneset (*Eupatorium fortunei*).

Kikyō – Bellflower or ballon flower (*Platycodon grandifloras*), which is sometimes replaced with *asagao* (morning glory).

Susuki – Pampas grass or Chinese silver grass (*Miscanthus sinensis*). Pampas grass is sometimes also called *obana* in Japanese and is closely linked to moon viewing traditions. These golden feathery plumes are often displayed as an offering to the moon, due to their visual similarity to ripening stalks of rice, making *susuki* symbolic of a good harvest. In Japanese art, when a full moon hangs low in the sky, viewed as if rising from an ocean of swaying pampas grasses, it refers to a place called Musashino Plain – an area of Tōkyō known for its expanse of autumn grasses.

Akizakura
Cosmos

✹ September–November ✹

A lesser-known example of vibrant pink flowers that are also popular in Japan are cosmos or *kosumosu*. They're also affectionately called *akizakura*, which means "autumn cherry blossom" (*aki* being autumn and *sakura*, blossom). Due to their delicate pink petals, they're dubbed the *sakura* of autumn. These cheerful pink and white flowers bloom from September to November and are synonymous with autumn in Japan. Originally native to Mexico, the cosmos is also known as the Mexican Aster and has spread throughout Japan's cities and countryside ever since the Edo period (1603–1868).

The word "cosmos" originally comes from the Greek *kosmos*, meaning harmony or an ordered universe. Visiting fields of these cheerful flowers is a popular autumnal activity in Japan. For a spectacular cosmos viewing experience, you can wander through Nara's Hannyaji, the so-called cosmos temple that's home to 30 different varieties and 150,000 blooms, which appears in the Japanese epic, *Heike Monogatari* (*The Tale of the Heike*).

Higanbana
Red Spider Lily

The vivid crimson spider lilies with their sharp little red tongues originally heralded from Nepal, China and Korea but are now an established part of Japan's autumnal landscape. Their Japanese name, *higanbana*, means "flower of Higan", which means "distant shore" in Japanese. *Ohigan* is a Buddhist celebration that takes place around Japan's autumnal equinox celebrations. It's a time when people pay respects to their ancestors and often visit their graves.

Each autumn, these blooms dye the banks of the Genji River in Ibaraki Prefecture red with their petals. Kinchakuda Manjushage Park in Saitama is famous for its annual spider lily festival, home to five million of these mythical flowers. The red spider lily (*Lycoris radiata*) is known by many names, such as the cluster amaryllis, fire flower or equinox flower, because it reaches peak bloom just in time for Higan, Japan's Autumn Equinox.

ALTERNATIVE NAMES FOR
THE RED SPIDER LILY

According to legend there are over 1,000 Japanese names for this crimson flower, which heralds the autumnal equinox throughout Japan.

Manjushage – Red Flower of Heaven

Kajibana – Fire Flower

Shibito Bana – Flower of the Dead

Yūrei Bana – Ghost Flower

Jigoku Bana – Hell Flower

Patches of *higanbana* grow wild each autumn along Japan's waterways, roadsides and on the grounds of temples and shrines. The roots of this flower are highly poisonous, so farmers often plant them as a protective boundary around their fields. It is an appropriate flower for the equinox season when many Buddhist families visit the graves of their ancestors. These blood-red lilies are sometimes called the flower of the afterlife (*Gokuraku Jōdo*) because they are said to guide souls to their next reincarnation.

In the Japanese artistic tradition, the beauty of autumn is tinged with sadness because it mirrors the poetry and pathos of spring. Just as the evanescent cherry blossoms shed their delicate petals, the trees put on a glorious display each autumn, splashing the hills and temples in luminous shades of scarlet before they shed their leaves. This is what the Welsh poet Dylan Thomas (1914–1953) called "the blood of October". Autumn is not the end. It's part of a return to the beginning. It's the start of a new chapter because, in Buddhism, death is not the end but the beginning of a new phase of existence. The world is reincarnated each spring.

CHADŌ

The Way of Tea

Tea is inextricably bound up with nature. Consider that the water in your tea bowl was once a cloud; the finely powdered tea was once vibrant green leaves in a field growing in the shadow of Mt Fuji and the clay that formed your tea bowl is the soil of Japan. Grand Master Sen Soshitsu XV, head of the Urasenke School of Tea, wrote in his book *Chadō: The Japanese Way of Tea*, "In my own hands, I hold a bowl of tea; I see all of nature represented in its green colour. Closing my eyes, I find green mountains and pure water within my own heart."

Japan is a kingdom of green tea. The tea world is a world within a world, with its own language, rituals, rules, traditions and annual celebrations. Tea has shaped the cultural landscape of Japan as we know it, so it's impossible to cover the tea ceremony's history, cultural significance and philosophies in just one chapter. However, I hope this will be a primer on a subject which is very dear to my heart.

My introduction to the world of Japanese tea and *Chanoyu* (usually "tea ceremony", literally "hot water for tea") took place during my first visit to Japan almost a decade ago. Everywhere I stayed, from the smallest *ryokan* (traditional Japanese inn) to the grandest hotel, Japanese green tea was served, and tea-making equipment was supplied in my room. My first tea ceremony experience was at a small tea house in Kyōto and this encounter ignited my interest in *Chadō* (the Way of Tea). I was immediately drawn to the understated elegance of the tearoom and the beauty displayed by the tea utensils.

Everything from the kimono worn by the *chajin* (tea people) to the delicate sweets in the form of seasonal flowers served with the vibrant green bowl of matcha was a feast for the senses. After years of independent study, it was an absolute joy to finally become a *chajin* myself and begin formally practising *Chadō* with my sensei in London. As I don't live in Japan, tea has become one of the many small ways I can connect with Japan, wherever I am.

At its heart, a tea ceremony is a celebration of nature. When attending a *chaji* or tea gathering, you meet nature at every stage and in several forms. First, in the *roji*, the dewy path or tea garden; next through the *kaiseki* meal served; then through the *chabana* (tea flowers) displayed; next through the *wagashi* (sweets) enjoyed before the bowl of tea; then through the *dōgu* (utensils) used to make the tea; and finally through the tea itself, the powdered whole leaf of the *Camellia sinensis* plant.

Ultimately, *Chadō* is an art form in and of itself, a series of carefully choreographed movements which result in an elegant and refined dance across the tearoom. The practice of *Chanoyu* cultivates an attitude of appreciation, quiet observation and gratitude. It reaffirms our connection to the natural world and teaches us to broaden our definition of beauty to include objects we might not have considered previously. The more I study *Chanoyu*, the more I value minimalism and understand the merits of a single bud over a bouquet.

THE HISTORY OF JAPANESE TEA

Ocha or *cha* is the Japanese word for tea. All *Nihoncha* (Japanese green teas) are made from the *Camellia sinensis* plant, but the term *cha* also covers tisanes and herbal teas. Tea is the world's most consumed beverage, second only to water, and we have been drinking it for over 5,000 years. According to legend, the mythical Emperor Shen Nong discovered tea in China in 2,737 BCE. Tea began as a form of medicinal herb and then, over time, developed into a drink consumed by Buddhist monks who used it to help them stay awake during long periods of meditation. Tea made its way to Japan during the Heian period (794–1185), carried by monks returning from China via the Silk Road.

Sharing tea and making ritual offerings of tea to the Buddha became one of the ways Buddhism spread throughout Japan. Tea-drinking culture spread beyond the temples and monasteries popularized by Eisai (1141–1215), the patron of Zen Buddhism in Japan, who brought tea seeds back with him from Song Dynasty China and introduced the matcha style of tea. In his book *Kissa Yōjōki (Drinking Tea for Health)*, the first Japanese treatise on tea, Eisai wrote about the health benefits of tea as well as how to grow and process tea leaves, calling tea the elixir of "mountain-dwelling immortals".

MATCHA

Matcha, the powdered green tea served during the tea ceremony, has taken the world by storm. It is made from *tencha*, the fresh new leaves of the tea bush grown in the shade, protected from sunlight for two to three weeks. Once they have been steamed, they are dried and eventually ground in stone mills. Apart from the stems, which are removed, the whole leaf is contained in this brilliant, fine green powder. Like all green teas, matcha oxidizes quickly, so keeping it in an airtight container away from strong sources of heat and light, is essential. If possible, keep it in your fridge.

All around, no
flowers in bloom
Nor maple leaves in glare,
A solitary fisherman's hut alone
On the twilight shore
Of this autumn eve.

FUJIWARA NO TEIKA (1162–1241)
TRANSLATED BY TOSHIHIKO
AND TOYO IZUTSU

WABI CHA

Tea of Quiet Taste

The celebrated tea master Sen no Rikyū (1522–1591) was instrumental in shaping the Japanese tea ceremony into the art form we now recognize as *Chadō* or *Sadō,* the Way of Tea. He was the father of *wabi cha* (tea of quiet taste), which promoted the use of humble and rustic pieces in the tea ceremony. There are three main schools of tea in Kyōto, also known as the *San Senke* (the three Sen families); they are Urasenke, Omotesenke and Mushakōjisenke, and all of them were established by the descendants of Sen no Rikyū.

The philosophy of tea that Sen no Rikyū pioneered involves making tea in a rustic, isolated setting, such as a modest thatched hut of rush mats and unpainted wood. The teahouse is a retreat from modern life, which blends seamlessly into its natural surroundings. *Wabi* is a spiritual way of life or philosophy that eschews the superficial and extravagant and instead honours emptiness, natural simplicity and imperfection. In Japanese Buddhism, understanding these principles is considered the first step to *satori* or enlightenment. *Wabi* is something you inherently feel deep within yourself, so it can be difficult to put into words because you subjectively experience it. As H E Davey wrote, the world of *wabi* "hints at a sort of beauty best exemplified by nature or natural surroundings". Whereas *sabi*, which is often uttered in the same breath, is an aesthetic ideal that can be applied to all art forms. What some might call imperfections, signs of age such as rich patina, rust, oxidization, and slowly creeping mosses, all of which show the effects of the passage of deep time, are all indicators of *sabi*.

WHAT IS THE JAPANESE TEA CEREMONY?

In 1872, the Japanese government officially recognized *Chanoyu* as a Japanese art form of great cultural significance. *Chanoyu*, usually translated as "tea ceremony", literally means "hot water for tea". It is the ritual of preparing and serving matcha, powdered Japanese green tea. There are four guiding principles of *Chadō*, according to Sen no Rikyū. These are *Wa, Kei, Sei* and *Jaku*.

Wa is the perfect harmony of all elements.

Kei is reverence and respect for all things.

Sei represents cleanliness, order and purity.

Jaku means calm or tranquillity.

Chanoyu also teaches art appreciation, showing reverence for the *chabana* (tea flowers), and the calligraphy scroll hanging in the *tokonoma* (display area for art, flowers and objects) is one of the first things guests do upon entering the tearoom. The last thing guests do before leaving the tearoom is called *haiken*, the viewing of the utensils. After the last guest has finished their tea, the first guest will enquire about the provenance of the utensils, including the *chashaku* (tea scoop) and *natsume* (tea caddy). Where was it made? Who was it made by? What is it called?

Gomei
Poetic Names

The tradition of naming beautiful art objects, especially those with an important provenance, such as tea utensils, originally comes from China. In Japan, they are called *gomei* or *mei*. These poetic names are given to the *dōgu* (utensils or equipment) used as part of the tea ceremony, such as tea bowls, tea scoops and tea caddies. The poetic names can be playful, metaphorical, historical, inspired by poetry or other works of literature, as well as seasonal phenomena. Here are a few examples of the most memorable seasonal *gomei* I've encountered.

Spring	*Summer*
Haru no Oto – The Sound of Spring	*Yūgao* – Moonflower
Hana Dayori – Herald of Flowers	*Tsuyu no Yado* – House of Dew
Kochō no Yume – Butterfly's Dream	*Taki no Oto* – Waterfalls Echo
Autumn	*Winter*
Miyamaji – Deep Mountain Road	*Yuki no Hana* – Snow Flower
Tsuki no Tomo – My Companion the Moon	*Kan Suzume* – Frozen Sparrow
Wakare Boshi – Departing Stars	*Ginchiku* – Silver Bamboo
All Year	
Kashō – Herald of Joy	
Kokoro no Tomo – Friend of the Heart	

THE FOUR GUIDING PRINCIPLES OF *CHADŌ*

Practising the Way of Tea is a humbling experience. We stoop to enter the tearoom through a low door. Everyone is equal in the tearoom; we all sit on the floor together; and no one person is higher than another, irrespective of age, title or means.

Wa

Wa means complete harmony between all elements, which includes the host and guests, as well as balance in the tearoom between the flowers, scroll, utensils and the season itself. When we drink a bowl of tea, we are at one with nature, which brings with it a sense of peace.

Kei

Kei or respect, is a profound sense of humility and reverence for all things: our fellow human beings, the natural environment, all living things, inanimate objects and those who crafted them. Out of sincere respect, I bow my head and give thanks before I drink a bowl of tea. No matter how many I may have consumed previously, I show my gratitude each time like it's the first time – conveying my appreciation for the privilege of being able to participate in a tea gathering and respect for the host and my fellow guests.

Sei

Sei is a purity of heart and mind, encompassing orderliness and cleanliness. The simple acts of sweeping the tea garden, dusting the tearoom and cleaning the tea utensils is a discipline that represents clearing the dust of the world from our hearts and minds. Once these tasks are complete, we have restored order to both the physical space and our state of mind.

Jaku

Jaku means tranquillity and calm. In the quiet of the tearoom, tucked away from the concerns and demands of the everyday and living in tune with the rhythms of nature, we can reach a state of tranquillity.

ROJI

The Dewy Path

Inspired by Zen principles, such as *mu* (nothingness), the *roji* (dewy path or dewy ground) is the most modest and deceptively simple of all Japanese gardens. It leads guests from the garden gate to the tea house. As you journey through the tea garden, you enter the realm of lush foliage in myriad shades of green. Here, Japanese yew, pine, oak and cedar trees mingle with ferns, grasses and mosses in naturalistic configurations, emulating a stroll through a secluded mountain landscape. Writer and curator of Asian art Rand Castile (1938–2017) described the *roji* as a "partnership with nature".

You may note the absence of any brightly coloured or fragrant flowers. This is because the *roji* is designed to help soothe the mind and prepare you to enter the world of tea. Guests enter through a gate and travel through the tea garden along a stone path. This journey is meant to symbolize leaving behind the outside world and all your worldly concerns before entering the teahouse. A key feature of the *roji* is the *tsukubai*, a water feature carved from stone, where guests purify themselves by washing their hands and mouths before they enter the tearoom, mirroring the steps of entering a Shintō shrine.

The next time you visit a Japanese garden, count how many shades of green you can see in the garden. How many different types of moss are there? What shapes do the rocks remind you of? What images do they call to mind?

CHASEKI

The Tearoom

The *chaseki* (tearoom) is a modest organic space containing only natural elements, which anchors it in the wider natural world. The kimono worn by your host, the rush grass mats you sit on and every utensil refer to nature directly or indirectly. As Sen Soshitsu XV eloquently explains, "In our everyday struggle to survive in this world, polluted and preoccupied with materialistic concerns as the world is today, nature is the one retreat where we can discover our real selves."

The tearoom is a sanctuary from the modern world, echoing the monastic lives of those who first drank tea. It serves as the perfect, minimal exhibition space to showcase the myriad Japanese art forms and aesthetics visible during a tea gathering. It is also the only place outside a museum or private residence where you can see all these Japanese art forms in one place. Moreover, these items are alive and actively used in the tearoom, just as they were during Sen no Rikyū's lifetime.

The *chaseki* is a modest space; many resemble small huts only large enough to contain four-and-a-half tatami mats.[13] They are designed to be a sanctuary, built using only natural elements, like wood and bamboo, anchoring them in the natural world. The *chaseki* is without ornament, which – like the white walls of an art gallery – provides the perfect stage for the tea ceremony and allows the beauty of the few carefully chosen decorative elements to shine through. Art critic Okakura Kakuzō (1863–1913), author of *The Book of Tea*, believed that the tearoom was the only place where one could engage in the "adoration of the beautiful", undisturbed by the aggravations of modern life. Even though he was writing in 1900, his words seem more appropriate than ever. The three hours a week I spend at *keiko* (tea ceremony practice) are a tonic to living in a world where we can rarely disconnect. When you are focused solely on the procedures for making tea and the objects in front of you, everything becomes quieter, and you can appreciate the beauty of each item.

---

[13] A standard tatami mat is twice as long as it is wide and measures 0.9m x 1.8m (3ft x 6ft).

Tokonoma
Alcove

In every tearoom, you will find a *tokonoma*; this alcove is a space dedicated to showcasing art. It houses the seasonal *chabana* (tea flowers) and the hanging scroll, the only two decorative elements in the otherwise bare room. You may not have a *tokonoma* at home, but you can still create a dedicated space within your home to showcase your seasonal celebrations. Your *tokonoma* might be a small table, a windowsill or a bookshelf. Each micro season, each month or each season, you can refresh your flowers and decorations for the season ahead. In the tearoom, every design element and implement carries messages and meaning.

Chabana
Flowers for Tea

Chabana (tea flowers) are flowers chosen explicitly for a tea gathering. Unlike ikebana, this minimalist arrangement usually only includes one or two stems of seasonal flowers in a bamboo basket or ceramic vase. As a member of the tea family, *tsubaki* (camellias) are also closely associated with the tea ceremony. They are often used in both ikebana and its cousin, *chabana*. However, they only feature in *chabana* before the buds have fully opened, as for the tea ceremony the flowers should look like they have just been picked – fresh from the field. The singular bloom in the tearoom is the distilled essence of the season's flowers.

As Professor Haruo Shirane explains, in Japan, "a flower arrangement can be an offering to a God portrayed in a hanging scroll, a greeting from a host to a guest, a salute to the seasonal moment, and or part of a social or religious ritual". When a host carefully selects flowers for the tearoom, they need to find the right flowers for that gathering – traditionally they would go out into the fields or mountains. Several factors need to be considered: harmony within the tearoom, the feeling they wish to create and the current season, all of which will help set the tone of the tea gathering.

You won't find exotic or strongly scented flowers in the tearoom because they would disrupt the delicate balance of this quietly beautiful space. Flowers that bloom for only one day are ideal for the tearoom because they remind us that our brief lives are as transient as the flowers themselves. Each moment of our existence is precious, like the buds that bloom in the midday sunshine but quickly fade and wilt by dusk. Tea master Ii Naosuke (1815–1860) put it perfectly when he stated that the flowers in the tearoom are an expression of the "exquisite evanescence of nature".

CALLIGRAPHY FOR THE TEA CEREMONY

Another one of the art forms showcased during the tea ceremony is calligraphy, often composed by a celebrated priest or tea master known for their brushwork. This critical element of *Chanoyu* is in the form of a *kakemono* (hanging object). These are vertical Japanese scroll paintings or calligraphy mounted onto brocade fabric so they can be easily rolled and stored. The host takes time to select a suitable *kakemono* for each tea gathering, depending on the teaching and the seasonal feeling they want to convey. This artwork is the first thing guests see when entering the tearoom, and in combination with the *chabana*, it will set the mood of the tea gathering. Sometimes, this may only be a single character. For example, in June, my sensei chose a scroll which read *taki* (waterfall) to suggest feelings of coolness on a hot day. This kanji has a long, sweeping tail that flows down like a waterfall.

TORIAWASE

Curated with Care

A 17th-century Spanish priest once called the *dōgu* (Japanese tea ceremony utensils or equipment) the crown jewels of Japan. These items vary depending on the season and formality of the tea gathering. Still, the following items will always be present: a tea bowl, a tea caddy, a tea whisk and a scoop. These are carefully purified in front of the guests before each bowl of tea is made, using a folded square of silk or *fukusa* and a white piece of folded hemp cloth called a *chakin*. This shows reverence for the utensils and deference to the guests.

Japanese aesthetics prize asymmetry over the symmetrical and odd numbers over even, so ideally, no one colour or design is repeated when all the objects are assembled. (Cherry blossom season is the main exception to this rule.) Instead, the *dōgu*, combined with the *chabana* and *kakemono*, will suggest an overall seasonal theme. This practice is called *toriawase*: the art of skilfully selecting tea utensils to suit a particular occasion or to achieve the desired seasonal atmosphere, bringing together lacquerware, bamboo crafts, ceramics, textiles, calligraphy, *wagashi* and flowers to create a seasonal tableau. Much like the French *art de la table*, the art of entertaining includes creating place settings and choosing linens, silverware, china patterns, stemware and flowers. Just as in the tea ceremony, the flowers are the living, breathing element of the *art de la table*. Both are creative endeavours that allow the individual to express their aesthetic sensibilities and personal taste. Just like *toriawase*, the ultimate aim of *art de la table* is creating harmony.

TEA AND THE SEASONS

How does *Chadō* teach us to cultivate an awareness of the seasons? Studying the art of tea awakens your sensitivity to the seasons. Over the course of the year, the tea you drink, the sweets you consume, the flowers you select and the utensils you use change with the passing seasons. *Temae* (tea-making procedures) also change to reflect the seasons. To celebrate *Tanabata* (see page 146) in July, some tea schools use a verdant green mulberry leaf sprinkled with drops of water as a lid for the *mizusashi* (cold water container). This practice is unique to the summertime and is called *habuta temae* (leaf lid procedure). The mulberry leaf brings a sense of freshness to the tearoom but also echoes the mythology of the Star Festival because mulberry leaves are the only source of food for Japan's silkworms and the festival celebrates the love story of the famed weaver Orihime.

Each summer I take out my *natsu chawan* (summer tea bowl), a low open bowl of solid clear glass painted with a swirl of green maple leaves. Summer *chawan* are wider and shallower than their winter cousins, cooling the hot tea more quickly. In the winter, however, you can feel the comforting weight of a thick, heavy *raku* tea bowl, black as midnight. Shaped by hand, it's taller and narrower than a summer *chawan*, designed to keep the tea warm during the coldest months of the year.

CHAWAN

Tea Bowl

As the 15th *Raku* master, Raku Kichizaemon, wrote in *Raku: A Legacy of Japanese Tea Ceramics*, the tea bowl is "a universe held in the palms". In the tearoom, Japan's rich history of ceramics is represented by the *chaire* (container for thick tea) and the *chawan*. The tea bowl is the most iconic tea utensil and because both the host and the guest handle it, it is also considered the most important. Like great works of art, each tea bowl has its own poetic name. The most prized tea bowls are *raku*, meaning enjoyment or pleasure. *Raku* bowls are usually black or red. These pieces are made in the kiln of the *Raku* family, whose lineage stretches back to the 16th century.

CHASEN

Tea Whisk

Bamboo is an instantly recognizable element of Japanese art and design. In *Chanoyu*, it is represented by the *chasen*. The *chasen* (tea whisk) is one of the essential tools necessary to perform the tea ceremony and perhaps the most well known after the *chawan*. It has existed for over 500 years and, like the *chashaku* (tea scoop), is carved from bamboo and its form has remained unchanged for hundreds of years. The village of Takayama in Nara has been the *chasen*-making centre of Japan for centuries, and this is where 90 per cent of Japanese tea whisks are made. Traditionally crafted bamboo *chasen* are made entirely by hand; it takes 2–3 years to season the bamboo ready to carve it into *chasen*. Each whisk is made of a single piece of bamboo split into 80–120 strands. According to legend, the form of *chasen* now used was designed in the 1500s by the Japanese poet Takayama Soezei (d.1455). When you enter a tearoom, you will notice several bamboo utensils, including flower containers, water ladles and incense boxes, which are all used in *Chanoyu*.

Mitate
To See Anew

One of the concepts at the heart of *Chanoyu* is *mitate*, "to see with new eyes". This is the Japanese practice of replacing an item with a repurposed one that was not initially intended for that purpose but which fulfils the need beautifully.

Try disconnecting from what the intended purpose for the object might have been. In your hands, what could it become? A vessel for flowers, perhaps? An object to contemplate while you enjoy your quiet tea moment? Inspiration for a haiku? Tea Master Sen no Rikyū did this with humble everyday objects used by farmers, such as fishing baskets and water pails, which he turned into *chabana* vessels – seeing the simple bamboo baskets and buckets with fresh eyes and appreciating their beauty in a new way. He took them into the tearoom and elevated them into art, transforming them from their humble origins by perceiving their potential and allowing their inherent beauty to shine through.

I'm especially drawn to the concept of *mitate* because it gives us an opportunity to look at things in a new light. Letting go of preconceived notions encourages us to be creative and see the potential in things others walk past. You don't need to practise the tea ceremony to practise *mitate*. When you place freshly picked flowers into a jam jar instead of a vase, that's *mitate*. Repurposing an item or finding a new purpose for something that might have been previously overlooked or discarded is the spirit of *mitate*.

WAGASHI

Sweets for the Tea Ceremony

We can awaken the five senses through tea by admiring the beauty of calligraphy and the host's graceful movements and feeling the glaze of a *chawan* beneath our touch. *Wagashi*, the Japanese sweets served before tea, are designed to stimulate both our sight and taste. When we enjoy the food, tea and sweets served during the tea ceremony, we engage *sanmai* (the three tastes) using our eyes, tongue and heart.

Japanese confectionary has a history spanning thousands of years. The term *wagashi* was coined during the Meiji era (1868–1912), *wa* meaning "Japanese" and *gashi* meaning "sweets". Its three primary influences are Chinese sweets, *Chanoyu* and the arrival of westerners in Japan. Sugar was once a luxury item, only enjoyed by the aristocracy. However, once Spanish and Portuguese merchants arrived, refined sugar became more readily available. From the Edo period (1603–1868) onward, *wagashi* came into its own and demand exponentially increased. At the same time, *Chanoyu* was also growing in popularity, and these two art forms supported each other's development.

THREE KINDS OF *WAGASHI*

Serving tea and a seasonal sweet to guests is a quintessential part of *omotenashi* or Japanese hospitality that you'll encounter nationwide, not just in the tearoom. As with tea utensils, *wagashi* are also given beautifully poetic seasonal names. Kyōto, Japan's ancient capital, is the nation's *wagashi* mecca, where countless traditional sweet shops offer a veritable treasure chest of edible jewels to choose from. The selection changes with each micro season, representing Japan's changing landscape and some sweets are only available once a year for ten days or less.

HIGASHI

Dry sugar sweets called *higashi*, are made with a finely powdered sugar called *wasanbon*. They are pressed into wooden moulds in the shapes of seasonal plants and flowers and served just before the guests enjoy their *usucha* (thin tea) during the tea ceremony. They melt on the tongue like snowflakes; their sweetness lingers in the mouth and provides the perfect foil to the *umami* (delicious savoury flavour) of freshly whisked matcha.

NERIKIRI

Nerikiri are a type of *namagashi* (fresh, moist sweets) made from red and white bean paste and sculpted by hand into the form of seasonally specific flowers and leaves. These are served before *koicha* (thick tea) during the tea ceremony. These sweets are designed to be paired with tea, and their delicate sweetness is the ideal foil for *koicha*. These exquisite edible works of art represent one of the best examples of Japan's seasonal confectionery.

YOKAN

Yokan is a traditional Japanese sweet made from a base of red adzuki beans, agar agar and sugar; it's similar in texture to a very firmly set jelly. There are many seasonal varieties, including summer *yokan* decorated with sliced lemons and autumnal *yokan* studded with dried fruit and nuts. It's usually sold in blocks, ready to be sliced when served to guests. *Yokan* makes a great *omiyage* (gift) because it keeps for a long time, and the packaging is often as beautiful as the sweet itself.

A SEASONAL GUIDE TO JAPANESE TEA

Rand Castile, ex-director of the Asian Art Museum in San Francisco and dedicated student of *Chanoyu*, wrote in his seminal book *The Way of Tea*, that although "Tea has no mind, no intention, yet across its bright green surface, virtually the whole of Japan can be seen."

Spring Teas

SHINCHA – NEW TEA

Shincha, meaning "new tea", is harvested during the very first tea harvest of the new year, which starts on the 88th day after the Spring Equinox in the lunar calendar. This day is called *Hachijū Hachiya*, meaning the "88th night". Tea harvested on this date is considered auspicious and will bring those who drink it good health and fortune.

Japanese tea is harvested four times a year. First flush tea, also called *ichibancha* or first tea, is picked from late April to late May. Depending on the region the harvest traditionally begins around the middle of April and goes on for approximately three weeks. This first picking or first flush is the most prized because it produces the highest quality *sencha*, rich in nutrients such as catechins and amino acids, which have built up in the plants and are stored over the winter. *Shincha* is only available for a brief period in the spring – after July it is no longer considered new tea.

SAKURA CHA – CHERRY BLOSSOM TEA

Although it's called a tea, this is a tisane made from preserved Japanese cherry blossoms of the later blooming *kanzan* variety, which are pickled in salt and plum vinegar just before the buds open entirely. *Sakura cha* is technically a tisane not a tea because it is not made from any part of the *Camellia sinensis* plant. It is traditionally served at joyous celebrations, such as weddings.

FUKAMUSHICHA – DEEP-STEAMED TEA

This luminous green liquor, which to me is the distilled essence of spring, is called *fukamushicha* or *fukamushi sencha*, which means "deep-steamed tea". *Sencha* is Japan's everyday green tea, served throughout the country. All Japanese green teas are traditionally steamed as part of their manufacturing process, unlike Chinese green teas, which are lightly pan-fried. However, *fukamushicha* is steamed for longer than the usual standard of 30 seconds to one minute. This more intense steaming increases the sweetness and gives the tea its eye-catching vibrant green colour.

Summer Teas

GYOKURO – JEWEL DEW

Less than 1 per cent of all Japan's tea production is *gyokuro*, Japan's most expensive tea. It is primarily harvested by hand and, like matcha, grown in the shade for three weeks before harvest. This gives it a distinctive rich green colour and slight sweetness, making it perfect for the summer practice of *kōridashi* or "ice brewing".

KŌRIDASHI – ICE-BREWED TEA

Kōridashi or ice-brewed tea is more mellow in flavour than traditionally brewed tea, because ice brewing still extracts the l-theanine from the leaves but pulls less caffeine and catechins from them, removing any bitterness or astringency from the tea. You can ice brew any tea of your choice by filling a *kyūsu* (one-handled Japanese teapot) with ice, adding one-and-a-half teaspoons of tea leaves, and leaving the lid off to aid the melting process. Once the ice has completely melted your tea is ready to drink. This brewing process requires patience and can take several hours, depending on the room's ambient temperature. The purity of the water will affect the taste of your tea, so it's best to make your ice cubes with filtered water.

MUGICHA – BARLEY TEA

Mugicha is a roasted-grain-based infusion made from barley. Like *hōjicha* (roasted green tea – see below), it's served cold throughout the sweltering Japanese summertime. *Mugicha* is caffeine-free and popular across East Asia. You might also encounter it in China, Korea and Taiwan. *Mizudashi* or cold brewed tea, infused overnight or in the fridge for several hours, is a summer staple in Japan.

Autumn Teas

GENMAICHA – BROWN RICE TEA

Genmaicha, sometimes called popcorn tea, is a tea blend of either *sencha* or *bancha* tea leaves combined with grains of toasted brown rice. It has a slightly nutty taste and low caffeine content. *Bancha* is made from the same tea plants used for *sencha*, but harvested from the older, more mature leaves during the last tea harvest of the year, which is why it contains less caffeine than *sencha*.

HŌJICHA – ROASTED TEA

For me, autumn means it's *hōjicha* season. The warming roasted liquor with its toasted and slightly smoky caramel tones is autumn in a cup. *Hōjicha* is wonderful because it contains almost no caffeine due to the roasting process involved in its production. *Hōjicha* is made from roasted *bancha* or *kukicha* tea leaves; it is naturally soothing, low in caffeine and aids digestion, which makes it a popular digestive and the perfect after-dinner or cosy autumn evening drink, blanket optional. The roasted aroma and colour of *hōjicha* can vary depending on the level of roast, from light to dark.

Winter Teas

YUZU CHA – YUZU TEA

This wonderfully fragrant tea is a popular drink in both Japan and Korea. *Yuzu cha* (*yuzu* tea) is an infusion made with finely sliced *yuzu*, a golden yellow Japanese citrus and rock sugar or honey. This syrup is added to hot water for a warming winter drink full of vitamin C.

ŌBUKUCHA – GOOD FORTUNE TEA

This Japanese green tea is enjoyed exclusively during the first days of the New Year. *Ōbukucha* sometimes includes fine flakes of edible gold leaf to make it more celebratory. After the tea is poured, a dried Japanese plum (*ume*) and a piece of dried kelp (*kombu*) tied into a knot for good luck are added. Drinking *ōbukucha* is based on a centuries-old tradition that began at Rokuharamitsu Temple in Kyōto. This auspicious tea is believed to bestow good health and luck on those who drink it.

TAKING TIME FOR TEA

Just like selecting a vinyl record to play, when you carefully remove it from the sleeve and place it onto the record player, making a bowl of tea at home can be a ritual. Taking time out of our hectic lives to make a simple bowl of matcha has innumerable mental[14] and physical[15] health benefits.[16,17] Once we slow down, we notice the subtle changes in the weather and the season. Making the time to perform a seasonal tea ritual is one of the ways I do this. It doesn't take long or require much space, so you can do it anywhere, anytime. All you really need is your favourite tea and a mug or cup.

[14] Mancini E, et al. (2017). "Green tea effects on cognition, mood and human brain function: A systematic review". *Phytomedicine: International Journal of Phytotherapy and Phytopharmacology*, 34, 26–37.

[15] Zhao, T., Li, C., Wang, S., & Song, X. (2022). "Green Tea (Camellia sinensis): A Review of Its Phytochemistry, Pharmacology, and Toxicology". *Molecules*, 27(12).

[16] Khan, N., & Mukhtar, H. (2018). "Tea Polyphenols in Promotion of Human Health". *Nutrients*, 11(1), 39.

[17] Prasanth, M. I., Sivamaruthi, B. S., Chaiyasut, C., & Tencomnao, T. (2019). "A Review of the Role of Green Tea (Camellia sinensis) in Antiphotoaging, Stress Resistance, Neuroprotection, and Autophagy". *Nutrients*, 11(2), 474.

CREATE YOUR OWN TEA RITUAL

STEP 1. Select your tea.

STEP 2. Take it out of the tea caddy and measure out the leaves. Notice the colour, shape and aroma of the dry tea leaves.

STEP 3. Heat the water. Make sure you use filtered water for the best tea experience and select the right temperature for the tea you are brewing.

STEP 4. While the water is warming, choose your teaware. Is it an autumnal evening that calls for a big comforting mug of *hōjicha*? Or is it a fresh spring morning, so instead you select a delicate flower-shaped glass cup to enjoy the vibrant grassy green of your *sencha*?

STEP 5. Assemble your tea tray. Choose a teapot and a small treat to enjoy with your tea. I like to share my tea with a vase of seasonal flowers in bud.

STEP 6. Find a comfortable spot on the floor or in your favourite chair – somewhere you can relax, clear your mind and ideally see trees or a garden from your window.

STEP 7. Finally, you are ready to pour the tea. (Depending on your teapot you might also need a tea strainer.) Now, sit back, relax and enjoy every last sip.

ICHIGO ICHIE

Once in a Lifetime

Ichigo ichie is a Japanese idiom that means "one lifetime, one encounter". This saying encapsulates the idea that because our entire human existence is so brief, nothing is certain and tomorrow is not promised, so each moment is precious. This moment right here, right now, can never be repeated. Just as two leaves of the same tree are not identical and no two snowflakes are alike, no two moments in time can ever be exactly the same, even if the same people are present at the same location. Time passes and the people are no longer the people they were. As the Greek philosopher Heraclitus once said, "No man ever steps in the same river twice, for it's not the same river and he's not the same man."

Much like the tea ceremony, *ichigo ichie* is an invitation to cultivate gratitude, slow down, forget about our past mistakes and future concerns and be completely present in the moment that is unfolding around us. If every moment is unrepeatable, then surely we should try our best to cherish them. Each singular moment is like a shining pearl or drop of morning dew. I collect mine in my mind, stringing precious memories together like a necklace of invisible pearls.

What We Can Learn from *Ichigo Ichie*

- Stop, slow down, look around and take everything in.

- Practise gratitude for our one incredible life.

- Savour every moment, every last bite, every bloom, every sunrise, whatever the season.

- Cultivate joy by celebrating our wins and joyous experiences, big and small.

- Be present, whether in the company of our friends and family or alone, giving each moment our full attention.

NEW YEAR IN THE TEA ROOM

The *ro* is a square-shaped opening installed below the floor of a tearoom, snuggly protected in a fitted wooden surround and lined with the same clay that covers the walls of a traditional tearoom. It is a dedicated naturally insulated space for a charcoal fire. The *ro* or sunken hearth season typically begins in the tearoom on the Day of the Boar in the traditional Japanese calendar, which now translates approximately to the beginning of November. Sen no Rikyū (1522–1591), the 16th-century tea master, began using the *ro* only once the *yuzu* fruit turned from green to yellow. *Ro* season lasts from November until April, followed by the *furō* (portable brazier) season from April to October. Therefore, the tea calendar can be divided into these two distinct seasons. The first use of the *ro* each year is marked by a celebration called *Robiraki,* when charcoal is laid in the sunken hearth for the first time.

In November, the *chatsubo* or *tsubo* (tea-leaf storage jar) is displayed in the *tokonoma* (display area for art, flowers and objects) for all guests to see as they enter the tearoom. Later it's removed from its silk cord netting and shown to the gathered party, who watch as the seal on the earthenware jar is broken; this is part of *kuchikiri chaji*, the opening of the tea jar during a formal tea gathering. Since the jar was sealed, it has been carefully storing young tea leaves picked during the spring harvest. The tea leaves for the day's ceremony are removed and freshly ground into *koicha* (ceremonially prepared matcha), and then the jar is resealed. At this time of the year, the *shōji* (paper screens) are re-covered, and pine needles are spread in the tea garden over areas of moss and bare earth where frost might form. In many senses, for tea devotees, this is already the beginning of a new year.

November themes in the tearoom are pine needles, charcoal, wild boars, *momiji* (maple leaves), ginkgo nuts and roasted chestnuts. These are all reflected in the *chabana*, the hanging scroll, the tea utensils used and the accompanying *wagashi*. During *aki* (autumn), a hanging scroll depicting scenes of deer and maple leaves hangs in the alcove.

NODATE

The Japanese Tea Picnic

My memories of childhood summers in the UK bring to mind strawberries and cream, freshly picked tomatoes eaten straight from the vine, warmed by the sun, and, of course, picnics. Japan has its own beautiful picnic tradition in the form of *nodate*. This is the Japanese term for an informal tea gathering that takes place outdoors – a much more relaxed al fresco version of the formalized setting of *Chanoyu*. *Nodate* is a tea picnic, enjoyed outside to celebrate and contemplate the beauty of the changing seasons.

Nodate settings are dictated by the seasons – in the spring, the ideal picnic setting might be under a grove of blooming cherry trees; in the summer, by a flowing stream or shining lake. Later in the autumn, ideally, they take place somewhere with a view of Japan's spectacular autumnal scenery, where the foliage of golden gingkoes and burned orange maples dominate the landscape.

You don't need to travel far from home to find a lovely place for a tea picnic. A local park, forest, river, field or garden are all ideal options. It only needs to be somewhere quiet with a sense of space, where you can ground yourself and take root in nature, whether that's by the water or in the woods.

For a high autumn *nodate*, my friend and I found a beautiful, sheltered spot in an old churchyard. The trees formed a canopy above us, and all manner of fallen leaves created a carpet beneath us. As my friend prepared our matcha, I watched as grey squirrels perched on nearby branches and scampered around the base of the trees seeking out acorns.

Have you ever taken your tea outside in nature? Where was your favourite *nodate* experience?

Nodate Essentials

Nodate can be as simple or as elaborate as you choose to make it. Some days, making a flask of your favourite tea and taking it with you on a walk, finding a fallen log and simply sitting down and enjoying the view is more than enough.

If you'd like to enjoy a bowl of matcha out in the wild, you'll need a few supplies.

Chabako

A *chabako* (tea box) can be a bag, a box or a basket that you'll use to pack and transport all your items in. I use a vintage French wicker basket for mine because I wanted something with some gentle age and wear to it. Most importantly, I knew instinctively that it had to be made of natural materials so that it would feel like a part of the natural landscape wherever I went.

Chawan

Your *chawan* is your tea bowl. I tend to bring my less precious *chawan* out into the world, but it's entirely up to you! You can also experiment with wooden, bamboo or coconut shell *chawan*, which are lighter and less fragile than the traditional ceramic ones. I recommend wrapping your *chawan* in a seasonal *furoshiki* (traditional wrapping cloths, see page 105) for an added layer of protection.

Natsume

This is your tea caddy or container of matcha. The traditional version of this is a *natsume*, but any small, airtight vessel will do if you want to avoid transporting your fragile or precious *natsume*. Some brands now supply matcha in airtight metal tins, which is ideal.

Chasen

A *chasen* or bamboo matcha whisk is essential so that you can whisk your matcha to perfection, no matter where you are.

Chashaku

A *chashaku* or bamboo tea scoop is traditionally used to measure a portion of matcha. If you don't have one, then a 1tsp measure works, too!

Mizusashi

In the tearoom a *mizusashi* is the vessel that holds the pure water for cleaning and purifying the tea utensils. Its water is also used for boiling and making the tea. In its place for your *nodate* outings you can use a small thermos flask or a metal water bottle, which will keep your cold water cool in the summer and retain the heat in your hot water the rest of the year.

Chakin

A soft cloth or *chakin* (tea napkin) is a useful item to have in your *nodate* set, even if you are not using this in the strict *Chadō* ritual sense. Wipe your bowl and implements clean both before and after you use them.

There are a couple of additional optional extras I usually take along, too. The first is a mini tea strainer, which I like to include in my kit so that my matcha is always free of lumps and whisks more smoothly. And the second is some small Japanese *wagashi* sweets to enjoy alongside the matcha. Something small and portable like *konpeitō* (colourful sugar candy), *higashi* (dry sugar sweets, see page 264) or even some summer berries are perfect.

MOMIJIGARI

The Ritual of Leaf Hunting

Forests cover one-third of our planet and almost 70 per cent of Japan, making it one of the most densely forested countries in the world, a land of immense ancient trees, broad-leafed woodlands and coniferous forests. The iconic trees of Japan are the *sakura* (cherry blossom), the *sugi* (cedar), the *momiji* (maple), the *ichō* (ginkgo), the *hinoki* (cypress) and the *matsu* (pine). Japan's special relationship with trees stems from Shintō, or the Way of the Gods (see page 17) – Japan's ancient indigenous faith, which heavily influences the country's relationship with the natural world. The worship, protection and appreciation of trees is a central tenet of Shintō. This gives Japan a unique appreciation of ancient trees, which play a vital role as a conduit and home for the gods. These trees are called *shinboku*.

Trees are our constant companions. They inspire us, feed us, help us to breathe and heat our homes. They provide shelter to us and all manner of wildlife. Despite the fact that over 4 billion people – that's 56 per cent of the world's population – now live in cities, we continue to be drawn to the woods. Japan's autumnal tradition of *momijigari* (red-leaf hunting) is just one example of this. We go in search of balance, to discover ourselves, to find peace and to try and tap into the magic of these ancient trees. By spending time in their presence, we can reconnect to the wonders of the natural world throughout the seasons of the year. It's no wonder that the mysterious and ancient forest is a leitmotif that repeats around the world. Undisturbed by time, these ancient woodlands are liminal spaces between worlds where supernatural creatures dwell and fairytales unfold.

In the western storytelling tradition, an enchanted forest outside Athens was the setting for Shakespeare's *A Midsummers Night's Dream* (c.1595), a tale of lovers manipulated by the forest's resident fairies. Author Charles Perrault and later the brothers Grimm told the fairytale of Little Red Riding Hood's adventures in the woods and her encounters with the local wolf. Japanese animator Hayao Miyazaki delighted children and adults alike by creating two of the most magical forest environments ever seen on screen in *My Neighbour Totoro* (1988) *and Princess Mononoke* (1997).

Both films are infused with elements of Shintō, folklore and animism, which brought the ancient beliefs of the Way of the Gods to life on screen. Animistic belief systems like Shintō are found the world over, including in the culture and traditions of Aboriginal Australians, Native Americans and the Maori of New Zealand. The word animism comes from the Latin word *anima*, meaning "spirit" or "soul". The foundation of animistic faiths is the respect, veneration and appreciation of nature's innumerable and diverse spirits.

In an interview with the *Japan Times*, Hayao Miyazaki, the beloved director of Studio Ghibli, once said, "In my grandparents' time, it was believed that *kami* [spirits] existed everywhere – in trees, rivers, insects, wells, anything. My generation does not believe this, but I like the idea that we should all treasure everything because spirits might exist there, and we should treasure everything because there is a kind of life to everything."

CHINJU NO MORI

Shrine Forests

In Shintō, the forest is the realm of the Divine, the sacred home of gods. Sadasumi Motegi, Professor of Shintō Studies at Kokugakuin University, wrote that "This is where the voices of the gods (*kamigami*) sound in your ears. This is where our ancestors lived, humbly, in harmony with nature." Trees purify and sanctify the land around them. Although there are Shintō shrines throughout major cities like Tōkyō, many of Japan's shrines are still surrounded by small groves or forests. *Chinju no mori* are the forests that encircle Japan's sacred Shintō shrines. These trees are decorated with a *shimenawa* (sacred rope) woven from rice straw and decorated with white paper streamers. The most famous example is the enormous five-ton *shimenawa* at the entrance to the Grand Shrine of Izumo. This twisted cord encircles venerated trees and hangs above the entrance to Shintō shrines, indicating that you are entering a sacred space that's home to *kami* (spirits, gods or deities). These nature guardians also dwell in other places of outstanding natural beauty, such as mountains and waterfalls.

There is no distinction in Japanese between singular and plural, so *kami* can refer to a singular divinity, or a sacred essence that can manifest in multiple forms. According to ethnologist Fosco Maraini (1912–2004), these divine beings can be local deities, mythological heroes or great sages, but they "may also be thunder, an echo in the forest, a fox, a tiger, a dragon – or a mere insect".

The first recorded mention of tree spirits is in Japan's oldest known book, the *Kojiki* (*Record of Ancient Matters*), which mentions the ancestor of all trees, Kukunochi, the Tree Trunk Elder. The God of Trees is the second son of Izanagi and Izanami, the mythical creators of Japan. Kukunochi is sometimes called Ki no Kami or Spirit of the Trees. Another Japanese name for tree-dwelling spirits is *kodama* and belief in *kodama* is an archaic one that predates Japan's written language. The earliest known use of the term *kodama* dates back to a Heian-period dictionary, *Wamuryorui Jyusho Japanese (Names for Things)*, c.931–938, which lists *kodama* as the Japanese word for "spirits of the trees".

Sakaki (Cleyera japonica) is an evergreen tree considered sacred to followers of Shintō. Its name means "tree on the border". It exists on the very edge of our world and the world of the *kami*. In a country of dynamic and distinct seasons, evergreen trees that are seemingly unchanged by the passage of time were considered sacred because they possessed an immortal life force. These trees acted as conduits that allowed deities to travel between worlds. The *kami* used especially large evergreen trees to travel back and forth from their home, *Takamanohara* (the High Plain of Heaven) and the mortal plane. These trees represent the centre of the world, and the *kami* exercise their power beneath these trees, nurturing everything underneath their canopy. Bonsai or dwarf trees are symbolic miniatures of the universe itself. If you had to choose, what kind of tree would you make your home?

SHINBOKU

Sacred Trees

It is said that when a tree reaches the age of 100, it gains a *kami*. There are still shrines throughout Japan, especially in the mountains and the countryside, surrounded by primeval forests, that venerate these spirits and the ancient trees they inhabit. In these sacred places, we may feel a sense of what the Japanese call *yūgen*, which Dr Qing Li, Chairman of the Japanese Society of Forest Medicine, describes as a profound sense of the beauty and mystery of the universe – something we innately feel but cannot wholly comprehend.

Beneath our feet, the forest is connected by an underground network of roots and tiny threads of fungi called mycelia, which weave an invisible tapestry connecting all the trees in the woods. This is called the mycorrhizal network, which is how trees communicate: sharing water, minerals and nutrients. A forest is a living, breathing thing. It exhales oxygen and inhales carbon dioxide, cleaning the air as it breathes. Trees release their natural oils in the form of phytocides. When we breathe these in, we experience forest aromatherapy. You can recreate these smells using essential oils such as *hinoki*, the iconic

Japanese cypress. Add a few drops to an oil burner, light a scented candle or use a reed diffuser.

One of the world's oldest tree species is the *Jōmon sugi* (Jomon cedar), which can be found in the primeval forest of Yakushima, an island at the very southern tip of Japan, off the coast of Kyushu. This World Heritage Site is home to some of Japan's oldest living trees, which are thought to be 2,000–7,000 years old. It was this forest that inspired Miyazaki's forest in *Princess Mononoke*. These older trees are called mother trees because they have the most mycorrhizal connections and can detect signs of distress in the trees around them, sending water and vital nutrients to young saplings.

There's a lot we can learn about community from trees; they may appear to be separate, but they are always supporting each other invisibly, sending help and nourishment to those in need through their network. Perhaps we could follow suit and support each other a little more by checking on the vulnerable people in our own networks and communities.

SHINRIN YOKU

The Ritual of Forest Bathing

According to Dr Qing Li, *shinrin yoku* (forest bathing) can help us bridge the gap between humanity and nature. *Shinrin* means "forest", and *yoku* means "bathing". The term "forest bathing" is relatively new. It was coined in 1982 by Tomohide Akiyama, Director of the Japanese Ministry for Forestry in the Akasawa Forest in Nagano, but it speaks to the much older and more profound relationship to trees that Japan has maintained for thousands of years.

Unlike hiking, it's a gentle activity that everyone can take part in, no matter their age, level of fitness, physical limitations or mobility issues. It involves surrounding oneself with the atmosphere of the forest and using all five senses to bathe in its beauty. You can bask in the sight of trees so tall it's almost impossible to see the sky; hear the sound of leaves as they crunch underfoot in autumn; feel the verdant silken mosses at the base of ancient trees; and smell the damp earth on the breeze. It is truly a way to tune in and immerse yourself in the forest.

The Benefits of *Shinrin Yoku*

American naturalist and environmental philosopher John Muir (1838–1914) believed that "The clearest way into the universe is through a forest wilderness." What we have always innately known deep down is now backed up by science,[18] as the green healing powers of forests have now been scientifically proven.[19,20] You can tap into this by experiencing *shinrin yoku* for yourself anywhere in the world. All you need is to spend some time in the company of trees – and a park will do if you don't live within reach of a forest. In my case, I love to walk in the ancient woodland of the New Forest in Hampshire, England where I can feel the cortisol levels in my body dropping with every step I take. My whole body slowly relaxes, and a feeling of calm settles over me. I forget the world beyond the forest. I find that spending time amid the greenery also enriches my inner world, which in turn feeds my creativity.

These are just some of the proven benefits of *shinrin yoku*. It can:

- Lower stress levels and promote relaxation.

- Reduce blood pressure.

- Help to alleviate anxiety and depression.

- Boost the immune system.

- Improve concentration and energy levels.

---

[18] Barton, J and Pretty, J (2010) "What is the best dose of nature and green exercise for improving mental health? A multi-study analysis", *Environmental Science & Technology*, 44(10), pp. 3947–55.

[19] Berman, M G et al (2008) "The cognitive benefits of interacting with nature", *Psychological Science*, 19(12), pp. 1207–12.

[20] Schertz, K E and Berman, M G (2021) "Understanding the affective benefits of interacting with nature", *Nature and Health*, pp. 7–22.

HOW TO PRACTISE
SHINRIN YOKU

We can easily miss the subtle seasonal changes taking place just outside our window when we spend all day at our desks and forget to look up. Making time to take a walk in your lunch break or before work if you're an early riser will improve your whole day and immediately ground you in the current season. The more we appreciate our woodlands, the better care we take of them, making their protection a priority and preserving them for future generations.

It's a good idea to familiarize yourself with local forests and woodlands within easy reach of where you live and work. You can take things one step further by researching ancient woodlands in your area or planning a pilgrimage to visit some that are further afield. In the UK, I love to visit the New Forest, Tremenhere Gardens in Cornwall and Hampstead Heath in London, which is a little closer to home.

So, get outside, surround yourself with the rich colours of the forest whatever the season and bathe in nature.

STEP 1. Prepare for your walk. Make sure you have good walking shoes, a water bottle, warm layers depending on the season and anything to enhance the experience you'd like to bring with you. I like to take my camera, a flask of Japanese tea to enjoy and sometimes a small sketchbook.

STEP 2. Take a gentle walk through the woods at your own pace. Be brave and stray from the well-trodden path. Follow your curiosity.

STEP 3. Be present in this unrepeatable moment. Let any intrusive thoughts pulling you away float by.

STEP 4. What seasonal changes have you noticed in the forest? Are there fresh buds and shoots signalling the arrival of spring? Or is there a lush green summer canopy overhead? Is there a thick carpet of autumnal leaves on the forest floor? Or do the bare branches of the trees seem to shiver in the winter wind?

STEP 5. Tune out the rest of the world and tune in to the sounds of the forest. Beyond your own footsteps, what can you hear?

STEP 6. Engage your other senses. What can you smell?

STEP 7. Stroke the velvet soft mosses and explore the gnarled bark of the ancient trees.

DOMESTIC *SHINRIN YOKU*

Bringing the Outside Inside

Even if you live in a city far from any forests or woodlands, there are still ways for you to engage in the ritual of *shinrin yoku*. You can bring the outside inside in a variety of ways. Here are a few suggestions.

- Use essential oils to bring the beneficial scents of the forest into your home. Take inspiration from the list of Japanese woodland botanicals at the end of the chapter.[21] (See page 299)

- Make or buy a *kokedama*. These Japanese moss balls contain miniature plants and trees, bringing a little greenery into your home and adding a little Japanese aesthetic to your space.

- Instead of lavender, try using a sachet of *hinoki*-scented wood chips, so you can enjoy the scent of the Japanese forests at home.

- When you go for walks, look out for interesting fallen branches to bring home and place in a vase. Unlike flowers, these are almost everlasting and can add a little of nature's poetry to your home.

- You can enjoy the view outside your window even if you don't have a garden. Just being able to see the trees on your street or in your neighbour's garden will lift your spirits.

- Burn some incense; again, look for scents of the forest.

- Print your favourite photos from forest walks and lush green places you've visited or support the work of an artist you admire. Surrounding ourselves with images of trees boosts our wellbeing.

- You don't have to wait till the Christmas holidays to bring

---

[21] Chen, C-J (2015) "Effect of Hinoki and Meniki Essential Oils on Human Autonomic Nervous System Activity and Mood States", *Natural Product Communications*, 10(7).

evergreen trees into your home. The harsh lines of modern spaces can be softened by decorating with sprigs of elegant pine and other evergreen trees –which means that there is always something green within your eye line.

- Burn a pine- or fir-scented candle and let the fresh, clean scent clear your mind.

- Grow some indigenous Japanese trees in pots on your patio or your garden. I especially love Japanese maples, which can easily be grown in the UK, Europe and the United States. Just be sure to double-check that they're suitable for your garden's soil type.

SIX BEAUTIFUL JAPANESE WORDS ASSOCIATED WITH TREES

Kaede – This means "frogs' hands". It describes the leaves of the Japanese maple, which are a vibrant green in the spring/summer, but each autumn *kaede* transform into beautiful *momiji*.

Momiji – Although this term is used interchangeably to describe all maple leaves in all the seasons, it also refers specifically to them in their iconic autumn guise.

Komorebi – Rays of sunshine filtering prismatically through the leaves of trees.

Somabito – Someone who works with the forest and the bounty it produces.

Yakusugi – An ancient cedar tree from the island of Yakushima.

Ochiba and **Kuchiba iro** – The colour of fallen leaves – *ochiba* means "fallen leaf", and *iro* means "colour". This autumnal shade is a warm orange.

MOMIJIGARI

Red-leaf Hunting

Autumn is a time of anticipation, promise and transformation. There is so much colour, beauty and poetry in nature to look forward to. Each autumn, it feels like we are entering not just a new season but also a new phase. Autumn sets Japan on fire; the fires engulf every tree until each leaf becomes a flame. November is called *Jūichigatsu* in Japan's ancient *Tenpō* calendar, meaning "the month of frost". The weather is mild and ideal for sightseeing and hunting for the most beautiful landscapes as autumn dyes Kyōto shades of red and gold. At this time of the year, Japanese food is elevated even further by the tastes of autumn's bountiful harvest and marked by the russet colours of the changing leaves. Many consider autumn to be the best time to visit Japan and the ideal time to try *kaiseki ryōri*, Kyōto's seasonal haute cuisine, for the first time. Both spring and its counterpart autumn remind us of the evanescence of life. The cherry blossom and the autumn leaves are both exceptional in their beauty as they fall.

Momijigari is the ancient Japanese custom of going in search of the changing colours of the autumnal foliage. The phrase *momijigari* literally means "red-leaf hunting", a compound of *momiji* (red maple leaves) and *kari* (hunting). Each autumn, when the ginkgos and Japanese maples begin to turn from green to shades of golden yellow, burned orange and brilliant fiery scarlet, people all over the country participate in this tradition. Making excursions out into the countryside to hunt for the best views of the changing leaves is a Japanese pastime that dates back to the Heian period (794–1185).

This quintessential autumnal activity is so popular that Japan produces the *kōyō zensen*, the annual autumn foliage forecast, to help people plan their leaf-hunting activities. The first leaves begin to change in September in Hokkaido, Japan's northernmost island. This "front" then moves south, working its way down the length of the country. In Japan, the *momiji* is to autumn what the *sakura* (cherry blossom) is to spring.

Momiji has been a favourite theme for Japanese poets since the Nara period (710–794), surpassed in popularity only by *sakura*. The *Kokin Wakashū*, a 10th-century *waka* poetry anthology, includes poems describing the exceptional sight of 3,000 maples in the grounds of Eikando Temple in Kyōto. *Waka* was the form of Japanese poetry that preceded the better-known haiku.

GO LEAF HUNTING

As a child, I don't think I ever came home from an autumnal walk with empty pockets. Instead, I would carefully carry back the treasures of autumn: conkers (horse chestnuts), seed pods and a handful of especially beautiful leaves that I couldn't bear to leave behind. Then, once I got home, I would carefully press the leaves and paint my precious finds.

STEP 1. Get outside and go hunting for autumn leaves in rainbow hues. Look out for golden gingkoes and fiery maple trees.

STEP 2. Try visiting your closest Japanese garden, arboretum or favourite place for an autumnal walk and admire the splendour of the changing autumnal landscapes. In the UK, Kew Gardens, the RHS Garden Wisley and the Westonbirt Arboretum all have stunning collections. In the USA visit the New England village of Stowe in Vermont, famous for its autumn foliage.

STEP 3. Collect some precious fallen leaves and bring them home.

STEP 4. You could either try pressing them between heavy books, with a sheet of white paper on either side, or sketch and paint them to capture their vivid colours.

AKI MATSURI

Autumn Festivals

Culture Day – Bunka no Hi
❧ *3 November* ❧

Bunka no Hi (Culture Day) is a national holiday in Japan that started in 1948. Culture Day aims to promote the arts and traditional Japanese culture, so typically there are lots of beautiful exhibitions, parades and festivities taking place around Japan on this day.

If you are lucky enough to find yourself in Asakusa on Culture Day, you can see the *Shirasagi no Mai* (White Heron Dance), which takes place outside the main hall of Sensōji, Tōkyō's oldest temple. The heron, like all white creatures, represents purity so the white makeup worn by the young dancers symbolizes their purity. Both the *sagi* (white heron) and the *tsuru* (white crane) are popular recurring images in Chinese and Japanese culture, often used interchangeably. The white heron dance's original purpose was to drive out plague and purify spirits before their journey to the netherworld. According to Pure Land Buddhism, white cranes dwell on the Isle of the Blessed, carrying souls to Western Paradise. The white heron is also a symbol of good fortune and longevity, revered for its natural affinity with the three elements earth, air and water. This thousand-year-old dance was revived in 1968 as part of Tōkyō's 100th anniversary celebrations and dates to the Heian period (794–1185). It is only performed on the second Sunday of April and 3 November.

Shichi Go San – The Seven, Five, Three Festival
❧ *15 November* ❧

This festival honours girls aged three and seven, and boys aged five. Their parents pray for their health, happiness and future wellbeing. All over Japan children are dressed in *haregi* (their best clothes) to visit Shintō shrines and pray to Ujigami, the Shintō guardian deity of good health. Afterwards, children indulge in long sticks of red and white sweets called *chitose ame* (1,000-year candy), made from sugar cane, which represent longevity.

This festival dates back to the Muromachi period (1336–1573) when samurai would celebrate their growing families. The practice became increasingly popular and spread to the townspeople during the Edo period (1603–1868). For the three-year-old girls this will often be the first time they wear kimono and this is also when they begin to grow long hair. For young boys, age five is the first time they wear *hakama*, the formal pleated trousers worn with men's kimono. At age seven, young girls switch their *tsukehimo* (children's kimono fastener) for an women's formal *obi* (sash).

Tori no Ichi – The Lucky Rake Festival
⊱⁓ *Rooster Days* ⁓⊰

Tori no Ichi begins at the stroke of midnight on the so-called "Rooster days" of the month, which occur every 12 days, meaning that there are two or three each November. In the *Jikkan Jūnishi* (Ten Stems and Twelve Branches system), each hour of the day and day of the month is allocated to one of the animals of the zodiac, such as the *tori* or rooster. These days change each year according to the lunar calendar of the Chinese zodiac.

Tori no Ichi, which began as a harvest festival, has been celebrated in Tōkyō since the Edo period (1603–1868). Each year food stalls line the surrounding streets of Otori shrines, named for Ōtori Sama, the deity of good fortune and business success. Crowds of people attend sites such as Chōkokuji in Asakusa and visit the Rooster Market to browse the array of colourful stalls and buy *kumade* (lucky rakes). These elaborately decorated bamboo rakes are talismans loaded with auspicious symbols. Designed to help your business "rake in" luck and bring happiness to your home, these are part of the practice of *kakiatsumeru*, or collecting good luck and economic good fortune.

This November event is the first celebration in the run-up to *Oshōgatsu*, the Japanese New Year. People begin preparations for the upcoming end of the year and focus on the promise of a happy and prosperous New Year. Traditionally, businesses start by buying a small, modest rake and buy an increasingly large rake each year. The larger the rake, the more luck it will bring in. There are hundreds of different varieties of *kumade* (lucky rakes*)*, each decorated with different *engimono* (Japanese lucky charms), which include *maneki neko* (beckoning cats), assorted treasures, coins, cranes, tortoises, *Okame* masks and small portable shrines. Once you have purchased a rake, your name is written on a wooden plaque and added into the arrangement of decorations. The purchase is brought to a close and celebrated with a custom called *tejime*, during which the stallholders will exclaim loudly and rhythmically clap their hands in unison. *Tejime* is an abbreviation of *teuchi de shimeru* – *teuchi* meaning "to strike a deal" or "to come to an agreement", and *shimeru* meaning "to fasten" or "to close".

JIKKAN JŪNISHI

Ten Stems and Twelve Branches

In both China and Japan, the *eto* (animals of the Chinese zodiac) are used to measure hours, days and years. They are known as the Twelve Terrestrial Branches or *Junishi* and each of the twelve branches is named for a different animal. They're a popular choice for *omikuji* (fortunes) that you can buy at Shintō shrines. In Japan, these animals are the *ne* (rat*)*, *ushi* (ox), *tora* (tiger), *usagi* (rabbit), *tatsu* (dragon), *mi* (snake), *uma* (horse), *hitsuji* (sheep), *saru* (monkey), *tori* (rooster), *inu* (dog) and *inoshi* (boar).

AKI KIGO

Seasonal Words for Autumn

Aki no Nishiki – This means "autumn brocade". *Aki* is the Japanese word for "autumn", and *nishiki* means "brocade". *Nishiki* is an area in Kyōto famous for its textiles.

Kōyō – Japan's autumn colours, a vivid fiery palette of red, orange and yellow.

Aki no fukei – Autumn scenery, temples and mountains awash with red *momiji*.

Arisugawa – A textile design of deer in combination with autumn flowers and leaves.

Unkin – Meaning "cloud brocade", this popular multi-seasonal motif combines Japan's two most iconic motifs, the cherry blossom and the maple leaf. The *sakura* are the clouds, and the *momiji* are the brocade.

Tatsutagawamon – The poetic sight of maple leaves floating down the Tatsuta River in Nara.

JAPANESE MICRO SEASON NO.54
MOMIJI TSUTA KIBAMU
Maple Leaves and Ivy Turn Yellow
2–6 November

Autumn has opened her paintbox once again and according to the Japanese micro seasons, we are now officially in the glorious season of changing leaves. This magnificent phenomenon begins in Hokkaido, Japan's northernmost island. Then, it travels down the country, turning Japan's iconic maples from green to red. The spectacle is so fantastic it can even be seen from space. During this micro season, the change has already begun.

You may not be able to find many Japanese maple trees in your neighbourhood but there are numerous other stunning trees to enjoy at this time of the year. I delight in seeing the Virginia creeper turning redder with every passing day, and the golden autumn light dancing across her leaves. Have you spotted the changes in your local landscape and are you enjoying the changing palette of the leaves yet this year?

SIKA

Deer

Japanese maple leaves are closely associated with deer (*Cervus nippon*), another ancient symbol of autumn. They appear together in a kimono motif called *arisugawa*, meaning "deer combined with autumnal leaves". Since prehistoric times, *sika* deer have been intertwined with the Kasuga Grand Shrine, part of the Kofukuji Temple complex in Nara. They inhabit the surrounding woods of Kasugayama Primeval Forest, which is now a UNESCO heritage site. The deer are symbols of the shrine and are considered good omens because they are the sacred messengers of its Shintō deities. According to medieval records c.768, Takemikazuchi no Mikoto, the first of the shrine's four deities, arrived in Nara on the back of a white deer. Paintings from this period depicting the deer as sacred are called *Kasuga* mandalas.

In Japanese art and literature, the appearance of deer signifies autumn, considered the most melancholy of the four seasons in the Japanese poetic tradition. Rinpa artists, such as Mori Tetsuzan (1775–1841), used deer to evoke loneliness because of their plaintive call, which can be heard during their autumn mating ritual. The stag's cries are an archetypal seasonal motif that expresses love in *waka* poetry.

Deer are also traditionally associated with longevity because, according to Taoist legend throughout East Asia, deer are one of the only creatures capable of detecting the Fungus of Immortality. This illusive cloud-shaped mushroom only grows high up in the mountains where the immortals reside and grants eternal life to those who consume it.

SHICHI FUKUJIN

Japan's Seven Lucky Gods

The *Shichi Fukujin* (Japan's Seven Lucky Gods) are Ebisu, Daikokuten, Benzaiten, Bishamonten, Fukurokuju, Jurōjin and Hotei. Although they all have different roots originating from Shintoism, Buddhism, Confucianism and Taoism, they are often protagonists in Japanese art and folk songs. They demonstrate the many threads woven together to form the Japanese belief system. The first images of them as a group date back to the 16th century, which depicts them aboard their *takarabune* (treasure ship). Pictures of them are auspicious and popular in businesses and restaurants. They remain one of Japan's most common religious icons.

Deer also act as the messengers for the gods of longevity, Fukurokuju and Jurōjin, two of the *Shichi Fukujin*. Originally of Chinese origin, Fukurokuju was once a Taoist sage and became the god of wisdom and longevity. His Japanese name is a compound of the traits he is associated with: happiness (*fuku*), wealth (*roku*) and longevity (*ju*). He is depicted as a short man with a high forehead and is believed to have the power to resurrect the dead.

Fukurokuju is often confused with his peer Jurōjin, who is also of Chinese origin; likewise, he is also a god of longevity. Depicted in Japanese art as an elderly scholar with a white beard, he carries a staff and is often accompanied by a stag and a crane. Attached to his staff is a scroll containing the secret to everlasting life.

AKI WAGASHI

Autumn Sweets

Fukiyose – This term means "blown" or "fused together". This exquisite medley of sweets resembles the way autumnal leaves and plants are blown together by the wind. Shaped like leaves and seasonal fruits, they represent the bounty of autumn.

Momiji Manjū – The traditional *wagashi* of Miyajima Island, famous for its beautiful maple trees, floating *torii* gate and free roaming local deer. *Momiji* means "red maple leaf", and *manjū* are a particular variety of Japanese confectionery created by Chef Takastu Tsunesuke in 1906. Shaped like a maple leaf, they are made from light, fluffy Castella cake dough, traditionally filled with red bean paste or – my personal favourite – custard. Castella cake, named for Castile in Spain, came to Japan from Portugal in c.1573. These delicious little cakes make excellent souvenirs from Miyajima and nearby Hiroshima, but nothing beats eating them fresh and warm.

Momiji Tempura – A popular delicacy made in the town of Minoh City in northwestern Osaka. Minoh is famous for its stunning waterfall surrounded by maple leaves, which is the inspiration behind this delicious autumnal snack created over 1,300 years ago. The idea of making tempura out of the delicate maple leaves was first conceived by *Shugendō* practitioners, mountain-dwelling priests who meditated beneath waterfalls and were so moved by the outstanding natural beauty of the area that they created this sweet.

Momiji tempura is a regional delicacy. It is made by pickling yellow maple leaves for a year and then coating them in flour, sugar and sesame seeds and deep-frying them, transforming the star-shaped leaves into a crunchy, slightly nutty and very addictive snack. Takido Street, the road that winds up toward Minoh Falls, is lined with small stands where you can watch women skillfully making fresh *momiji tempura*, coating the leaves in batter and then frying them. They float on the surface of the oil like *ochiba*, fallen leaves on the surface of an autumnal lake. They are the perfect snack for your walk through the park. You can purchase a bag to take with you on your hike, and then follow the path that weaves upward toward the waterfall.

Making maple leaves into tempura is a way to honour their ephemeral beauty. *Momiji tempura* is something you eat with all of your senses. You can enjoy the preserved shape of the delicate leaves, the sweet smell of the fried batter and the sesame seeds' nutty taste – and finally, the satisfying crunch as you pierce the outer shell, reminiscent of the crunch of fallen autumn leaves beneath your feet.

ICHŌ

Lessons from the Ginkgo Biloba

Called the *ichō* in Japanese, the Ginkgo biloba, also known as the maidenhair tree, is a truly magical entity, a living fossil. It is a member of an ancient genus that dates back 270 million years and has no living relatives, making it the oldest surviving species of tree known to exist on Earth. Ancient ginkgo trees can often be found in the grounds of temples and shrines and encircle those of the Imperial Palace in Tōkyō. The trees are viewed as protectors because of their high moisture content, making them resistant to fires. The ginkgo is the official tree of Tōkyō, and every autumn they paint the city gold.

In Japan, gingkoes are admired for their green, jewel-like nuts and beautiful fan-shaped leaves, which turn a golden yellow in the autumn. Only female ginkgo trees produce *ginnan* (ginkgo nuts), a sought-after seasonal element in *kaiseki* dishes (see page 75). Ginkgo nut season begins in mid-October. The nuts are an autumnal delicacy often served roasted and salted at festivals, which is how I first encountered them after a visit to *Tori no Ichi* (the Lucky Rake Festival).

Ginkgo trees are also known for their tenacity. The six gingkoes that grew near the 1945 atom bomb blast site in Hiroshima, Japan were among the few living things in the area to survive the explosion. Although almost all other plants and trees in the area were destroyed, miraculously, the gingkoes survived and recovered. People then began calling them *hibakujumoku* (survivor trees). These trees became a symbol of strength, resilience and hope. I hope you can find something of beauty to take away from the story of this remarkable tree.

Ginkgo trees are especially precious to members of the Urasenke School of Tea, which uses an *ichō* leaf as its emblem. Legend has it that when Sen Sōtan (1578–1658), the grandson of Sen no Rikyū (the father of the Japanese tea ceremony) retired, he planted a ginkgo in the grounds of Konnichian, the modern-day home of Urasenke in Kyōto. The *sōtan ichō*, as it's known, is said to have shed all its leaves during one of Kyōto's many fires to protect the tea houses nestled beneath it.

TATSUTAHIME

The Goddess of Autumn

Tatsutahime, the Goddess of Autumn, dwells in the west of Nara, Japan's ancient capital on Mt Tatsutayama, a mountain so famous for its autumnal foliage that the mere mention of it conjures up images of red maple leaves. Often depicted dressed in a crimson kimono, Tatsutahime can be identified by her scarlet sleeves, and is renowned for her dying and weaving skills.

According to legend she weaves Japan's *aki no nishiki* (autumnal brocade). Each year she dyes silk threads with the palette of autumn, weaving them into a magnificent autumnal tapestry. Then, later in the season, she becomes a strong gust of wind and blows the coloured leaves away, scattering them across rivers, mountains and shrines all over Japan. Each April and July, the princess is honoured during the festival *Tatsuta kaze no kami Matsuri*, also called the *Kazamatsuri* (wind festival), where people pray for gentle breezes and a bountiful harvest.

Tatsutahime is also celebrated in *Tatsuta*, a late autumn noh play by Zeami, Japan's most celebrated playwright. In the play, Tatsutahime appears to a travelling monk and implores him not to cross the Tatsuta River for fear that he might tear the divine brocade of crimson leaves she has carefully woven across its surface, which is protected by a fine sheet of ice.

The goddess introduces herself as a *miko* (shrine maiden). She guides him to the nearby Tatsuta Myojin Shrine via an alternate path. There, she reveals a single tree still aflame with crimson red foliage, long after the other trees have shed their leaves. She explains to the monk that this tree and its scarlet leaves are the shrine's sacred treasure and regales him with ancient poetry and a proverb about the dangers of crossing the river and tearing the autumnal brocade, which will offend the local deity he has come to pay his respects to. Finally, the Tatsuta Lady reveals herself to the holy man in all her glory, then she blazes with an inner light and vanishes into the shrine.

A GODDESS FOR EVERY SEASON

Four goddesses guard each of Japan's cardinal directions. Mt Tatsuta in the west, the home of the Autumn Princess Tatsutahime is twinned with Mt Saho in the east, where Sahohime the Spring Princess lives. According to the teachings of *Gogyo Setsu* or the theory of five elements which came to Japan from China with Buddhism in the 6th century. Spring is affiliated with the east, summer with the south, autumn with the west and winter with the north (see Chapter 6).

- The Spring Princess Sahohime dwells in the east.

- The Summer Princess Tsutsuhime lives in the south.

- The Autumn Princess Tatsutahime, who dyes the leaves red, resides in the west.

- The Winter Princess Utsutahime naturally occupies the north.

JAPANESE WOODLAND BOTANICALS

Yoshino Hinoki – A conifer native to Japan, the Japanese cypress or *Chamaecyparis obtusa*, has been used in temples since ancient times. Its deep woody perfume with a hint of spice, has notes of cedar, sandalwood and cardamom.

Kōyamaki – The Japanese umbrella pine (*Sciadopitys verticillata*), a conifer unique to Japan, is often used as an offering on Kōyasan, the sacred Mt Kōya. It has a fresh green scent that is extracted from its leaves and twigs.

Hida Sugi – Cedar is the national tree of Japan. This variety of cedar (*Cryptomeria japonica*) comes from Gifu Prefecture, known for its harsh winters. This resilient tree has a delicate, refreshing and fruity fragrance.

Aomori Hiba – Known as the tree of life, *Hiba arborvitae* is one of the largest trees in the cypress family. It is indigenous to Japan and has historically been used to build temples and shrines throughout the country. Perhaps this is because its oil, which has a distinctive crisp woody aroma, acts as an insect repellant and has natural antibacterial properties.

OSHŌGATSU

The Fifth Season

The old calendar
fills me with gratitude
like a song.

YOSA BUSON
TRANSLATED BY ROBERT HASS

Oshōgatsu, or Japanese New Year, defines Japan's first chapter of the year. In fact, the New Year is such an important holiday in Japan that it's sometimes called the fifth season. Haiku expert R H Blyth once wrote, "The New Year is a season by itself" and, in the haiku tradition, New Year is considered a separate season. Much like Christmas or Yule, there are many established practices about what foods to eat, evergreen decorations to hang and lots of activities specific to this festive season in Japan, and people travel home from all over the country to celebrate it with their families.

New Year is a season of firsts, defined by the first sunrise, the first dream and the first temple visit. According to the old calendar, Japan starts the world anew in January or *Mutuski*, "the month of harmony or friendship".

After the celebration of *Shōgatsu* or Big New Year, which, according to the western Gregorian calendar is on 1 January, on 15 January rural Japan marks *Koshōgatsu* or Small New Year, which takes place on the first full moon of the year in accordance with the much older lunar calendar. On this date, people often eat *azuki gayu*, a slightly sweet rice porridge made of red beans, believing that the red colour acts as a protective talisman against evil. This practice originated in ancient China.

Fuyu, or winter in Japan, begins in December and lasts until February. According to the lunar calendar, another ancient name for February is *Yukige-zuke*, meaning "when the snow starts to melt". December is spent preparing homes, minds and bodies for a happy and healthy New Year.

Preparations for the Japanese New Year start early. They begin on 13 December, when it's traditional to deep-clean your home in preparation for the end of the year. This is called *ōsōji*, "the biggest clean-up". The purpose of this is to cleanse your home and make it fit for welcoming in the gods of the New Year. Just as you would purify yourself before you entered a Shintō shrine, once your home is ready to receive the gods, you can hang up your New Year's decorations. People usually put these up on or around 28 December and take them down around 7 January to be burned. The ritual fires held at this time at local shrines help to light the way home for the visiting deities.

SHIMEKAZARI

Tied Rope Ornament

If you visit Japan at the end of the year or in early January, you will see beautiful handmade Japanese New Year's decorations called *shimekazari* (tied rope ornaments). You'll find them both inside and outside Japanese homes and businesses. They're designed to welcome Toshigami, the *kami* of the New Year, who watches over the house and the family, protecting them for the following year. The word *toshi* now means "year", but it originally meant "rice"; this makes the god of the New Year also the god of rice, which is logical as Japanese culture was once centred around growing and harvesting rice.

There are several varieties of New Year decorations, each with a different function. The *shimekazari* (tied rope ornament) is designed to be hung above the door or entrance to your house. It acts like the *shimenawa* (boundary ropes) at the entrance to Shintō shrines, keeping evil spirits at bay and inviting good spirits (*kami*) to descend and dwell in your home.

Most importantly, the base of the Japanese New Year's wreath is a rope made from rice straw. Traditional decorative elements and *engimono* (Japanese lucky charms) are then added to the base, which can include a *suehiro*, a *washi* paper fan that symbolizes ever-increasing good fortune and a *tsuru* or crane made of *mizuhiki* (*washi* paper cord), *tawara* (rice bales) and *shide* (zigzag-shaped paper strips), as a token of wealth.

Shimenawa are one example of *yorishiro*, objects that can attract and house *kami*. *Yorishiro* can be swords, mirrors, *kumade* (lucky rakes), unusually shaped rocks, trees and many natural elements found in nature. For example, *kadomatsu* (gate pines) made with evergreen plants and trees are the *yorishiro* of the *kami* of the New Year.

ENGIMONO

Japanese Good Luck Charms

Engimono is the collective name for Japanese good luck charms: *engi* means "luck", and *mono* means "thing" or "piece". They originate from folklore but have a basis in Buddhist and Shintō practices too. Amulets or talismans are holy objects in Buddhism. Generally, Buddhists will have at least one sacred item. Shintō is rooted in animism, and Shintō amulets are sold at shrines and are usually dedicated to particular *kami*. Japanese art and literature are replete with animals that can bring luck to those they encounter, and many popular *engimono* use animal imagery. Each charm represents a different kind of fortune: love, health or financial success. There are several kinds of *engimono,* and some are regionally specific. Typically, *engimono* are associated with a particular person, sacred place or historical event.

KADOMATSU

Gate Pine

The word *matsuri*, which means festival or holiday, comes from the Japanese word *matsu* or pine tree, which symbolizes courage, endurance and longevity. It refers to the ancient connection between evergreen trees and Japanese festivals. In the West, the Celtic Druids, the ancient Romans and the Vikings all brought evergreen trees such as spruce, pine or fir into their homes, just as we do to celebrate Christmas, one of our most important annual holidays. Like them, we decorate a Christmas tree and add garlands of greenery to our mantlepieces.

In Japan, people decorate their homes for New Year with evergreen *kadomatsu* or gate pines, placed in pairs on either side of the entrance. *Kadomatsu* are made of three pieces of green bamboo bound together with straw, each cut to a different height. The tallest represents Heaven, the shortest represents the Earth, and the middle-sized one represents humanity. They act as a dwelling place for Toshigami (God of the New Year) throughout the holiday period, and in January they are burned in a special ceremony at a Shintō shrine. *Kadomatsu* are also sometimes decorated with plants such as branches of *ume* (flowering plum) or sprigs of nandina bearing red berries (*nanten* in Japanese).

In Kyōto, instead of a pair of *kadomatsu*, sometimes a single branch or sapling of an evergreen tree is nailed to the doorpost. The branches come from trees and shrubs such as pine, camellia or the sacred *sakaki (Cleyera japonica)*, and is the continuation of a courtly tradition that dates back to the Heian period (794–1185) when courtiers would pull up small pines by their roots on 7 January as a kind of prayer for longevity to lengthen the year.

OSECHI RYŌRI

Foods for the New Year

Osechi ryōri is a tradition that dates back over 2,000 years and began as an offering to the God of the New Year. Traditional Japanese

New Year's Day cuisine is made up of a combination of lots of small colourful dishes that are eaten for good luck. This New Year tradition resembles eating black-eyed peas in America, *pelmeni* (dumplings) in Russia or *tteokguk* (rice cake soup) in Korea. *Osechi* also contains lots of *sunomono*, preserved or fermented dishes that can be prepared in advance and kept for several days. *Osechi* is the most important meal of the year. It's traditionally served beautifully presented in an elegant *jūbako*, a three or five-tiered box made of black or red lacquerware decorated with seasonal motifs, such as plum, pine and bamboo. Each decorative element of *osechi* is symbolic or has a special significance because these are *iwai zakana* (lucky dishes).

The top tier of the box is filled with strongly flavoured sweet and salty hors d'oeuvres designed to be enjoyed with sake. These dishes are called *kuchitori* (appetizers). They include *kuromame*, sweet black soybeans, and *kamaboko*, a thinly sliced steamed fish cake in shades of red and white. This colour combination is called *kohaku*, which is thought to ward off evil, and the semi-circular shape represents the first sunrise of the new year. A popular *osechi* dish is *kuri kinton* (chestnut golden mash), a sweet paste made from Japanese sweet potatoes studded with whole candied chestnuts. This dish is golden yellow, representing wealth and prosperity.

Much like making mulled wine during the festive season in Europe, for the Japanese New Year, people make a special celebratory drink called *otoso*, a mulled sake, which is infused with medicinal herbs for eight hours and served warm. It's designed to ward off illness throughout the new year. It reminds me a little of mulled wine, and there are definitely some similarities. The mulling herbs for both are available to buy in small sachets in supermarkets towards the end of the year and use a *tososan*, a blend of herbs and spices, which, depending on the recipe, includes cinnamon, cloves, *sanshō* pepper (Japanese prickly ash) and mandarin orange peel.

The second tier of the *jūbako* is filled with *yakimono*, grilled or broiled meat and fish dishes. The third is filled with *sunomono* (vinegared dishes), which includes pickled or marinated vegetables such as *surenkon* (vinegared lotus root), crunchy and refreshing *namasu* (pickled white radish and carrot), again in celebratory shades of red and white. Another lovely seasonal and decorative element is *kikka kabu*, which are pickled turnips cut into the shape of white chrysanthemums. This dish is a *hashiyasume*, a palate-cleansing side dish served between courses, similar to an *intermezzo*. The *kiku* or chrysanthemum is another iconic Japanese flower, the seal of the Imperial family and a symbol of longevity and rejuvenation (see Chapter 8). The fourth tier is filled with *nimono*, simmered dishes, such as meat, fish and vegetables cooked in soy sauce, mirin, sugar and sake. The fifth and final tier is called *hikaenoju*, and is intentionally left symbolically empty, leaving space for future development and prosperity.

Ōmisoka
New Year's Eve
31 December

The last day of the year is called *Ōmisoka,* and before midnight, people often enjoy a bowl of steaming hot *toshikoshi* soba (year-crossing noodles). This dish contains thin buckwheat noodles in a light *dashi* broth. Enjoying them on New Year's Eve is a tradition that is said to have started in the Edo period (1603–1868). The idea is that the healthy buckwheat noodles get your new year off to a good start, especially because the long thin noodles symbolize longevity. People hope to have a life as long as a soba noodle. Consuming auspicious foods such as *toshikoshi* soba means that you start the new year as you mean to go on – happy and healthy.

Japanese soba noodles are now readily available in supermarkets and from specialist grocery shops, so why not give them a try?

HATSUYUME

The First Dream

Hatsuyume, the first dream of the New Year that takes place on the first night of January, gives a hint of what might be to come in the year ahead. In Japan, dreaming of Mt Fuji is considered to be the luckiest dream.

So, if you remember your first dream of the New Year when you wake up, write it down before you forget. What did you dream of?

HATSUHINODE

The First Sunrise

People often stay up through the night to see *hatsuhinode,* the first sunrise of the year. This is a beautiful ritual that you can take part in no matter where you are. Think back over the past year and contemplate your hopes for the year ahead while you watch the sun rise on *gantan,* the first morning of the New Year.

What a wonderful ritual to incorporate into your life to start the New Year in an intentional way!

HATSUMŌDE

The First Shrine Visit

On *Ganjitsu,* the first day of the New Year, people flock to their local temples and shrines to participate in *hatsumōde,* their first visit to a shrine of the New Year, which usually takes place sometime between midnight on 31 December and 7 January.

On the first morning of the New Year, the bells of the Buddhist temples all over Japan ring out 108 times; this is called *Joya no Kane* (midnight bell). Each ring of the bells represents the renunciation of one of the 108 earthly desires that humanity is believed to possess and hearing the bells toll allows us to start the year anew. Once the last bell has rung, the New Year can begin.

HATSUGAMA

The First Tea Kettle

⁂〜 *1–11 January* 〜⁂

Hatsugama is a compound word made up of the kanji for "first" or "new" and "kettle", the utensil used to heat water for the tea ceremony. This phrase refers to the first bowl of tea of the New Year. For *chajin* (tea people), the New Year begins with the first *chaji* or formal tea gathering, when we come together and enjoy the first *wagashi* of the year, *hanabira mochi* (flower petal *mochi*).

Japanese New Year's traditions and foods often refer to symbols of longevity. Last year for *hatsugama*, my sensei displayed a calligraphy scroll that read *Shōju Sennen no Midori*, meaning "the pine tree is one thousand years green". The scroll refers to the unchanging nature of the evergreen pine or *matsu*, which is said to live for a thousand years and is believed to be immortal.

NENGAJŌ

New Year Cards

A key part of *Shōgatsu* is the tradition of sending *nengajō* (New Year cards) to colleagues, friends and family. This tradition dates back to the Heian period (794–1185) when the Japanese nobility started to write letters to those who lived too far away to visit for in-person New Year greetings.

These greeting cards are often decorated with elaborate knotted cords called *mizuhiki*, which are used to embellish cards and gifts. Each colour and design has a specific purpose. For example, red and white are the most popular combination for decorating New Year cards. The ends, which point upward, symbolize growth, prosperity and abundance.

MAKE YOUR OWN NEW YEAR CARDS

People in Japan often make their own New Year cards. If, like me, you also love snail mail, why not make some yourself and send a postcard or a note to your friends at the beginning of the year? Here are a few tips and ideas.

THEMES

If you want to use traditional Japanese New Year's imagery, you could include images of the Chinese zodiac animal of the New Year, a red rising sun and flying cranes, snow-covered landscapes or the Three Friends of Winter (the plum, the pine and bamboo).

MESSAGES

Take some time to compose your message, sending your best wishes for the year ahead and thank your friends, family, colleagues and teachers for their kindness and support over the past year. I like to wish people health and happiness for the coming year.

METHODS

There's no limitation to how you create your cards. Over the years, I've tried my hand at collage, painting, drawing and using decorative stamps. The choice is entirely up to you – have fun!

YUKI USAGI

The Snow Rabbit

When it snows, Japanese children make snow rabbits instead of snowmen. Rabbits are popular protagonists in Japanese folktales, and white rabbits in particular are the embodiment of the moon's purity. They also symbolize long life and fertility.

HOW TO MAKE
A SNOW RABBIT

❄ ❄

This is a sweet activity that you can do anywhere that has snow. So instead of making a snowman with your friends and family, why not try making an adorable snow rabbit?

STEP 1. Shape some fresh snow into the form of a rabbit by cupping your hands together to make an egg shape (the traditional shape for snow rabbits).

STEP 2. Add red berries for eyes. In Japan, these would be nandina berries, but any small locally available red berries, such as holly or hawthorn, will work just as well.

STEP 3. Add the ears. These would traditionally be nandina leaves, but any long narrow evergreen green leaf will do.

STEP 4. Finally, traditionally the snow rabbit is placed onto a black lacquered tray so it can be transported and enjoyed closer to the house. This step is entirely optional, of course.

SHŌCHIKUBAI

The Three Friends of Winter

In Japan *ume* (plum blossom), *matsu* (pine) and *take* (bamboo) make up the triad known as the Three Friends of Winter. They act as heralds for the coming spring and for decorations for the New Year. This grouping of plants is an ancient auspicious motif imported to Japan from China. When these three longevity symbols appear in combination, they represent steadfastness, perseverance and resilience because they thrive in harsh winters and flourish in the face of adversity.
What local plants and trees represent winter for you?

Ume (plum) – The plum (*bai* in Chinese) demonstrates strength by overcoming adversity and by blooming in the most unlikely season – at the end of winter.

Matsu (pine) – The pine (*sho* in Chinese) symbolizes winter and the New Year. As an evergreen tree, it represents longevity, eternity and unchanging fidelity.

Take (bamboo) – Japan is home to over 400 varieties of bamboo (*chiku* in Chinese). This fast-growing grass is a durable and elegant material that is a ubiquitous part of life in Japan. It's used for everything from building materials to a source of food. When used as a decorative motif, bamboo represents flexibility, resilience and great strength because it won't break even under heavy snow.

Ume
Plum Blossom

An enduring image of winter in East Asian art, the *ume* or plum blossom has been cherished in China and Japan for thousands of years for its sweet fragrance and delicate flowers. They bloom in the harsh climate of winter, often under snow and in spite of icy winds, making them a symbol of perseverance, purity, hope and great beauty. Long before cherry blossoms became the unofficial flower of Japan, people held plum blossom viewing parties to admire the delicate and fragrant *ume*. The most famous representation of *ume* in Japan is a pair of gold folding screens depicting red and white plum trees on either side of a flowing river, painted by Ogata Kōrin (1658–1716).

In English, *ume* is translated as plum, but it's actually a kind of apricot brought to Japan from China in the Nara period (710–794). It's said that the first *ume* to come to Japan were as white as freshly fallen snow. *Ume*, or plum blossoms, have several beautiful Japanese names, including *hana no ani*, meaning "the elder brother of the flowers" (the flowers in question being cherry blossoms) and *harutsugegusa*, or "spring announcing plant". The *ume* is also the source of *umeboshi* (pickled plums), a staple of *washoku* (Japanese cuisine) which is traditionally added to *ōbukucha,* the celebratory tea of Japanese New Year.

KITSUNEBI

Fox Fire

Animals play a crucial role in Shintō, and several Shintō deities have animal attendants. White animals in particular, such as cranes, herons and white foxes, are considered to be good omens.

Since ancient times fleet-footed *kitsune* (magical shapeshifting foxes) have been worshipped in Japanese folklore and mythology as the divine messengers of Inari, the Shintō god of rice, fertility and agriculture. *Kitsune* statues grace the grounds of some 30,000 Inari shrines throughout Japan, where they represent abundance, making them a popular choice for *hatsumōde*, the first shrine visit of the New Year. The most famous Inari shrine in Japan is Fushimi Inari Taisha in Kyōto, where Inari has been worshipped since the Heian period (794–1185).

Each New Year's Eve, the *kitsune* of Eastern Japan gather beneath a huge tree and visit the Oji Inari shrine in Tōkyō to pay homage to Inari. They illuminate their procession with *kitsunebi* (fox fire). When mysterious flames of light appear in the sky without warning, these lights signal the presence of *kitsune*, a sight famously depicted in the woodblock print *New Year's Eve Foxfires at the Changing Tree, Oji,* by the artist Utagawa Hiroshige (1797–1858). According to legend, the greater the fire in the sky and the longer the procession, the better the new year's rice harvest will be. But beware, these colourful lights have been used to confuse travellers, sending them off the beaten path into the wilderness.

FUYU KIGO

Seasonal Words for Winter

Yukizuri – Before the first snow in late November/early December, *yukizuri* (snow hanging) ropes are put in place to support the branches of ancient trees, protecting them from snapping after heavy snowfall. Trees nestling inside the conical shapes made by the ropes are a feature of the exceptional Kenrokuen Garden in Kanazawa, famous for its pine trees.

Hatsugōri – The first ice of the season. When you see ice on the surface of the water for the first time, then you know winter has truly arrived.

Yuki Usagi – A snow rabbit, often made by children in Japan instead of a snowman.

Fuyu no tsuki – The winter moon.

Hatsuyuki – The first snow of the year.

Kazahana – In Japan, snowflakes are called *kazahana* (wind flowers), because they dance through the air like petals.

SETSUGEKKA

The Three Beauties

In Japan, three things are celebrated for their beauty above all others. They are known collectively as *setsugekka*, the Three Beauties of Nature – a triumvirate that includes three cherished elements: Snow, the moon and flowers. Originally inspired by the work of the Chinese Tang Dynasty (618–907) poet Bai Juyi (772–846 CE), who famously wrote, "At the time of snow, moon and flowers, I think of you." His poem established the connection between these three ephemeral seasonal elements as a reminder of the transience of all living things. Just as winter's snow-capped landscapes eventually melt and vanish, the lovely face of the moon is forever changing, and the delicate sakura will bloom all too briefly and shed their petals onto the river below. In Japanese, this sense of impermanence is called *utsuroi*.

The fleeting beauty of these three natural elements, which illustrate the seasonal beauty of Japan, has become a theme, inspiring countless Japanese artists. These three motifs repeat endlessly, both separately and together, throughout Japanese literature and art. The Three Beauties represent the best scenery of each season. Their ephemeral nature is an inextricable part of what makes them beautiful. Perhaps instead of mourning their loss, we could choose to focus on how lucky we are to witness their evanescence and look forward to their return the following year.

YUKIMI

Snow Viewing

Every season has its own ephemeral beauty, and winter is no exception. Winter is prized for its pure white snow, so clean that people use it to make tea. Parts of Japan, especially the north, see spectacular snowfall each year, resulting in stunning snow-covered landscapes each January. Vermillion red *torii* gates punctuate their cold beauty.

Just as people love to picnic beneath the cherry blossoms in spring, there is also a tradition of enjoying Japanese tea while admiring the snow's beauty in winter: *yukimi*. My favourite Japanese snow-related tradition is *yukimiburo*, the magical experience of indulging in an outdoor hot spring while the snow falls all around you.

YUKI MATSURI

Snow Festivals

In Japan, the phrase *yukiguni* (snow country) refers to anywhere that sees heavy snowfall annually. In places like Akita, where the Yokote Snow Festival is held, people build *kamakura*, the Japanese word for "igloos". Originally these small candlelit huts were dedicated to the Shintō gods of water. Villagers would come to pray and ask the gods for clean water, plentiful harvests and the safety of their local community. Now there are dedicated *kamakura* festivals where entire villages made of snow appear for a brief period in February.

Guests can visit hundreds of *kamakura* and eat, drink and even shop inside these temporary snowy structures. Inside you'll be greeted by flickering candlelight and served freshly grilled *mochi* and warm *amazake*, a naturally sweet fermented non-alcoholic drink made from rice, water and *kōji* (fermented cooked rice). It can be served hot or cold, but it's especially comforting when served warm to celebrate the New Year.

In Japan, snow country refers to areas such as Niigata, Nagano and Hokkaido. Outside Japan, we might use it to describe Colorado in the USA, the Cairngorms in Scotland or the Swiss Alps. Do you live in snow country?

Tips for Snow Viewing

- Wrap up warm and wear shoes with good grip or snow chains if you plan to do some hiking.

- Be sure to take a flask of steaming tea, coffee or hot chocolate with you; you'll thank me later.

- Get out early; the earlier, the better. You can catch the sunrise over the quiet, snow-covered landscape and enjoy the snow before it starts to melt.

- Count how many shades of white you can see.

- In Japan, seeing the bamboo groves and stone lanterns covered in snow is an iconic winter image. Is there a Japanese garden you can visit locally to experience this feeling?

- Make a snow rabbit (see page 311).

- Look at the trees around you. What shapes do the snowy branches remind you of?

- Cast your eyes around the snowscape. What natural features can you spot half hidden beneath the snow, making them all the more magical?

YUKI ONNA

The Snow Maiden

The people of snow country tell tales of *yuki onna*, the ghostly snow woman. She is a kind of *yōkai* (supernatural entity) called a *yurei*, a ghost or spirit from Japanese myth and legend. On snowy nights at the edge of the woods, you might catch sight of this ephemeral beauty, the spirit of the snow. In her thin white kimono, she's camouflaged and almost impossible to see against the snow. Her beauty is unnatural; her pale skin is said to be translucent, her lips blue from the cold. She leaves no footprints, only her long raven-black hair is visible against the bleak winter landscape, and if threatened, she will disappear, transforming into a flurry of snowflakes. Myths about *yuki onna* vary from region to region, but my personal favourite is that she represents all those who have perished, lost in the snow.

TSURU

Cranes

Cranes are the most sacred birds in Japan, ridden by sages and immortals. They are iconic because of their pure white feathers, elegant lines and graceful dances. Cranes are a *zuiju*, an auspicious animal. Revered in Japanese folktales, art, literature and textiles, cranes symbolize longevity, fidelity and authority. Red-crested cranes arrive in Japan every October, stay for the winter and fly north each spring. In Japanese art, cranes, in combination with a red rising sun, represent *Shōgatsu*, the beginning of the New Year.

Senbazuru
One Thousand Cranes

Legend says that if you fold *senbazuru* or 1,000 paper cranes, your wish will be granted by the gods. In Japan, cranes are considered mystical or holy creatures, and it is said they can live for 1,000 years, which is why

1,000 cranes are made, one for each year of a crane's long life. In some stories, it is believed that the 1,000 cranes must be completed within one year, and they must all be made by the person who will make the wish at the end. Japanese school children learn how to fold their first paper cranes in kindergarten. *Senbazuru* are also often made by friends and loved ones as gifts for the seriously ill.

A symbol of hope, people often donate *senbazuru* as a prayer for world peace. The Atomic Bomb Museum in Nagasaki displays thousands of cranes gifted from all over Japan – a nation's prayer that past atrocities will never be repeated. The cranes are left hanging, exposed to the elements. Their colours slowly fade and they become more tattered, eventually disintegrating and, releasing their wish into the world. In this way, they are reminiscent of Tibetan prayer flags.

THE SMALL SEASONS OF WINTER

Rittō – Sekki No.19
The Beginning of Winter
7 November

Although it may still feel very much like autumn, winter has officially begun according to the ancient lunar-solar calendar. This is based on the waxing and waning of the moon and the sun's position in the sky, so the dates can change each year. *Rittō* is the 19th of the 24 *nijushi sekki* or small seasons, as I like to call them. These 24 solar terms originally came from ancient China and are used to divide up the Japanese agricultural year. In Japan, winter lasts from *Rittō* till *Shunbun*, the spring equinox.

Shōsetsu – Sekki No.20
Lesser Snow
⊰──── 22 November ────⊱

The skies are bright and clear and the last autumn leaves are falling from the trees, leaving their branches bare. During this season, Japan's many fragrant citrus fruits, such as *yuzu* (see page 322) and *mikan*, are ripening and ready for harvest. Soon the *daidai* (bitter orange) will be ready to use in New Year's decorations.

Taisetsu – Sekki No.21
Heavy Snow
⊰──── 7 December ────⊱

Taisetsu means "greater or heavy snow". It feels as though winter has well and truly arrived, and snow is forecast in some parts of the country. Frost glitters in the morning sunlight, and the evenings have turned cold.

Tōji – Sekki No.22
The Winter Solstice
⊰──── 21 or 22 December ────⊱

At this point in the year, yin energy is at its highest, and yang energy begins to return. In Japanese, this celebratory moment is called *ichiyō raifuku*, meaning "the return of spring". Once we pass this point in the year, the days get longer and the promise of spring is close at hand. Despite the short days of winter and the lack of sunlight, this hopeful moment offers comfort.

On 22 December, Japan celebrates *Tōji* or the Winter Solstice, the shortest day and the longest night of the year. Traditionally, every *Tōji* Japanese people flock to their local *onsen* (hot spring) and *sentō* (public bathhouses) to enjoy *yuzuyu* (*yuzu* baths). These fragrant aromatherapy baths full of yellow citrus fruits help elevate the mood and revitalize the mind during the dark winter months. They are also believed to ward off malevolent spirits. Bathers say *"ichiyō raifuku"*, which means that the sun is regaining its strength so winter will soon be over and fortunes will change with the return of spring. After bathing, when they have washed away all their bad luck from the previous year, people can move forward into the next year with only good fortune.

Eating *unmori*, auspicious foods and vegetables that end in the letter N in Japanese, such as *ginnan* (ginko nuts), *nankin* (pumpkin), *daikon* (white radish), *udon* (noodles) and *ninjin* (carrots) are considered especially lucky. This is firstly because the "un" sound in Japanese means "good luck" and secondly because the letter N is the last character in the *hiragana* alphabet and the winter solstice signals the end of shorter days.

The custom of taking *yuzu* baths is part of Japan's long tradition of adding seasonal plants to their bathwater, enjoying their beauty and medicinal properties. This dates back to the Edo period (1603–1868). *Yuzu* baths have several documented health benefits. The baths warm the body, improving circulation, easing rheumatism, arthritis and aching muscles, boosting immunity and mood. The sight of the bright yellow fruits also acts as a form of colour therapy. By bathing in its fruits, people hope to embody the qualities of strength and resilience that *yuzu* has, to overcome bad luck and harsh winters.

Shōkan – Sekki No.23
Lesser Cold
❀⁓ *5 January* ⁓❀

Shōkan marks the beginning of midwinter or *kanchu,* the season of cold winds and snow. At this time of the year, people often send winter greeting cards, which are distinct from *nengajō*, New Year cards. Another name for *shōkan* is *kan no iri* ("entering the cold"), indicating that this is the beginning of the cold season.

Daikan – Sekki No.24
Greater Cold
❀⁓ *20 January* ⁓❀

Daikan is the last of the 24 *sekki*, the solar terms used to punctuate the year in traditional East Asian calendars. January can be bitterly cold here in the UK, Europe, the USA and Japan. In England, from 1600 till 1814, the River Thames would freeze over so completely in January that "frost fairs" were held on its ice-covered surface. Londoners could skate across the frozen Thames and attend street markets held on the river surface during the coldest month of the year. This tradition is alive and well in Northern Japan. In Hokkaido, when Lake Shikaribetsu freezes over each January, the annual Lake Shikaribetsu *Kotan* festival is held on the surface of the frozen lake, where an entire *kotan* (the Ainu word for village) is constructed from ice.[22]

Daikan, meaning "greater cold", takes place 15 days after midwinter. It's the coldest time of the year, when we awaken to frost-covered landscapes and frozen rivers. Meanwhile, at the same time in Japan, the *ume* (plum blossoms) begin to bloom in January, reminding us that spring is close at hand. The 30-day period that extends from midwinter until the first day of spring on 4 February, is called *Kan no Uchi*, which means "the coldest season". This period is considered to be the best time of the year to make *kanshikomi* – fermented foods such as miso, soy sauce and sake traditionally prepared during the cold season – which make the most of the pure winter water and cold weather to ferment slowly and gently over several months.

YUZU

Citrus Junos

Citrus trees flourish in Japan and there are more than 40 kinds native to Japan, some of which you may have heard of, such as *yuzu*, *mikan* and *sudachi*. *Yuzu* (*Citrus junos*) is a member of the Rutaceae family of tart citrus plants such as oranges, grapefruit, lemons and limes. It arrived in Japan from the Yangtze River region of China 1,200 years ago, during the Asuka period (538–710). The remote village of Mizuo in Kyōto Prefecture is believed to be the home of Japan's first *yuzu* cultivar. Originally prized for its medicinal properties and later for its culinary versatility *yuzu* look like small knobbly grapefruits that ripen from a dark green to vibrant sunshine yellow, and each part of the fruit can be used, from the peel to the seeds. *Yuzu* has been prized in Japan

---

[22] The *Ainu* are the indigenous people of Hokkaido, the Northernmost Island of Japan. They have a rich cultural heritage which is distinct from Japanese culture.

for over 1,000 years and has finally made its way to Europe, the UK and the United States, much to my delight because I'm a devotee of this fragrant citrus fruit.

Yuzuyu
Taking a *Yuzu* Bath

Traditionally from 20–23 December, people in Japan take a *yuzuyu* or *yuzu* bath. Bathing with these sunshine-yellow citrus fruits is said to boost both immunity and mood during the dark winter months and ward against evil spirits. In 2019 I took my first *yuzuyu* (*yuzu* bath) with organic *yuzu* grown in Kochi Prefecture. The smell was incredible!

Scent is another way to connect to the season. Even if you can't have your own *yuzuyu* experience in Japan, you can still enjoy this aromatic tradition. Try adding a few drops of *yuzu* essential oils or *yuzu*-scented bath salts to your bath and create your own winter solstice bathing ritual at home.

If you can't find anything *yuzu* scented, try another uplifting citrus oil, such as lemongrass, mandarin or grapefruit. Or try another iconic Japanese scent like *hinoki* cedar wood, which is used to make Japanese soaking tubs.

Make Your Own *Yuzu* Exfoliating Scrub

If you live somewhere where fresh *yuzu* is hard to find, you can always use *yuzu* essential oils to make a *yuzu* exfoliating scrub. This scrub is a fantastic way to clean and exfoliate your hands after painting or gardening, and it makes a lovely gift too.

Ingredients

400g (2 cups) granulated sugar
55g (¼ cup) coconut oil
6 drops *yuzu* essential oil

Method

1. Combine all the ingredients in a large bowl.
2. Mix them together and make sure they're evenly distributed.
3. Spoon your scrub into a sterilized glass jar with a secure lid. A recycled glass jar works perfectly.
4. You can store it for up to three months in an air-tight container.

SUISEN

Daffodils

Daffodils are one of the first flowers to bloom at the end of winter, announcing the arrival of spring both in Europe and Japan. They bloom from the end of December till late February.

Daffodils came to Asia and arrived in Japan via trade on the Silk Road. The kanji *suisen* is made up of the symbols for water (*mizu*) and wizard or hermit (*sen*). This refers to the riverbanks where daffodils often grow and the Greek myth of Narcissus, who was bewitched by his own reflection and fell in love with the image he saw in the water. Their poetic name is *setchuka*, meaning "flower in the snow". In Shimoda city, on the Suzaki Peninsula, 3 million narcissi bloom every January, filling the air with their sweet scent; they are celebrated during the Tsumekizaki Narcissus Festival.

JAPANESE MICRO SEASON NO.55
TSUBAKI NAJIMETE HIRAKU

Camellias Bloom
❧ ⟋ **7–11 November** ⟍ ❧

Yukitsubaki are winter-blooming camellias. *Yuki* means "snow", and *tsubaki* is the Japanese word for "camellia". These hardy plants thrive under blankets of snow. Their dark green glossy leaves and vivid pink and red flowers are always welcome in the depths of winter. This variety of camellias usually reaches its peak at the same time as the plum blossoms, the first flowering trees of the new calendar year. You can see them combined in a spectacular display at Jonangu Shrine in Kyōto, which is famous for its camellias and weeping plum trees.

FUYU WAGASHI

Winter Sweets

Tsubaki mochi – Camellia *mochi* is a sweet rice cake served in early spring, filled with red bean paste sandwiched between two evergreen camellia leaves. This sweet appears in *The Tale of Genji*. It has been eaten since the Heian period (794–1185), making it one of the oldest forms of Japanese confectionary and possibly the origin of Japanese *wagashi*.

Hanabira Mochi – Meaning "flower petal rice cake", this sweet is assembled between flattened sheets of white *mochi* to look like a flower petal. Inside the folds are a piece of sweetened burdock root and soft pink *mochi* filled with miso-flavoured *anko* (sweet bean paste).

Ume – A sweet shaped like an open plum blossom, which anticipates the first flowers of the New Year.

Kagami Mochi

Kagami mochi is an essential ingredient of the Japanese New Year. In the past, on *mochi tsuki* (25–28 December), whole families would get together to pound the rice to make their *mochi* for the upcoming holidays. This tradition still takes place in some places, now as a lovely community event, but most people in contemporary Japan buy rice cakes for the holidays.

Kagami mochi is an offering made to the gods. It is made up of two pieces of disc-shaped *mochi* placed on a sheet of white paper and stacked on top of each other in ascending order of size. A *daidai*, a small bitter orange citrus fruit used in New Year decorations, is then placed on top of them. It symbolizes longevity because the fruits remain on the tree for years unless picked, turning green in the summer and orange in the winter. The orange is accompanied by persimmons, which represent joy. The decorated offering is finally placed on a small stand on the *kamidana*, a Shintō household altar.

On 11 January the final part of the New Year's celebration takes place. This is called *kagami biraki* (opening the mirror), when the *kagami mochi* offering from the New Year is removed from the family altar and broken into small pieces. These are lightly grilled and added to *zenzai* (or *oshiruko* as its called in the east of Japan), a kind of sweet soup made from azuki beans. It's served warm and garnished with either toasted *mochi* or *shiratama dango*, dumplings made from glutinous rice flour.

FUYUGOMORI

Hibernation

Winter is a period of rest for the natural world. Plants and animals withdraw and become dormant during this season, and we accept this without question or complaint. It's only natural for us to do the same. Our culture of continuous production and productivity is not sustainable. Human beings also need periods of rest. As Casper ter Kuile identified in his book, *The Power of Ritual*, our "culture of incessant activity" is pushing us to breaking point.

Instead of becoming trapped in what he calls "cycles of performance", what about immersing ourselves in the cycles of the seasons, which allows for the ebb and flow of productivity and includes time for recuperation and rest?

SHITAMOE

Sprouting Beneath the Snow

We can take comfort in the cycles of the year because they remind us that no matter how dark things may get, nothing lasts forever – every winter eventually ends and spring always returns. Meanwhile, beneath the cold and sometimes bleak landscapes of winter, things are percolating beneath the frost and snow, while we take a step back and gather our strength to re-enter the world in the spring. Then when it's time, we can emerge full of life, energy and new ideas, just like the slender leaves of the first daffodils and snowdrops, piercing the damp earth like jade swords.

FINDING THE FIRST SIGNS OF SPRING IN WINTER

One of the first signs of spring is called *yuki ma gusa* in Japanese, which describes a young sprout or shoot (*gusa*) poking its head out from under a snow drift. This makes me think of the first snowdrops and daffodils we see in the UK each February. The first sightings of these new shoots and buds I see on freezing winter walks remind me that spring is not as far away as it may sometimes feel.

So here are a few ways to reconnect with nature during the winter while we're waiting for cherry blossom season to arrive.

- Keep a look out for shoots, buds and any signs of life and new growth all around you, especially on trees and roses. Maybe you'll even see some snowdrops.

- Plant some bulbs, such as fragrant paperwhite narcissi or *suisen* – daffodils – which are a popular motif for early spring in Japan. If you pot these up in December, then by January you'll have fresh green shoots to enjoy and flowers to anticipate while the darkest month of the year passes by.

- On your winter walks watch and listen out for the birds. Can you hear them singing? Try looking up any you spot but don't recognize or whose song you don't know.

- Care for a house plant. Ferns are easy to look after and come in lots of beautiful varieties. They're a popular choice in Japanese gardens and ideal for *kokedama* (hanging plants with their roots wrapped in moss).

- Gaze at the moon from your window. Observe its cycle and watch as it waxes and wanes over the course of the month.

- Think about what you'd like to grow on the windowsill or in the garden this spring, then order some seeds.

RESOURCES

ACKNOWLEDGEMENTS

Countless people have supported me in nurturing this book from a tiny seed of an idea through the long winters of writing, editing and querying until it finally blossomed into the book you now hold in your hands. I would like to sincerely thank all the Japanese cultural experts, guides, translators and locals who graciously gave their time to talk to me and recommend museums, books, poems and beautiful places to visit throughout my research.

In the world of tea, I would like to thank my endlessly patient sensei Yasuhiro Yamaguchi, tea ceremony instructor Bruce Sosei Hamana, who welcomed me into his tearoom in Kyōto, and my dearest tea friends, Dr Sarah Stewart in London and Elsa Derrez in Uji.

In Kyōto, my gratitude goes to the ceramic artist Shinichi Miyagawa and his family who kindly welcomed me into their home; my excellent *obanzai* teachers Yoshie Ishiguro, Susumu Fujikake and translator Jason Davidson; Matt Joslin, who helped connect me with master indigo dyer Shōji Shimura; and my guide Kazumi Tsuji.

In Yamagata, I'd like to thank Sarah Nishina and Derek Yamashita who helped me realize my *sansai* foraging dreams with local guide Bridgitte Kayasith (also known as Brigitte Bardot) and the warmest hosts you could possibly imagine – expert foragers, Michi and Yoshi Suzuki.

Kylie Clark, the Mizu to Takumi team and the West Toyama Tourism Promotion Association were instrumental in organizing my research trip to Toyama, as was my delightful local guide Kyoko Takano, who showed me all of Toyama's hidden cultural gems. I'm also grateful to Curator Hideo Shintani, translator Joey Zhu and all the staff of the Takaoka Manyo Historical Museum.

In Tōkyō, I especially want to thank Japanese subculture legend and folk-art expert Manami Okazaki for her ongoing friendship and encouragement.

I am forever grateful to my loving partner, my parents, friends, mentors and teachers in the UK, Europe and beyond, as well as my earliest supporters, very first proofreaders and editors Elizabeth Stormfield, Lindsay McSporran, Anna Pivovarchuk, Zarry Bizeva, Jon Crabb, Wanda Proft and Akiko DuPont. And a special mention goes to my university dyslexia tutor, Alex Wilkinson, without whom I could never have completed my Master's, let alone written a book.

I'm also indebted to the members of the vibrant Anglo-Japanese community in London and beyond who have followed me on my Japanese seasonal adventures for years and have been incredibly supportive of this project – in particular, cherry blossom expert Naoko Abe and vintage kimono dealer Sonoe Sugawara.

I would like to thank Etan Ilfeld and the whole team at Watkins. From the moment we met I knew I had found the right home for my book. My particular thanks go to my warm, curious and always constructive editor Ella Chappell, copy editor Ingrid Court-Jones and our exceptional illustrator, Inko Ai Takita.

I also want to acknowledge the important work of two female anthropologists whose work has been a great source of inspiration to me: Liza Dalby, whose books have lined my shelves for many years, and the invaluable Beth Kempton, without whose enthusiasm and sage advice my book dream could never have been brought to life.

Finally, I would like to mention my beloved Uncle Stuart, who was a great reader and a fellow bibliophile – he always thought I should write a book, I'm just heartbroken he left us before he could see it.

NOTE ON THE USE OF JAPANESE NAMES

For legibility and ease of reference we have used the English naming system, which puts the given name first, followed by the family name, without macrons, as opposed to the Japanese system which traditionally puts the family name first, followed by the given name. The only notable exceptions are famous historical figures such as the poet Matsuo Bashō.

When the word sensei appears in the text it refers to a teacher or instructor.

JAPAN'S 24 *SEKKI* (DIVISIONS OF THE SOLAR YEAR) AND 72 *KO* (MICRO SEASONS)

Risshun (The Beginning of Spring)

4–8 February	*Harukaze kōri o toku*	The east wind melts the ice
9–13 February	*Kōō kenkan su*	Bush warblers start singing in the mountains
14–18 February	*Uo kōri o izuru*	Fish emerge from the ice

Usui (Rainwater)

19–23 February	*Tsuchi no shō uruoi okoru*	Rain moistens the soil
24–28 February	*Kasumi hajimete tanabiku*	Mist starts to linger
1–5 March	*Sōmoku mebae izuru*	Grass sprouts, trees bud

Keichitsu (Insects Awaken)

6–10 March	*Sugomori mushito o hiraku*	Hibernating insects surface
11–15 March	*Momo hajimete saku*	First peach blossoms
16–20 March	*Namushi chō to naru*	Caterpillars become butterflies

Shunbun (The Spring Equinox)

21–25 March	*Suzume hajimete sukū*	Sparrows start to nest
26–30 March	*Sakura hajimete saku*	The first cherry blossoms bloom
31 March–4 April	*Kaminari sunawachi koe o hassu*	Distant thunder

Seimei (Pure and Clear)

5–9 April	*Tsubame kitaru*	Swallows return.
10–14 April	*Kōgan kaeru*	Wild geese fly north
15–19 April	*Niji hajimete arawaru*	First rainbows appear

Kokuu (Grain Rains)

20–24 April	*Ashi hajimete shōzu*	First reeds sprout
25–29 April	*Shimo yamite nae izuru*	Last frost, rice seedlings grow
30 April–4 May	*Botan hana saku*	The first peonies bloom

Rikka (The Beginning of Summer)		
5–9 May	*Kawazu hajimete naku*	Frogs start singing
10–14 May	*Mimizu izuru*	Worms surface
15–20 May	*Takenoko shōzu*	Bamboo shoots sprout
Shōman (Lesser Ripening)		
21–25 May	*Kaiko okite kuwa o hamu*	Silkworms start feasting on mulberry leaves
26–30 May	*Benibana sakau*	Safflowers bloom
31 May–5 June	*Mugi no toki itaru*	Wheat ripens and is harvested
Bōshu (Grain Beards and Seeds)		
6–10 June	*Kamakiri shōzu*	Praying mantises hatch
11–15 June	*Kusaretaru kusa hotaru to naru*	Rotten grass becomes fireflies
16–20 June	*Ume no mi kibamu*	Plums turn yellow
Geshi (The Summer Solstice)		
21–26 June	*Natsukarekusa karuru*	Self-heal withers
27 June–1 July	*Ayame hana saku*	Irises bloom
2–6 July	*Hange shōzu*	Crow-dipper sprouts
Shōsho (Lesser Heat)		
7–11 July	*Atsukaze itaru*	Warm winds blow
12–16 July	*Hasu hajimete hiraku*	The first lotus blossoms
17–22 July	*Taka sunawachi waza o narau*	Hawks learn to fly
Taisho (Greater Heat)		
23–28 July	*Kiri hajimete hana o musubu*	Paulownia trees produce seeds
29 July–2 August	*Tsuchi uruōte mushi atsushi*	Earth is damp, air is humid
3–7 August	*Taiu tokidoki furu*	Great rains sometimes fall
Risshu (The Beginning of Autumn)		
8–12 August	*Suzukaze itaru*	Cool winds blow
13–17 August	*Higurashi naku*	Evening cicadas sing
18–22 August	*Fukaki kiri matō*	Thick fog descends

Shōsho (Manageable Heat)

23–27 August	*Wata no hana shibe hiraku*	Cotton flowers bloom
28 August–1 September	*Tenchi hajimete samushi*	Heat starts to die down
2–7 September	*Kokumono sunawachi minoru*	Rice ripens

Hakuro (White Dew)

8–12 September	*Kusa no tsuyu shiroshi*	Dew glistens white on grass
13–17 September	*Sekirei naku*	Wagtails sing
18–22 September	*Tsubame saru*	Swallows leave

Shūbun (The Autumn Equinox)

23–27 September	*Kaminari sunawachi koe o osamu*	Thunder ceases
28 September–2 October	*Mushi kakurete to o fusagu*	Insects hole up underground
3–7 October	*Mizu hajimete karuru*	Farmers drain fields

Kanro (Cold Dew)

8–12 October	*Kōgan kitaru*	Wild geese return
13–17 October	*Kiku no hana hiraku*	Chrysanthemums bloom
18–22 October	*Kirigirisu to ni ari*	Crickets chirp around the door

Sōkō (Frost Falls)

23–27 October	*Shimo hajimete furu*	The first frost
28 October–1 November	*Kosame tokidoki furu*	Light rains sometimes fall
2–6 November	*Momiji tsuta kibamu*	Maple leaves and ivy turn yellow

Rittō (The Beginning of Winter)

7–11 November	*Tsubaki hajimete hiraku*	Camellias bloom
12–16 November	*Chi hajimete kōru*	Land starts to freeze
17–21 November	*Kinsenka saku*	Daffodils bloom

Shōsetsu (Lesser Snow)

22–26 November	*Niji kakurete miezu*	Rainbows hide
27 November–1 December	*Kitakaze konoha o harau*	The north wind blows the leaves from the trees
2–6 December	*Tachibana hajimete kibamu*	Tachibana citrus tree leaves start to turn yellow

Taisetsu (Greater Snow)		
7–11 December	*Sora samuku fuyu to naru*	Cold sets in, winter begins
12–16 December	*Kuma ana ni komoru*	Bears start hibernating in their dens
17–21 December	*Sake no uo muragaru*	Salmons gather and swim upstream
Tōji (The Winter Solstice)		
22–26 December	*Natsukarekusa shōzu*	Self-heal sprouts
27–31 December	*Sawashika no tsuno otsuru*	Deer shed their antlers
1–4 January	*Yuki watarite mugi nobiru*	Wheat sprouts under snow
Shōkan (Lesser Cold)		
5–9 January	*Seri sunawachi sakau*	Parsley flourishes
10–14 January	*Shimizu atataka o fukumu*	Springs thaw
15–19 January	*Kiji hajimete naku*	Pheasants start to call
Daikan (Greater Cold)		
20–24 January	*Fuki no hana saku*	Butterburs bud
25–29 January	*Kiwamizu kōri tsumeru*	Ice thickens on streams
30 January– 3 February	*Niwatori hajimete toya ni tsuku*	Hens start laying eggs.

SELECTED BIBLIOGRAPHY

Ashkenazi, Michael (2003) *Handbook of Japanese Mythology*. Bloomsbury: Santa Barbara (CA)

Bailly, Sandrine (2009) *Japan: Season by Season*. Harry N Abrams: New York

Baird, Merrily (2001) *Symbols of Japan: Thematic Motifs in Art and Design*. Rizzoli: New York

Ball, Katherine M (2004) *Animal Motifs in Asian Art: An Illustrated Guide to their Meanings and Aesthetics*. Dover Publications: New York

Bickford, Maggie (1985) *Bones of Jade, Soul of Ice*. Yale University Art Gallery: New Haven (CT)

Bird, Winifred (2021) *Eating Wild Japan*. Stone Bridge Press: Berkeley (CA)

Blyth, Reginald H (2021) *Haiku (Volume I): Eastern Culture*. Angelico Press: New York

Carpenter, John T (2012) *Designing Nature: The Rinpa Aesthetic in Japanese Art*. Metropolitan Museum of Art: New York

Castile, Rand (1979) *The Way of Tea*. Weatherhill: New York

Dalby, Liza (2007) *East Wind Melts the Ice: A Memoir through the Seasons*. Chatto & Windus: London

Dalby, Liza (2001) *Kimono: Fashioning Culture*. University of Washington Press: Seattle (WA)

Davey, Hiseki E (2007) *The Japanese Way of the Artist*. Michi Publishing: Albany (NY)

Davis, Frederick Hadland (1912) *Myths & Legends of Japan*. George G Harrap & Company: London

De Visser, Marinus (2008) *The Dragon in China and Japan*. Cosimo Classics: New York

Ekiguchi, Kunio and McCreery, Ruth (1990) *A Japanese Touch for the Seasons*. Kodansha International: Tōkyō

Gluckman, Dale Carolyn and Takeda, Sharon Sadako (1992) *When Art Became Fashion: Kosode in Edo Period Japan*. Los Angeles County Museum of Art: Los Angeles

Gygi, Fabio (2018) "Things That Believe: Talismans, Amulets, Dolls, and How to Get Rid of Them", *Japanese Journal of Religious Studies*, 45(2)

Hamana, Bruce (2020) *100 Beautiful Words in the Way of Tea*. Tankosha: Kyōto

Hass, Robert (2013) *Essential Haiku: Versions of Basho, Buson and Issa*. Bloodaxe Books Ltd: Hexham, Northumberland

Hendry, Joy (1997) *Wrapping Culture: Politeness, Presentation and Power in Japan and Other Societies*. Clarendon Press, Oxford

Hibi, Sadao (2000) *The Colours of Japan*. Kodansha: Tōkyō

Hibi, Sadao (1987) *Japanese Tradition in Colour and Form*. Graphic-sha: Tōkyō

Higginson, William J (1995) *The Haiku Seasons: Poetry of the Natural World*. Kodansha International: Tōkyō

Hori, Ichiro, Kitagawa, Joseph and Miller, Alan (1968) *Folk Religion in Japan*. University of Chicago Press: Chicago

Illustrated Festivals of Japan (1992). Japan Travel Bureau: Tōkyō

Ingram, Cherry (1948) *Ornamental Cherries*. Country Life: London

Introduction to Japanese Cuisine: Nature, History and Culture (2015). Shuhari Initiative: Tōkyō

Isao, Kumakuro (1998) *Flowers and Wagashi: Traditional Japanese Confections*. Toraya: Tōkyō

Ishige, Naomichi (2011) *The History and Culture of Japanese Food*. Routledge Taylor & Francis Group: New York

Jefferies, Richard (1947) *The Life of the Fields*. Lutterworth Press: London

Katoh, Amy Sylvester (2003) *Japan: The Art of Living*. Tuttle: North Clarendon (VT)

Kawabata, Yasunari (1969) *Japan the Beautiful and Myself*. Kodansha International: Tōkyō

Keane, Marc Peter (2014) *The Japanese Tea Garden*. Stone Bridge Press: Berkeley (CA)

Kempton, Beth (2019) *Wabi Sabi: Japanese Wisdom for a Perfectly Imperfect Life*. Harper Design: New York

Kemske, Bonnie (2017) *The Teabowl: East and West*. Bloomsbury: London

Kenkō (1967) *Essays in Idleness: The Tsurezuregusa of Kenko*. Translated by Donald Keene. Columbia University Press: New York

Kirker, Constance and Newman, Mary (2021) *Cherry*. Reaktion Books: London

Koren, Leonard (1994) *Wabi-Sabi: For Artists, Designers, Poets & Philosophers*. Stone Bridge Press: Berkeley (CA)

Kuile, Casper ter (2021) *The Power of Ritual: Turning Everyday Activities into Soulful Practices*. William Collins: Glasgow

Kyoto Journal: Flora & Kyoto (2023). Kyotojanaru: Kyōto

Li, Qing (2018) *Forest Bathing: How Trees Can Help You Find Health and Happiness*. Thorndike Press: Waterville (ME)

Liddell, Jill (1989) *The Story of the Kimono*. Dutton: New York

Matsuhara, Iwao (1964) *On Life and Nature in Japan*. Hokuseido Press: Tōkyō

Maraini, Fosco (1973) *Japan: Patterns of Continuity*. Kodansha USA: New York

McCullough, Helen Craig (1996) *Kokin Wakashū: The First Imperial Anthology of Japanese Poetry*. Stanford University Press: Stanford (CA)

De Mente, Boye Lafayette (2011) *Elements of Japanese Design*. Tuttle: North Clarendon (VT)

Mitsukuni, Yoshida (1985) *The Culture of Anima: Supernature in Japanese life*. Mazda Motor Corp: Hiroshima

Miyazaki, Yoshifumi (2021) *Walking in the Woods: Go Back to Nature with the Japanese Way of Shinrin-Yoku*. Aster: London

Mizobuchi, Hiroshi (2016) *The Kagai in Kyoto*. Mitsumura Suiko Shoin: Kyōto

Morishita, Noriko (2021) *Wisdom of Tea: Life Lessons from the Japanese Tea Ceremony*. Allen & Unwin: Sydney

Morita, Kiyoko (2018) *The Book of Incense: Enjoying the Traditional Art of Japanese Scents*. Kodansha USA: New York

Murata, Yoshihiro (2012) *Kaiseki: The Exquisite Cuisine of Kyoto's Kikunoi Restaurant*. Kodansha USA: New York

Nakamura, Hajime (2013) *Wagashi*. Kawade Shobo Shinsha: Tōkyō

Pictorial Encyclopedia of Japanese Culture: The Soul and Heritage of Japan. (1987) Gakken: Tōkyō

Okakura, Kakuzō (2023) *The Book of Tea*. Translated by G C Calza. Officina Libraria: Rome

Ono, Sokyo and Woodard, William P (2004) *Shintō: The Kami Way*. Tuttle: Tōkyō

Plutschow, Herbert (1996) *Matsuri: The Festivals of Japan*. Japan Library: Surrey

Reider, Noriko T (2009) "Animating Objects: Tsukumogami Ki and the Medieval Illustration of Shingon Truth", *Japanese Journal of Religious Studies*, 36(2)

Sadler, Arthur Lindsay (2019) *The Japanese Tea Ceremony: Cha-no-yu and Zen Art of Mindfulness*. Tuttle: Tōkyō

Sanmi, Sasaki, McCabe, Shaun and Iwasaki, Satoko (2011) *Chado: The Way of Tea: A Japanese Tea Master's Almanac*. Tuttle: Boston

Sen, Soshitsu (1979) *Chado: The Japanese Way of Tea*. Weatherhill: New York

Sen, Soshitsu (1997) *Tea Life, Tea Mind*. Weatherhill: New York

Seigow, Matsuoka (2004) *Flowers, Birds, Wind, and Moon: The Phenomenology of Nature in Japanese Culture*. JPIC: Tōkyō

Shōnagon, Sei (2007) *The Pillow Book*. Translated by M McKinney. Penguin: London

Shigematsu, Soiko (1981) *A Zen Forest: Sayings of the Masters*. Translated by G Snyder. Weatherhill: New York

Shimura, Fukumi (2019) *The Music of Colour*. Translated by M Treyvaud. JPIC: Tōkyō

Shirane, Haruo (2012) *Japan and the Culture of the Four Seasons: Nature, Literature, and the Arts*. Columbia University Press: New York

Shiro, Usui (ed.) (1999) *The Chanoyu Quarterly: Tea and the Arts of Japan No.1–88*. Urasenke Foundation: Kyōto

Stamm, Joan D (2010) *Heaven and Earth Are Flowers: Reflections on Ikebana and Buddhism*. Wisdom Publications: Boston

Stamm, Joan D (2023) *The Language of Flowers in the Time of COVID*. Wisdom Publications: Boston

Sugiura, Miki (2018) "The Mass Consumption of Refashioned Clothes: Re-dyed Kimono in Post War Japan" in *Business History* 61, 1–19

Takano, Noriko (2010) *A Visual Guide to Annual Events in Japan*. Ehon House Publishing: Tōkyō

Takei, Jiro. and Keane, Marc P (2008) *Sakuteiki, Visions of the Japanese Garden*. Tuttle: North Clarendon (VT)

Takeuchi, Seiichi (2019) *Flower Petals Fall, but the Flower Endures: The Japanese Philosophy of Transience*. JPIC: Tōkyō

Tanizaki, Junichiro (2019) *In Praise of Shadows*. Vintage Publishing: London

Taylor, Harriet (1912) *Japanese Gardens*. Methuen: London

The Kodansha Bilingual Encyclopedia of Japan (1998). Kodansha International: Tōkyō

Thoreau, Henry David (2012) *October, or Autumnal Tints*. W W Norton & Company: New York

Tokuoka, Kunio and Sugimoto, Nobuko (2010) *Kitcho: Japan's Ultimate Dining Experience*. Kodansha International: Tōkyō

Torrance, Robert M (1999) *Encompassing Nature: A Sourcebook*. Counterpoint: Washington

Tsuchiya, Yoshio (1985) *A Feast for the Eyes: The Japanese Art of Food Arrangement*. Kodansha International: Tōkyō

Tsuji, Shizuo (2006) *Japanese Cooking: A Simple Art*. Kodansha International: Tōkyō

Tyler, Royall (1992) *Japanese No Dramas*. Penguin: London

Way, Twigs (2020) *Chrysanthemum*. Reaktion Books: London

Weis, Robert (ed.) *Spirit of Shizen* (2022). Musée National d'Histoire Naturelle: Luxembourg

Williams, Florence (2018) *The Nature Fix: Why Nature Makes Us Happier, Healthier, and More Creative*. W W Norton & Company: New York

Uchiyama, Jun Ichi (2021) *Auspicious Animals: The Art of Good Omens*. PIE: Tōkyō

Yamaguchi, Shozo, De Garis, Frederic and Sakai, Atsuharu (1964) *We Japanese*. Yamagata Press: Yokohama

Yibin, Ni (2009) *Symbols, Art and Language from the Land of the Dragon*. Duncan Baird Publishers: London

Yumioka, Katsumi (2017) *Kimono and the Colours of Japan: Kimono Collection of Katsumi Yumioka*. PIE: Tōkyō

Zeami, Motokiyo (2006) *The Flowering Spirit: Classic Teaching on the Art of No*. Kodansha International: Tōkyō

PERMISSIONS

Every care has been made to trace copyright holders. The author would like to thank the following publishers, who have given permission to reproduce their material in *The Japanese Art of Living Seasonally* (2024).

Angelico Press: *Haiku (Volume I): Eastern Culture*, Matsuo Bashō, translated by Reginald Horace Blyth (2021).

Bloodaxe Books LTD: *The Essential Haiku: Versions of Basho, Buson and Issa*, Robert Hass (1994).

Imperfect Publishing: *Wabi Sabi: For Artists, Designers, Poets & Philosophers*, Leonard Koren (1994).

Japan Publishing Industry Foundation for Culture (JPIC): *The Music of Colour*, Fukumi Shimura, translated by Matt Treyvard (2019).

The Richard Jefferies Society: *The Life of the Fields*, Richard Jefferies (1884).

The William Morris Society: *Hopes and Fears for Art: Five Lectures Delivered in Birmingham, London, and Nottingham*, William Morris (1882).

The Wordsworth Trust: *The Tables Turned* by William Wordsworth (1798).

www.wakapoetry.net: *The Kokin Wakashū*, Ki no Tomonori, translated by Dr Thomas McAuley.